"I am really enjoying your book it has been amazing for me! The part that really stuck out to me was instead of focusing on the money (the number) focus on what you want with the money. I never really thought about that but I have a wonderful habit of manifesting what I want. For example, I really wanted NLP but didn't have the money and 2 years ago I won all 3 levels in a drawing. Now I want my dream wedding and I may be on a reality show to win it; so I wrote down what it is that I really want, instead of writing down the number that I want."

— Michelle Hastie, Total Body Health Solutions

"This book, which was great by the way, really opened my eyes and spoke in a way that I like. My favorite is *you need to treat money like a relationship*. I realized I was taking from money all the time and cutting its flow, but then never giving back to money or thanking it. If money were a person, they would have dumped me for sure! It was astonishing that I could treat something like money so poorly in my life because relationships are what I'm best at! So thank you for that reminder."

— Laura Bloomer, La Dorset

I have read other books about finances and didn't get much out of all the heavy and technical wording except a feeling of complete overwhelm. Pfennigwerth's take on finances is fresh and invigorating. He brings unique humor and empathy to financial issues many people struggle with. I felt I was having a conversation with someone who truly cared about my financial future. I never thought about the "relationship" I had with my finances. It makes a lot of sense that if you don't treat your money well it won't treat you well. This concept truly changed my life for better.

— Nichole Frechette, Zabel Belly Dance

Opening the Flow of Money

Create a Financial Breakthrough without Losing Your Heart

By Nick Pfennigwerth

Big Heart Publishing

Published by Big Heart Publishing

Art direction and cover design by http://fiverr.com/lolamaro

ISBN-13: 978-0615943374

ISBN-10: 0615943373

For my parents, Anne Pfennigwerth and Leroy Pfennigwerth. Thank you for teaching me that generosity is true wealth. You've showed me to never let go of my dreams, to never stop giving, and keep going no matter what. Without the both of you, this book and the teachings that come through would have never seen the light of day.

Table of Contents

Opening the Flow of Money

Prologue

If you're not careful, the pursuit of money will eat your entire life. Money will influence every decision you make: Should I get a job because it pays well? Or, should I start a business doing what I enjoy most? I can't have this or that because I don't have enough money. I want to give more, but I don't have enough money. I want to live in this town and in this house, but I don't have the money. I want to travel, but what about the money?

What if you did have the money, then what? Would you be free to do what you like? Would you never have to worry about money again? Would you retire, hang out all day, and never have to work? I mean, that's the point of money, right? The more money you have the more you can enjoy and live your life to the fullest—that's what you're told.

Current economic structures are not helping the situation. From the day you were born, the media, the government, schools, friends, and your family have been conditioning you that well-being equals money. You don't have to go any further than your closest screen and the power button to immerse yourself in the money culture we live in. Every day you're bombarded with corporate advertising telling you that you need their latest product for wealth and success. You observe the things and luxuries that money can buy, or the problems money solves. You agree to work almost an entire lifetime for the promise of retirement. And you see the mass population envy and worship those who have money, success, or fame.

I'm sure you've heard the phrases: "Money isn't everything, but it sure does help." "The more money you have, the more people you can help." "You need to work hard for a living." "Money will make you happy." The stories about money are endless, but the underlining theme is the same: money gives you power.

I'm willing to bet that your current relationship with money falls in one or two of these categories:

1. Money is a struggle and hard to get.

2. You feel like you don't have enough money; therefore, you are consumed with getting more.

3. You have enough money to pay the bills and have some money left over for leisure or saving, but barely enough, and you still feel insecure and worry about money?

You are not alone my friends. Thousands, if not millions, of people have the money conscious as discussed above.

What's going on here? Why are the economic promises of money *not* fulfilling you on a spiritual, emotional, and physical level? It's because you have not found your freedom in an unfree world.

You already *are* a free functioning human being, but...you have taught yourself to be unfree. You have learned to cling to material possessions and money for your happiness. You have learned to identify with what you do, your family history, and the things you've done in the past that supposedly define you today. Finally, you seek for salvation in the future, and attach to your thoughts and imagination to achieve your desires. You have chained yourself, thus giving away your power to some-thing-out-there to bring you happiness, fulfillment, and success. You are not free.

I'm not criticizing you, nor am I judging you. Both the co-author and I know firsthand what financial scarcity feels and looks like in our lives. I cannot speak for Steve, but for me, Nick Pfennigwerth, I began my power hungry and money seeking quest as a real estate developer. I heard about this law of attraction thing, that you can have anything you desire as long as you ask, believe, and receive.

Well, I was hungry for money, and that's what I wanted. So I set goals to become a millionaire (of course, because that's what society says you should strive for) and the next top real estate developer aside from Donald Trump. I was serious about my goal, and perhaps deluded.

Nonetheless, I began developing, building, renovating, and pursing my ideas for "green" sustainable real estate. In the beginning, I was good at earning money. Thousands of dollars were rolling in and my asset portfolio grew each year. But there was a problem: I was unhappy. The work was hard—twelve hour days, seven days a week; the overwhelm and pressure to pay down my debts hit the red line making me emotionally unstable.

Once the real estate bubble burst in 2008, however, my emotional bubble burst, too. I was exhausted, broke, in-debt, over-weight, and ruined a lot of relationships. My company crumbled to the ground and I felt lost and pathetic. I had nothing left, expect for a Father, Mother, Brother, Sister, and a load of debt society wasn't going to forgive.

Looking back, it was a beautiful time in my life. I didn't realize it then, but I was free. I didn't have any possessions, or any commitments, or any relationships, and I was still okay. I was at the bottom of the mountain dirty and broken, but I was alive. I remember the turning point, when that moment of freedom hit me. I was sitting in my truck wondering what to do next. My houses were in foreclosure, I didn't have construction jobs, and my real estate days were over. All I had was this question: "Who am I?" Then the cloud of thoughts parted, and the skies turned blue. I had no idea who I was, and it was the most peaceful moment in my life.

For three years I journeyed across "the other shore" not worrying too much about the relative side of life—possessions, money, status, jobs, etc. Now today, much of my journeying has been integrating the two: the absolute and relative into a free functioning human being. The irony is you already are a free functioning human being, regardless of how in-debt, broke, unhappy, or pathetic you think you are.

WHO YOU ARE

I have an idea of who you are. You've picked up this book because you're a person active in personal growth and spirituality. You're tired of feeling stuck in your finances. You know that you deserve better (and you do). You want financial security, a vibrant life, and abundance. Unfortunately, money cannot provide that for you. And the more you think that money can solve your problems and bring you abundance, the more stuck you become.

Do you want the truth? Money is a function of the economy—nothing more. It's a resource to make the exchange of goods and services easier and more economical. If there wasn't a monopoly over the legal tender of money, I could make my own and print a million copies—though, I would have to convince the majority population that my money is the best commodity to use. The point is money is worthless and only has value because you and I give it value.

Money is not power. Power is power, just like a stick is a stick, a cat is a cat, Nick is Nick, firewood is firewood, and ash is ash. Like I said earlier, we are confused; we think money is power. So, if you're anything like me, you've attended many workshops and seminars, and you've read countless books on how to attract money and have power over money. You've done affirmations, goal cards, vision boards, and tried to *act as if*. Now, I'm not saying those activities do not have value, what I'm saying, however, is that you're still stuck. Whatever you've tried is still not working and you need more growth, more truth, love, and power.

Here's another sobering truth: money is probably the most important commodity in the world. Because of its importance, money needs attention. On one hand money is nothing more than an economic function. But on the other hand money enables you to make more choices, express your specialized knowledge and skills, make a difference, and have a higher standard of living. You don't need money, and you can opt-out of the system, but you've decided that is not an option for you.

Your option is to have a financial breakthrough and a healthy relationship with money that is aligned with your heart, purpose, and deepest values.

WHAT YOU REALLY NEED

To open the flow of money, you need understanding, a way to stretch yourself, to transform (not change), and patience. In practical terms, and during my six year quest for a financial breakthrough, I have found four things that give you a healthy relationship with money.

UNDERSTANDING HOW MONEY WORKS.

Most of us have false assumptions about money, and we were never taught the practicality of money through the public education system.

That's because the public education doesn't teach the true essence and practicality of money. I'm not even sure if the ones in charge of creating the curriculum know what money *really* is.

This section of the book teaches the truth to money and what stands in the way of you and money. You'll discover the mental blocks to money and how to make a financial turnaround.

CREATING A HEALTHY RELATIONSHIP WITH MONEY.

Money has a huge influence in your life. There's no way around money. You need a certain amount to provide for the basic needs: food, shelter, common utilities, hygiene, and leisure. I guess you could opt-out of the money system, but that's not the goal here. You have the option to create a healthy relationship with money and regain your power. And that's what this section of the book is about.

The teachings in this section use money as a tool to look at the scarcity surrounding money that you have disowned. You will uncover the qualities that need embodying to have a healthy relationship with money and the next action steps or goals to exercise your power with money. By the end of this section, you'll realize that it's you and all of your unnecessary emotional, mental, and spiritual baggage about money that is the problem, not the economy, difficult people, or money itself. The goal is to mature your relationship with money so it's free flowing.

LIVING YOUR NEW RELATIONSHIP WITH MONEY.

This section of the book is about exercising your power. You can spend your days and evenings creating a healthy relationship with money, by knowing its truth and connecting with love, but if you do not take a sovereign position with money, your money relationship will never improve. You will read about ideas on how to design your life, overcome limiting beliefs, and achieve financial stretch goals.

LETTING IT FLOW.

This section is probably the most practical of them all. We go deeper into exercising your power so money becomes a consistent and healthy inflow and outflow. The ability to receive money is written as straight forward as possible: create and deliver value. It's that practical, but we complicate its simple nature. The goal of this section is to make it easy for you to learn how to create and deliver value so you get paid.

When you have embodied the four points above—understanding how money works, creating a healthy relationship with money, living your new relationship with money, and letting it flow—you will have a financial breakthrough and open the flow of money. This means, you will have the capacity to earn the income you desire, to live a vibrant life, to direct your attention to love, and to be free from overwhelm and the tyranny of scarcity.

Having this capacity and functioning as a human being does not remove you from the laws of cause and effect and the cycles of life. You will experience circumstances when the inflow of money is much greater than its outflow, you'll experience cycles of financial stagnation, and you'll experience times when the outflow or giving of money is greater than its inflow (though, this will be minimal). But one thing will always remain constant: whether money is coming in or out, it has little to do with your happiness and how powerful a human being you are.

You are already free. From this point forward reminds you of that truth and shows you how to open the flow.

Part I: Understanding How Money Works

1.
What's it Like to Enjoy Financial Abundance?

Honestly it's pretty much the same thing you'd experience in a virtual game world when your character has a lot of gold. When you have an abundance of gold, the nature of the game changes, doesn't it?

First, the price of items becomes less important because you can afford anything you want. You're less likely to whine, "I can't afford that!" If you have a million gold pieces and you're earning a thousand more each day, would you fuss about whether a potion costs 10 gold or 50 gold? You don't even have to think about it. What's cheap and what's expensive is relative to your assets, income, and mindset.

Second, in some ways the game becomes more fun, but in other ways it could be less fun. Your financial resources give you an edge. Your character is less limited and has more possibilities. It's easy for you to secure equipment, lodging, transportation, etc. It's easy to help out other characters. But you may have to change the way you play to keep it fun and engaging.

In the beginning it was challenging just to acquire gold, but now that you have so much, adding more to your stash may not be as exciting as it once was. You'll probably become more interested in other aspects of the game, such as socializing with the other players. The game becomes more of a social challenge than a financial one. This is an oversimplification, but my point is that when you have a lot of resources, your focus shifts away from acquiring more and toward something else that interests you and keeps the game fun. If the game stops being fun, you'll probably think about quitting.

Third, your social interactions with the other characters may change when you have more gold. When you're rich you can do more to help out other players, like buying them equipment and supplies.

Some people may appreciate the help. But for others it may not be a good thing. If someone is new to the game, and you artificially advance them, you may rob them of the early learning experiences; they may be a significantly worse level-30 player than someone who bootstrapped his way up from the bottom. You may also rob them of the fun of overcoming the game's challenges, via trial and error. However, when an experienced player is starting fresh with a new character, it makes more sense to give them some aid because repeating the early levels probably won't do much for them. It takes time to develop the wisdom to make financially and socially sound decisions, and not everyone will be pleased with your choices.

You may want to protect your gold because it took a lot of work to earn it, but you needn't be overly afraid of losing it because you know you could earn it back if necessary—this assumes you earned it in the first place. Those who are very skilled at earning money usually aren't too afraid of losing it, but those who aren't very good at earning money become more clingy and tight with what they have because they don't feel confident in their ability to earn it back quickly. The high achievers are still protective of their assets, but they don't live in fear of a big loss if they trust themselves; when they do succumb to playing too tight, the game becomes less fun, and they lose their drive and ambition.

I wouldn't say that the game is always better when you have a lot of gold, but in many ways it is. If you really enjoy the challenge of acquiring gold, then the early levels can be a lot of fun. If you remain in a state of financial scarcity for too long, however, you'll limit your avatar's growth. That doesn't mean you can't enjoy interesting growth experiences while in a state of financial scarcity, but the game typically gets boring, repetitive, or frustrating if you stay there too long. To keep it fun and interesting, you need to progress to different kinds of challenges.

If you've been stuck in a state of financial scarcity for longer than you'd like, it means you haven't yet put in the time to master one of *real* life's wealth building strategies. There are many to choose from, so pick a strategy that's fun for you, and run with it until you get good at it.

For example, you can create stuff and sell it. You can trade (buy low, sell high). You can get paid to support and/or optimize other people's wealth building systems. You can acquire income-generating and/or appreciating assets. You can bring people together for lucrative deals in exchange for a fair cut. You can become a performer or entertainer. The point is, *real* life has more wealth building opportunities than all the virtual worlds combined.

HOW WOULD YOU BECOME FINANCIALLY STUCK IN A GAME WORLD? WHAT CAUSES PEOPLE TO GET STUCK IN FINANCIAL SCARCITY?

Basically, you need to avoid doing those things that will bring in the gold.

For example, you could avoid going on income-generating quests. Stick with non income-generating activities like walking around aimlessly or socializing with other characters. This could still be fun and interesting, but don't expect to get paid for it.

Many times people will use the phrase "I don't know what to do" in order to justify their financial scarcity.

So you're going broke because you *don't know what to do*? Is that accurate? Your problems would be easily solved if you only knew what to do? All your financial problems can be traced back to not knowing what to do?
Seriously?

Is it perhaps more accurate to say that you're using this as an excuse to avoid accepting one or more of the quests that are *right in front of your face*?

I don't think I've ever met someone that claimed they didn't know *what to do* who wasn't butt up against the most obvious solution, staring them right in the face the whole time. They claim ignorance in order to prevent themselves from having to face that solution, which is often quite clear to everyone around them. They think that other people are actually buying their excuse, but the reality is that there's a whole gossip network around the person where friends and family keep asking, "Why won't s/he just do X?" But after dealing with years of denial, it's too hard for friends and family to be straight with that person and lay out the plain and simple truth because they expect the truth would kill the relationship.

If you're one of those people who goes around saying "I don't know what to do," please believe me when I tell you that no one around you actually believes your story. You're more transparent than you realize. To other people it just sounds like pointless whining.

If you're playing a game and you don't know how to earn gold, how would you figure it out? Is the solution to walk around complaining, "I don't know what to do"?

No, that would be stupid. You'd never do something like that, would you?

How could you figure out what to do?

You could start by reading the game's instruction manual: http://www.stevepavlina.com/personal-development-for-smart-people/
.

You could ask the other players who have a lot of gold or even a moderate amount of gold for advice. Chances are that anyone who has more gold than you has more of a clue than you do. If you really want to earn a lot of gold, make a study of how the game's resource system works. Try different ways of earning gold. Read books about gold mining. Experiment. Discover through trial and error what works best for you.

But for goodness sakes, if you sit around whining "I don't know what to do" while other characters are happily earning gold, don't be surprised when the armory guy comes to strip you of your sword and chain mail for being late on your payments.

CHOOSING GOOD QUESTS

To create a wealthy avatar, accept quests that will earn you some gold. Invest your time and energy into those quests, and you'll acquire gold.

This is an oversimplification because in real life there's more financial risk than in most games. Virtually anyone can get rich in a game world simply by playing long enough.

Let's consider some possible ways to choose a quest that will earn you some gold.

How about letting your parents or family decide for you?

Perhaps your family really wants you to become a healer because they know that healing pays big bucks. So they strongly encourage you to go to shaman school. You also believe that's a good way to earn a lot of gold, but you really don't want to be a healer. You don't think it would be fun for you. Should you ignore your feelings and take their advice?

Only if you're a total loon.

The point of the game is to have fun, right? So why on Azeroth would you try to acquire gold by committing to a long-term quest that you don't expect will be fun? What will happen? You'll become bored and frustrated, and you'll soon want to quit. You'll waste everyone's time and disappoint those who are counting on you.

Even if you can force yourself to succeed on this path, you'll end up hating your life. It will become a total grind. So what if you earn a million gold. Will spending it be any consolation for the sorry state of your emotional life?

It's okay to go on a short and dull mini-quest every once in a while, and that may be a necessary step for advancement sometimes. But if the bulk of your time is spent doing stuff you don't enjoy, the solution is obvious: quit and start over on a different path. And don't bemoan how far you've traveled down the wrong path. Let it be game over.

What if you accept only those quests that you expect will be the most fun?

That would certainly be interesting. You'd be enjoying the game and having a good time.

But maybe some of those quests wouldn't earn you any gold. Maybe you'd even have to pay for some of the experiences you'd like to have. Eventually you would get bored by the limited options available to you, and you'd feel anxious to progress to something more rewarding.

This hedonistic approach might work in certain games where every roaming monster carries a purse (yet you never see those monsters shopping in any of the stores), but it often falls flat in real life. Every analogy has its limits, so we have to be careful not to stretch this one too far.

Is there a better approach?

What if you played the game with the goal of balancing having fun and acquiring gold? Surely there are plenty of quests you could accept that are (1) fun and interesting, and (2) profitable.

From time to time you might do quests that are fun, but not profitable, or profitable, but not fun, or neither profitable nor fun. But suppose you aim to spend 80% of your game time on quests that are both fun and profitable.

Could you do it? Could you do that in real life?

After all, you're the one who chooses the quests. And there's a virtually limitless supply of quests available.

Writing this article is a mini-quest for me. I love writing, so it's fun for me to do this. This particular article probably won't be very profitable, but it could generate some extra traffic over the years, and I earn gold from web traffic in a variety of ways.

The point is that you're the one who's choosing these quests, aren't you? So if you're not having fun, whose fault is that?

I don't want to see you blaming yourself for picking lame quests, but it would make your life a lot better if you realized you're the one who's responsible for making those choices.

Sometimes the bad guy forces a quest on you, one that you wouldn't have chosen for yourself. When that happens, just accept it and get through the quest as quickly as you can. And remember that it's still supposed to be fun.

SKILL BUILDING

Just as there's an element of skill to playing games, there's also an element of skill to earning gold in real life.

Some players just plain suck at it, don't they?

If you're one of those sucky players, what's the solution? You need to find a way to suck less.

This means learning how to capitalize on your strengths and shore up your weaknesses.

Where is your character strong? Are you good at vanquishing monsters? Casting spells? Healing people? Motivating and inspiring your guild? Set yourself up in a role that plays to your strengths as much as possible. Do more of what you're good at and less of what you're bad at.

What about your weaknesses? Where are the chinks in your armor? How can you work around them? Can you educate yourself to become a better player? Can you recruit teammates whose strengths will compensate for your weaknesses? Most likely you'll need a blend of training and recruiting. Make your avatar as good as you can, but recognize that you'll still need help if you want to achieve your full potential.

Decide how you're going to develop your character. If you're a warrior at heart, don't go to mage school. If you're a cleric at heart, don't study lock picking. Train yourself to take better advantage of your strengths.

If you can't decide what kind of character you'd like to be, then make any choice and start pursuing it. You'll find out soon enough if you chose wrong, and then you can go back and start fresh with a new character and develop yourself along a different line. Often this is the only way you'll learn what your true strengths are. You may have to try on several gauntlets that don't fit in order to find the one that fits you like a glove.

When I played computer role-playing games, I almost always chose to be the fighter guy. I wasn't into casting spells or doing stealthy maneuvers. I didn't like to be subtle or sneaky. I was the kick-ass warrior guy who'd run into a group of monsters and start wailing on them. I must have thought RPG and FPS were synonyms.

Even when I did pen and paper role-playing, my favorite characters to play were the fearless warrior types. One of my favorite characters to play was called The Tackler. His special power was that he was exceptionally good at running headlong into groups of enemies and tackling them to the ground.

Often I like to control my real-life avatar in a similar manner. When communicating with people, I tend to be very direct and forthright. I'm not very subtle or sensitive. I'm disgusted by people who gossip behind people's backs. Is this the only way to play the game of life? Of course not. I like playing this type of character though, and when I try to behave too differently, it doesn't feel right; it feels like I'm out of sync with my avatar.

RECRUITING TEAMMATES

It's pretty hard to get ahead by playing solo because your options are more limited. Bigger teams can tackle bigger challenges and earn bigger prizes. Teammates can help compensate for each other's individual weaknesses. The social experience of interacting with other players and working together as a cohesive unit makes the game more fun.

As my primary teammate, I have Erin, who loves to play the healer. She's the perfect complement for my avatar. I run in first and get beat up, and she keeps me alive and tends to my wounds so I can return for another round. We've accomplished some interesting real-life goals this way.

Interacting with teammates can also help you develop a more well-rounded avatar without losing your sharp edge.

For example, sometimes I'm too aggressive, and I have to learn to tone it down a notch. Years ago, Erin and I were playing the game *City of Heroes*. I played a martial arts scrapper character (a tough fighter who inflicts a lot of damage), and she played a healer. While waiting for our teammates to arrive before embarking on a mission, I grew impatient and decided to run in solo and get a head start on bashing enemies. Erin's character remained in the street waiting for the rest of our group. She sees me enter a warehouse filled with enemies, and about 30 seconds later, my character comes running out the door and immediately falls flat on his face at her feet—dead. With my last virtual breath, I typed, "Do NOT go in there!"

How can you recruit teammates to help you out in real life? It's pretty much the same process you use in a game, albeit a bit less structured. Simply talk to people and invite them to do something fun and profitable with you.

That's how I recruited people to help out with my computer games business many years ago. I found people I thought would be a good fit for the team, and I asked them, "Hey, would you like to…?" Then we had a conversation about the possibilities of working together. I don't recall looking at many resumes. I just asked around. These days it's how I do joint-venture partnerships. It usually starts with a line like, "Hey, what do you think about this idea…"

That's how I started my latest mastermind group. I asked someone to join it, and he said yes. It's only three people so far, but it's off to a good start. It's a small team where we all help each other succeed. We had our third meeting recently, and all of us have benefited from it. Each of us is strong in areas where the others are weak.

Don't think you have to go it alone. Financial abundance is easier to achieve when you make it a social adventure, not a solo pursuit. You'll probably find that the social aspects make it more fun. Isn't it more interesting to tackle one of those dragons as a team instead of trying to take it on all by yourself? The best part of going on quests is the fascinating people you meet along the way.

COURAGE

Courage is an essential element for going on quests because good quests, especially those that are very lucrative, often involve some risk. You might die. You might get robbed. You might encounter a puzzle you can't solve and get frustrated.

So why do people take on those risks? Why do people keep fighting dragons and risking their character's lives to do it?

Mainly because it's a lot of fun. To play sheepishly makes the game boring and pointless. It's better to play full out and risk death now and then.

Nobody wants to get their character killed. But they understand it's a possible outcome, and they accept it. In the grand scheme of things, getting your virtual character killed is a minor setback.

It takes practice to find the right balance between playing too fast and loose versus playing too tight and timid. With practice you'll settle on a strategy that works for you.

How's your real life strategy working for you? Have you achieved the proper balance between courage and safety?

Most of the time, people play their real life characters way too tight and timid. Yes, some people are on the fast and loose side, but if you're reading this article, it's a safe bet that isn't your problem.

In real life people often exaggerate their fears. They run from things that are largely imaginary. I mean...how often do you have to risk death to acquire financial abundance these days? I guess that depends on where you live and what type of work you're doing. But where I live most people who choose to become wealthy can do so without substantially increasing their risk of death by dragon's breath.

What's the truth of your situation? Are you exerting the right amount of courage? Are you taking reasonable risks, or are you playing too tight?

Courage is what keeps you in the sweet spot of having fun. Courage isn't something you are or something you have, it's something you do. When you do courage, the game is fun. Real life is fun.

When you see a quest that scares you but also excites you, that's the best kind of quest to accept. Those are the really fun ones.

What are some of the quests that are right in front of you, waiting to be accepted? Have you been avoiding them because they require courage? If a quest requires courage, that's exactly why you should accept it. It will be fun!

YOUR WEALTHY AVATAR

The hardest part of building a wealthy avatar is adopting the right mindset. This is the mindset that people naturally adopt when they enjoy a role-playing game. The point of the game is to have fun and to advance your character. If you're not having fun, and other people are, you're probably doing something wrong. If you've been playing for a month and you're still stuck at level 3, you're probably doing something wrong. You're one of those clueless newbies who just doesn't get it.

When you have the right mindset, and you keep playing the game, it's only a matter of time before you have a wealthy avatar. Sure you'll have a few setbacks along the way, and your expectations won't always be met. But if you apply a sound strategy that fits the rules of the game and meshes well with the social landscape, in the long run you can expect to succeed.

Your financial challenges aren't there to beat you down. They're important training exercises. Your financial problems are solvable, but in order to solve them you must learn and follow the rules of the game. Are you following those rules, or are you violating them? Are you spending more than you earn? Are you racking up debt instead of creating value? Are you wasting your time on quests that aren't fun *and* profitable? Are you ducking the challenging quests that are staring you in the face because you're scared? Are you trying to do everything alone instead of building or joining a cool team?

2.
The Practicality of Money

How important is money? How much is enough? Is money a distraction from one's spiritual path? Is it a necessary evil? Is it unfair that some people have more money than others? Is poverty more noble than wealth? Is it possible to become an enlightened millionaire?

Even among highly conscious people, the subject of money is a contentious topic. As an individual you've probably wrestled with this subject on many occasions. Social attitudes towards money are so incongruent that it's no wonder people are confused.

Is money a positive resource or a consciousness-lowering distraction?

Like most people I grew up with mixed associations about money. In some ways money was a good thing; in other ways it was a necessary evil or a distraction from what was really important.

On the one hand, I saw evidence that money was good. It's not hard to recognize that money bestows certain advantages. Some problems can be solved by money very easily. Money can provide food, clothing, shelter, heat, transportation, education, technology, entertainment, medicine, and so on. Given the way our society currently functions, if you have a lot of money, you have a lot of solutions. Money surely won't solve all your problems, and it can create new problems of its own, but on balance it's safe to say that money is a powerful problem-solving tool. I think Earl Nightingale said it best: "Nothing can take the place of money in the area in which money works."

On the other hand, there are some things I don't like about money. I don't like that it's used as a gatekeeper for certain "privileges," like proper medical care, healthy food, or decent educational resources. I also don't like how it induces people to behave dishonorably to attain it.

While I admire the achievements of today's titans of industry, many of them acquired their wealth through means I couldn't stomach.

CONFLICTING BELIEFS ABOUT MONEY

For most of my life, I've been stuck with incongruent attitudes towards money. Objectively, material wealth seemed like a great thing—I should definitely pursue it. Subjectively it seemed like a giant distraction—why should I need it? Intellectually, wealth seemed good. Intuitively, wealth felt irrelevant. I hadn't yet figured out a way of thinking about money that was congruent across multiple perspectives.

Have you been struggling with a similar internal conflict? If so, you're certainly not alone because this conflict is largely the result of social conditioning. We have some influences telling us that money is very important, while other influences tell us it's not. Look at what happens during the holiday season. Advertisers tell us to spend, spend, spend. The more money we spend, the better our holidays will be. Buy your wife an (inherently worthless but nonetheless expensive) diamond necklace, and she'll love you forever. On the other hand, we might watch a classic holiday movie *It's a Wonderful Life* that tells us we need to keep money in perspective and that relationships are far more important. Mixed signals abound.

This social conditioning affects our relationships, too. What assumptions do you make about people based on their income or financial assets? If you know someone's financial status, but you've never even met him, do you prejudge that person by assigning other qualities that may or may not be true? What assumptions would you make about a millionaire? About someone who's totally broke? How would you feel dating someone who earned 10x as much as you? How about 1/10th as much as you?

I believe these mixed associations lead many conscious people to conclude that money itself is the problem. Maybe it's better to find a way to live without money at all…at least cut its presence down to the bare minimum. If money is truly a distraction from conscious living, wouldn't the most conscious choice be to shun money altogether? Maybe give up your worldly possessions and join a monastery?

Within the scope of religion, money often plays a confusing role as well. Supposedly Jesus wasn't a particularly wealthy individual, but today's Catholic Church is as wealthy as they come. According to United Nations *World Magazine*, the Church has several billion dollars *in gold alone*, and when you consider their massive worldwide real estate holdings, their artwork collection, and their tax exempt status, the amount of wealth controlled by the Catholic Church is staggering. While figures are hard to estimate due to the complexity and scope of the organization, some believe the Church is the world's wealthiest entity, with the Pope controlling more financial assets than any corporation or government on earth. Whether that's true or not, the Church's wealth certainly makes for an interesting contrast with the life Jesus supposedly lived. When it comes to your financial future, should you model Jesus or the Pope? Or someone else entirely?

We could go deeper into the quagmire of confusing financial beliefs, but I don't think that would be helpful, so let's put the social models aside for now and take a fresh look at money to see what role we would have it play in our lives.

WHAT IS MONEY?

Money is a social resource—the *primary* social resource. Money has no inherent value of its own, but we assign it value through social agreement. If I give you $100, you can withdraw $100 of value from society. The only reason this works is that we agree by consensus that $100 has a certain value. If we all agreed that money was worthless, then money would have no value whatsoever.

Because it's a social resource, money isn't a perfect medium of exchange. The value of anything, including money itself, is determined by social consensus. That may be the consensus of just two people, such as when you buy an item from another person. Or it may be the consensus of a large group, such as when you buy or sell stock in public companies.

When your personal valuation roughly matches the social consensus, you'll conclude that pricing is fair. When your personal valuation drifts from the social consensus, you'll conclude that certain items are either over- or under-priced.

Although there will be serious consequences to doing so, you're free to opt-out of the social contract of money. Most people would find this totally impractical, but you can choose to assign no value whatsoever to money if you wish. However, if you still want to take advantage of social resources, you'll need to create your own social contracts on a case-by-case basis. This could include barter or other forms of exchange, or it could involve leveraging relationships to meet your social needs.

For most of us, the social contract of money is far too advantageous to ignore. While the monetary system is far from perfect, it's more efficient than the alternatives. By assigning a monetary value to our social exchanges and by making it easy to transfer money from one person to another, social trades are performed with relative ease. Buying groceries, going to work, using electricity, or connecting to the Internet are all examples of social trades, and by social consensus, all of these are reducible to money.

Even money itself can be assigned a price, as anyone in debt can readily attest. If you want money today, you can purchase it by pledging a greater amount of money tomorrow.

So money is essentially social credit. It's an IOU from society, enabling you to extract a certain amount of social value whenever you want. The more money you have, the more society owes you, and the more value you can extract.

HOW TO EARN MONEY

Let's consider what it means to earn money. Since money is a social resource, earning money means acquiring more of that social resource. When you spend money, you convert money to value. But when you earn money, you convert value to money.

One way to earn money is to sell possessions. Take an item and sell it, and you'll receive money for it. Another option is to acquire items at one price and turn around and sell them for more than your costs. Companies dig up resources all over the planet and sell them for a profit. For individuals this approach might take the form of buying objects, stocks, or bonds at one price and selling them at a higher price. Sometimes value is added in the process (which may just be added convenience), while other times the money earned comes from market inefficiencies.

Perhaps the most common way to earn money is to sell your time. Get a job and trade hours for dollars. The greater your ability to personally deliver a high social value, the greater your earnings potential.

The difference between making $10/hour vs. $100/hour is that the latter work has much greater social value. This difference isn't anyone's "fault"—the difference is due to the social consensus about the value of certain work. Note the difference between absolute value and social value. Top athletes may not perform useful work in an absolute sense, but their compensation is based on the social value of their service, which is currently very high.

Another way to earn money is to create a system that earns money for you, such as a business. This is my personal favorite, since it can provide far more leverage than selling time. I also find it much less risky in the long run, since owning and controlling a money-generating system is more secure than trading hours for dollars at someone else's discretion.

You can also earn money by selling money itself…aka investing. By loaning your money or assets to someone else, you can earn interest and/or dividends. How you earn money depends on what you invest in. Investing in a new business is very different from investing in a criminal organization. One form of investing creates social value; the other steals it.

And of course a final option for making money is to steal it. Historically this has been a popular option, but I won't give it serious consideration here.

If you think about it, there are two basic ways to earn money: make a social contribution, and receive payment commensurate with the social value of your contribution. Or, take advantage of market inefficiencies to extract money without contributing any value.

Option 1 includes getting a job, running a business that provides products or services, reselling items with value added, or investing in any of these outlets. Option 2 includes reselling items without added value, gambling, mooching off others, crime, or investing in any of these.

Here's another way of labeling these two strategies: contribute or mooch.

Unless you've somehow opted out of the monetary system, you're using one or both of these two strategies right now. One strategy will likely be dominant in your life—either you're creating genuine social value and being paid for it, or you're mooching off the value created by others.

Note that #1 is essential for the monetary system to survive and thrive, but #2 is not. The only way moochers can survive is by extracting value from the contributors. But ultimately someone must contribute, or there can be no value for the moochers to extract.

Incidentally, Ayn Rand wrote a fascinating novel called *Atlas Shrugged* about what would happen if the world's contributors left to form their own society, leaving the moochers to fend for themselves. The contributor society became a paradise, while the moocher society fell to pieces. Rand suggested that a system that rewarded moochers at the expense of contributors was evil, and that contributors should be free to decide how their work is used (and whether or not they will support any moochers).

Some degree of mooching is to be expected. Children mooch off their parents. Those who are unable to contribute mooch off those who can. Whenever we enjoy the fruits of someone else's labor without paying for it, we're mooching. We all mooch off the hard work of our ancestors. But eventually we have to decide whether we're going to continue to mooch for the rest of our lives or begin making a genuine contribution. Will we remain moochers for life, or will we become contributors?

Obviously your life will include some contribution and some mooching, but what's your primary strategy for generating income today? Do you contribute social value? Or do you mooch off the value of other contributors?

Let's consider both possibilities.

THE MOOCHER MINDSET

Opting into mooch mode means you're extracting more social value than you're contributing. Your focus is on getting as opposed to giving, so you take more out of the system than you give back. The moocher mindset suggests you can always rely on others to pick up your slack. It's the mindset of unearned entitlement. Since you still need to extract value such as food, clothing, and shelter—value which others must provide for you—you live at the expense of others. Your burden may be shouldered by an individual such as a parent, or it may be shared by society at large, but either way you survive by suckling the social teat.

Sometimes mooching becomes so habitual it's easy to overlook. Many people who seemingly have contribution-based careers harbor an underlying moocher mindset. They aim to extract as much social value as possible while contributing as little as possible. They work to make money to the degree it's necessary, while mooching as much as they can get away with. Such people don't have inspired careers because work is only seen as a means to an end, not an outlet for genuine contribution. Take a look around and see if you can identify the moochers in your life. Who is there to get rather than to give?

Another name for the moocher mindset is the *scarcity mindset*. Since you aren't creating value of your own, the money you extract must come from someone else. It's a zero-sum game. Whatever you gain, someone else must lose.

The moocher mindset makes the attainment of financial abundance very difficult because in order to succeed financially with this mindset, you must embrace certain values that most people would consider negative. Your gain is someone else's loss, so getting rich requires taking advantage of more people. In order to gain by mooching, someone else must cover your extraction with real value. So the more wealth you accumulate, the more you steal from others.

Most people can't handle the thought of becoming wealthy at the expense of others, so usually the moocher mindset gives rise to self-sabotage instead. If you fall into this pattern, you'll experience a love/hate relationship with money. On the one hand, you may want more money, but on the other hand, you may feel disinclined to make too much, since you know that the more money you get, the more someone else has to pay for it. For example, if you make a living as a professional poker player, then you know that the more you earn, the more money others have to lose…not the best motivation for a highly conscious person to achieve financial abundance.

Some people are able to bypass this problem of financial self-sabotage by lowering their consciousness. They learn to make money without rationally considering the consequences of how they're earning it. They invent justifications to explain their actions while keeping their awareness from getting in the way. Ultimately this is the mindset of criminals.

The more you align yourself with the moocher mindset, the more difficult it will be for you to experience financial abundance *and* remain conscious. Ultimately you have to choose one or the other: be conscious or be wealthy. You can't have both if you subscribe to the moocher mindset. If you find yourself stuck at a certain level of income and unable to go any higher, an underlying moocher mindset is probably the culprit. This is the mindset that leads you to ask, "How can I *get* more money?" instead of, "How can I *contribute* more value?" It's also the mindset that says it's a bad idea to earn more money, since your gain is someone else's pain.

THE CONTRIBUTOR MINDSET

Now let's consider the contributor mindset. This mindset recognizes that the best way to make money is to provide fair value in exchange. Create genuine social value, and receive payment commensurate with that value. Due to market inefficiencies, sometimes you'll be underpaid, and sometimes you'll be overpaid, but the basic idea is that you earn money by contributing.

If you want to earn income as a contributor, you must contribute *social value*, not personal value. Many would-be contributors get stuck on this concept. Personal value is whatever you say it is—you're free to decide what has value to you personally, and it doesn't matter if no one agrees with you. Social value, however, is assigned by social consensus. If you believe your work has tremendous value, but virtually no one else does, then your work has high personal value but little or no social value. Here's the key point: **your income depends on the social value of your work, not the personal value.**

If you want to generate income from creative work, then your work *must* have social value. There's no getting around that. No social value, no income. If your skills and hard work are not in alignment with the creation of social value, then you will not be able to generate income as a contributor.

This isn't an unfair system—it's just how the monetary system works. Since money is a social resource backed by social value, it makes sense that you won't get paid much for providing something of little or no social value. The saying "Find a need and fill it" certainly rings true, assuming we're referring to a social need or desire.

This web site, for example, has a fair degree of social value. Whether you or I value it as individuals is financially irrelevant. It suc-

26

cessfully generates income because the overall social consensus is that this site has a certain level of value. And that social value makes it possible for the site to generate income. If there was no social value to this site, there would be no income potential.

Another name for the contributor mindset is the *abundance mindset*. This mindset says that wealth can be created from ideas and action. Your gain is a reflection of the social gain you've contributed. If you want to earn a high income, you must contribute a lot of social value. The more social value you create, the more money you can earn. This is a win-win mindset because you're putting value into the system for the benefit of others.

Under the contributor mindset, you receive money as payment for your social service. The money you earn is society's way of saying, "In exchange for your valued contribution, you are hereby granted the right to extract $X of value from society at a time of your choosing." This is a beautiful thing!

The only real limit on your income is how much social value you can create. If you want to earn more money, then develop your skills and talents to facilitate the creation of lots of social value. The best way to increase your income is to figure out how to deliver more social value. Focus on giving, and the getting will largely take care of itself. The systems to reward social service are already in place, so all you need to do is plug your service into the existing marketplace.

Generating income from social contribution is a very positive experience. Consequently, it won't lower your consciousness like the moocher mindset. With the contributor mindset, wealth and consciousness are not in conflict. In fact, they synergize extremely well, especially if you reinvest some of your income into expanding your contribution.

If you adopt the contributor mindset, just be aware that members of the moocher mindset will sometimes mistakenly count you among them. As you work to increase your social contribution and thereby earn a higher income, moochers will project their values onto you, concluding you've become greedy and must be taking advantage of others for personal gain. Don't let moochers dissuade you from your path though. Let your inspiration come from the desire to provide even more social value. It would be less honorable to withhold your value just because others misinterpret your motives.

PRO BONO CONTRIBUTION

Under the contributor model, you always have the option of making a contribution pro bono (i.e. for free). You don't have to receive the full social value for your work if you don't want to.

I like having this option because it means I can make my work accessible even to those who can't afford it. This web site represents a tremendous personal investment of time and energy, so it certainly isn't free from my point of view. But because I can leverage technology to keep my costs low, it's practical for me to provide abundant content without requiring an access fee for every visitor. Paying for the value received is entirely optional and is left to each individual visitor to decide for themselves.

Money is social credit, so when you decline to receive money for your work, you decline the social credit you've earned. While it's perfectly fine to decline the social credit you've earned, be sure to consider what you could do with that social credit if you choose to receive it. Could you re-invest it to make a bigger or better contribution? If so, then paid work makes more sense than pro bono work, since you can use the money to expand your mission and serve even more people. Money makes you more of who you already are, so if you're already a contributor, more money can allow you to expand your contribution.

You can also aim for a nice balance between paid work and pro bono work. It doesn't have to be either-or.

MAKING MONEY CONSCIOUSLY

Contributing social value is the primary strategy for making money consciously, but by itself it's still not enough. The problem with social value is that your personal values won't perfectly align with the social consensus. I'm sure that if everyone on earth were like you, the demand for certain products and services would shift dramatically. For example, if everyone were like me, fresh fruits and vegetables would have even higher social value, while factory farming would have none whatsoever.

When you attempt to provide social value without achieving congruence with your personal values, your motivation will be very weak. You won't be inspired because you'll be doing what you feel you should do, but not what you want to do. I often see this happen with people who jump into blogging on a topic they think will make them a lot of money, only to give up after a few months because they can't stomach it any longer. Please don't do this to yourself.

Alternatively, when you attempt to satisfy your personal values without providing any real social value, you get the starving artist syndrome. You may be inspired by work that totally fulfills you, but it won't pay the bills. Please don't do this to yourself either.

The solution is to find an area of overlap between your personal values and social values, and work within that area of overlap. This will allow you to do what you love and create something that others value as well. Don't force yourself to choose between your integrity and your income—choose both!

Social values and your personal values will fluctuate over time, so be prepared to adapt. In my early 20s, I launched my computer games business. At first it aligned perfectly with my personal values but not with social values—I loved the work, but I wasn't making any money. After several years I reached a point of balance, where I was enjoyed the work and making a nice living from it. Further down the road, my personal values changed, and the work no longer inspired me, even though it still had social value. So at that point, I opted to change careers and started this personal development business.

Personal development is a field which has high social value, and it also aligns beautifully with my personal values. Consequently, I can generate substantial income in this field and be very fulfilled at the same time. Don't underestimate the importance of alignment between personal value and social value. Both are essential if you want to make money consciously.

Unless you're really inflexible, it shouldn't be exceedingly difficult to envision a way for you to contribute social value that also aligns with your personal values. This is a problem that can be solved if you put some thought into it. For most people the more difficult challenge is how to transition.

For that I'll refer you to the article *The Meaning of Life Transitioning* (http://www.stevepavlina.com/blog/2005/06/the-meaning-of-life-transitioning/)

CONGRUENT CONTRIBUTION

Two simple realizations can help you achieve a congruent mindset about money and push beyond limiting financial beliefs. First, you must consciously adopt the contributor mindset and abandon the moocher mindset. And secondly, you must find a way to contribute social value while achieving alignment with your personal values. Once you've internalized those two mindsets, you'll be in a position to generate abundant income while serving the greater good.

If you want to generate income without lowering your consciousness, you have to get your limiting beliefs out of your way. Holding yourself back from earning more money doesn't serve anyone. Limiting your income only limits your contribution. The conscious reason to earn more money is that you can put those social credits to good use. Use them to expand your service to others. If you're living an honorable life, then it's a good thing for you to receive more money. You'll be a good custodian for it. The more money that flows through your life, the more resources you can invest into your life purpose.

3.
Living Paycheck to Paycheck

One of the traps people fall into, especially during an economic recession, is the trap of living paycheck to paycheck. You can't afford to switch jobs or get laid off because you're just barely making enough to squeak by.

Erin and I were in a situation like this about 10 years ago. We would sometimes end the month with less than $100 total. This was actually a big improvement over the situation we were in before that, at least we were no longer descending into debt.

To reduce our expenses, we moved into a cheaper apartment, not that we had a choice—we'd just gotten booted from our previous apartment after getting behind on our rent.

Unfortunately the new apartment was on a semi-busy street, and the traffic noise sometimes made it hard to sleep at night. The worst was when people would pull up to the curb outside our window at 1am with their car radios booming.

Technically since we were both self-employed, this wasn't quite a paycheck-to-paycheck situation, but it had the same effect. We were both working hard. We just weren't making much money...only enough to cover our basic expenses but not enough to build any safety net.

I remember feeling a bit stressed during that time. If anything bad happened, like if our car broke down and needed repairs, we were in bad shape.

We eventually got out of that situation and left it behind, not so much by taking certain actions but by shifting to a different mindset.

Here are some suggestions based on what we learned back then for others who struggle with similar financial challenges.

TAKE RESPONSIBILITY

The first step is to assume full responsibility for your current financial situation. It doesn't matter if someone screwed you, if an act of God put you there, or if you had a shoddy education that disadvantaged you. Sure those factors may have had a say in where you ended up, but it can't help you to dwell on them.

I got screwed over in some bad business deals, but as long as I focused on those past problems, I couldn't move forward. I had to let all of that go and forgive everyone and everything first.

You must assume 100% responsibility for your financial life. This doesn't mean 85% responsibility or even 99% responsibility. If you're going to improve your situation, you have to put the full burden of doing so squarely on your own shoulders. First and foremost, you must hold yourself responsible.

Even if you share your finances with someone else, you still have to claim 100% responsibility for your situation. There's no splitting responsibility 50-50. Responsibility is atomic. It's indivisible. You can multiply it, but you can't cut it into pieces. Either you have it, or you don't.

Think about that for a moment. If you put a fraction of the responsibility for your situation onto someone else, you're taking it off yourself. That's going to work against you down the road when you use it as an excuse to slack off in a moment of weakness. If you try to lay responsibility for your situation on anyone else, you're being irresponsible. It's all or nothing.

I can't emphasize this point strongly enough. I know the idea of assuming responsibility may sound a bit cliché at first, but seriously this is where the vast majority of people will fail. They'll claim 80% responsibility and figure that's enough. It isn't—not remotely. Get it in your mind right now that 80% is the same as 0% when it comes to responsibility. You can't allow yourself the "out" of blaming the world, the economy, your spouse's failings, or some other factor for their inability to get better results.

Responsibility isn't about blaming yourself or looking to the past. It's about taking control over your situation. It's about realizing that you always possess response-ability—the ability to choose your response.

It's about accepting the truth that if anything is going to change, your will must be the force that changes it.

Without 100% responsibility you are utterly powerless. If you want things to change, you have to step into your power fully and completely. And you can't do that if you remain in denial of even a smidgeon of your responsibility.

I'm not suggesting you can control every circumstance. I'm simply saying that you always have the ability to respond. Sometimes your responses may be limited or ineffective, but you still have the power to respond at all times.

I don't care if you're a housewife who relies on your husband for 100% of your family's income. If you want to change your financial situation, then the responsibility for making it happen is 100% your own—not your husband's. You aren't some weak and powerless being. You're a creative person. Never, ever put the blame on your spouse for not holding up his/her end of what you believe to be your financial bargain. If you don't like the situation you're in, then *you* change it. That may take the form of influencing your spouse to make some changes, or it may mean generating some income on your own. Either way, it's your will that must fuel this change.

Put yourself in the state of accepting that if your situation is to change at all, then it's all on you, or it will never happen.

CUT EXPENSES, BUT DON'T OVERDO IT

People who get themselves into a financial tight spot often focus on trying to cut their expenses. This only makes sense up to a point. I've seen a lot of people overdo it, which is a completely inept strategy.

If you've been living high on the hog, you may benefit from a round or two of cost cutting. Go ahead and eliminate the fluff. Perhaps you don't need designer clothes or cable TV. One thing I did was to cancel all magazine subscriptions, and I also started checking out self-help products (books, audio programs, DVDs) from the local library instead of buying them. These were reasonable cuts at the time.

Unreasonable cuts are when you start reducing your quality of life, thereby trapping yourself in a scarcity mindset. If you genuinely desire to live a minimalist lifestyle, that's fine, but don't delude yourself into claiming that minimalism is your choice if it isn't really what you want.

If you'd prefer a more abundant lifestyle, be honest and admit that to yourself. Never pretend to want something else just because you think you can't have what you really want.

How can you tell the difference between reasonable and unreasonable cuts? Reasonable cuts make you feel better: *Ahhh…nice to know I won't have these stacks of magazines and newspapers piling up anymore.* Unreasonable cuts make you feel worse: *Some people say being car-free is liberating, but I really hate riding the bus just to buy groceries.*

I know people that will spend two hours going out of their way just to save $5. That's lame. You could surely earn more than $2.50 per hour panhandling on a busy street. Don't waste your time just to save a few measly dollars. If you start doing things that would pay less than minimum wage (in terms of how much money you'll save relative to the time you invest) or if you're cutting your food budget to the point where you can only afford rice and beans, you're going too far.

Cut costs to give yourself some breathing room when possible, but don't set yourself up for long-term destitution by eliminating those things from your life that make you more effective, such as your kitchen appliances, your vehicle, and healthy food.

Take note that expenses are recurring items. When you cut expenses, you introduce long-term savings. This does not mean selling your assets to raise extra cash. Selling assets won't cut your expenses, unless you do something like selling your video game system to end your habit of buying new video games. It's fine if you want to cuddle eBay to raise extra cash by getting rid of stuff you really don't need— Erin and I had a couple garage sales—but raising extra cash won't necessarily help your ongoing cash flow situation. Unload the junk, but keep the stuff you still use.

Don't spend an excessive amount of time fussing over your expenses. It's not worth it. Some people really go nuts here. They buy the cheapest items they can find, and everything breaks. Going too cheap often ends up being more expensive in the long run.

You're going to run into a hard limit on the expense side because the best you can possibly do is to get your expenses down to zero, and for most people that's totally unrealistic and would create serious hardship. Think realistically about how much more you can actually save. There's no point in fussing over an amount you could earn in a few hours with a lemonade stand.

It's a lot easier in the long run to increase your income instead of cutting your expenses to the bone. You don't have hard limits on the income side. For all practical purposes, the sky is the limit.

Make reasonable cuts in your expenses, but don't go crazy. If you want things to improve, you'll be devoting most of your time and energy to the income side.

DECIDE YOU DESERVE BETTER

People essentially earn what they believe they deserve to earn. The main reason you aren't earning more is because you know you don't deserve it.

This is a tough thing to accept. Chances are your ego will very much dislike this idea. You may already be coming up with arguments to explain why this isn't true. Take a deep breath, and set them aside for the moment.

Take whatever hourly figure you're earning right now. Multiply it by 10. Then imagine yourself earning that much right now. Chances are it feels uncomfortable—maybe a bit scary, stressful, improbable, complicated, overly exciting, or just too "out there" for you to accept it as real. And that's precisely why you aren't earning that much. You're making that figure into way too big a deal.

The people who are earning 10x as much as you are don't think about that figure the same way you do. It just feels normal and natural to them. It's not a big deal at all. One reason you aren't there yet is that it's still a big deal to you. If you want to get there eventually, you must reach the point in your mind where that level of income is no longer a big deal. It's okay if it's mildly exciting, but it shouldn't seem so incredible that you can't accept it as real.

When I first met Erin about 15 years ago, she was earning $9 an hour doing secretarial work—filing, typing, and stuff like that. That's what she felt she deserved to earn. That felt normal and reasonable to her. You can see how much she earns today by looking at her intuitive reading prices. Suffice it to say that her rates are about 100x higher. She now earns in one hour what it used to take her almost three weeks to earn. And yes, her clients actually pay these rates and are happy to do so.

What's interesting is how people react to Erin's rates. Some people look at her rates and write to her, "I was interested in booking a reading, but when I looked at your rates, I thought, 'Whoa—no way I can afford that.'" Those people aren't a match for Erin's service; they can't afford it. They can't even imagine how Erin can charge that much. However, they can still be a match for reading Erin's blog, which is completely free.

But then there are Erin's actual clients. Those people simply go to her order form and book a reading—no complaining or attempting to get a price reduction. To them it's no big deal. They may have consulted with other psychics in the past and got great results from it. They may be used to these kinds of consultation rates. For the actual clients she serves, Erin's rates are normal and reasonable.

In order for Erin to earn these higher rates, she had to go through a mental process of giving herself permission to earn that much. One thing that helped was to realize that other top psychics in her field were earning sums around this level. She watched and learned from them, and she soon realized she was at least as good as they were for doing certain types of readings. But until she went through this mental process, it freaked her out to charge anything for a reading. She had a hard time getting into the headspace of giving herself permission to receive a certain level of compensation in exchange for the value she was providing.

I wouldn't call this a process of *justifying* higher incomes to yourself. It has more to do with giving yourself permission. You aren't trying to give yourself a sales pitch here. You're simply deciding that you want to earn more, and you're finding a way to accept that it's okay to do so.

When you raise your rates, you may price yourself out of one market, but you'll price yourself into another market. For example, Erin's clients don't want a $15 psychic reading. They wouldn't trust someone who only charged $15—they'd assume she was no good. They want a reliable, accurate reading they can trust. Erin's rates demonstrate that her work is pre-approved by the marketplace. Consequently, a reading with her is a lot less risky. Also, since Erin is attracting higher-income clients than when she first started, she now has more leverage to do good. If she can help a successful entrepreneur clarify his life purpose, that typically has a much greater rippling impact than helping a student decide where to go for summer vacation. The point is that you shouldn't feel that by raising your rates, you're providing less of a service. It's more likely the opposite is true.

Sometimes the process you go through to give yourself permission will be fairly elaborate. It can cause a lot of rippling changes in your life. You may feel you need to take some kind of action just to reach the point where you feel you deserve to be paid more.

When I wanted to go from earning four figures a month to five figures a month, I tried to imagine myself as a five-figure-a-month guy. This was back when I was running my computer games business. The problem was that I didn't feel I was providing a valuable enough service to deserve that level of income. I could only give myself permission by agreeing to increase my service. So I found a way to release more games in a shorter period of time, and shortly thereafter I reached my goal. It's important to understand that this process began with giving myself permission to earn that much. I told myself it was okay, and only after that did I permit myself to make the changes necessary to manifest it.

Thinking we don't deserve more than we're getting is a very common stumbling block. It's so common we don't even notice it most of the time. We just think it's normal to earn what we're earning right now. But it's only our thinking that makes it seem normal. Someone else would consider your current income a pathetic sum for the work you're doing. Can you accept that you're being grossly underpaid right now?

A speaker friend of mine got paid $75 for his first paid professional speech. When he was asked for his rates, that's the price he quoted. He thought that was a lot for an hour's work on the stage. He soon learned that pro speakers get paid a lot more than this, and he discovered that he could have asked for $1000 for that speech, and it would have been fine with the people who hired him because their budget was higher still. Last time I checked, his fees are now around $7500 per speech. But each time he raised his rates, when someone asked what his speaking fee was, it was hard for him to get the words out without choking.

Erin has the same issue with raising her rates. She never wants to raise them—I'm always the one to push her to do so. (So yes, I'm the one to blame if you can no longer afford her.) She's too close to the situation to realize how good she is and how much value she provides. Every time I suggest a price increase, she panics at first. She'll say something like, "But nobody will be able to afford me. How can I possibly charge that much?" We've been through this a half-dozen times now, and she still has the same reaction. If she never raised her rates, she'd probably have a five-year waiting list by now. Or she'd have to stop doing private readings completely like many other top psychics have done.

The point here is that it can be helpful to get a second opinion. Hang out with people who think you deserve more, and find out why they feel that way. I've been fortunate to have friends in my life who pointed out to me what I should be earning and why I was being grossly underpaid. This helped me step up my income at different times.

When I first started working as a game programming contractor, I charged only $10 per hour. I was still in college at the time, so in my mind I was "just a student" and didn't deserve anywhere close to full pay. But it turned out that I was really good at the work I was doing. Fortunately, the client company for which I was working voluntarily doubled my rate, and combined with the royalties from sales I received, I ended up earning closer to $50. You know you're charging too little as a contractor when your client offers to double your rate on your behalf...perhaps because they just can't stomach paying so little for quality work.

On the other hand, when I got into pro speaking, I earned several thousand dollars for my first paid speech. I didn't have to start at the bottom rung income-wise because I'd already given myself permission to earn that much. It wasn't a big deal to me—I allowed it to feel normal. Actually, it felt a little low compared to what I was already earning from blogging.

Top speakers get paid $20,000 per speech easy. Multiply that by 10 if you're an ex-President, by 15 if you're Bill Cosby. Do you think it's a big deal for Bill Clinton to earn six figures for a single speech? Do you think he freaks out about how much money he's making? Of course not. You and I might freak out about earning that much, but for him it's routine.

I happen to think it's a lot of fun to gradually raise my financial vibration. I like to go up a level, settle in for a while and fully experience it, and then work on going up the next level. I don't regret those times when I could barely afford a meal at Taco Bell. Even back then I considered my financial life as a challenging adventure. When Erin and I first moved in together, a luxury expense was to rent a movie for 99 cent, and maybe some cheap Two-for-One pizza. We used to balk about why anyone would pay $4 to rent a movie at Blockbuster. These days a luxury expense might be a fun trip, a show on the Vegas Strip, or a relaxing day at the spa. Somewhere down the road, we might step it up again. Every level is fun to experience.

At this point your attitude may be something like, "Yeah, yeah... give myself permission. Whatever. Alright, I give myself permission to earn more. Next." If that's all the effort you're going to put into this step, you can stop reading right now and give up. If you do this step correctly, it can seriously take weeks. It takes time to work through financial blocks and to give yourself full permission to step it up without clinging to excuses for holding back.

I recommend using a journal to work through this process. Start by listing why you believe you're not earning the amount of money you'd like. Put all your excuses down in writing. Ask yourself what it would take to let go of those limiting beliefs. Are they really true? Are other people earning more even with those same stumbling blocks? Are you turning minor challenges into full-blown excuses? Ask yourself if you're ready to experience a higher level of financial abundance. Do whatever you need to do to put yourself in a state of readiness. If you work through this mentally, it will help you get there emotionally.

Ultimately, giving yourself permission is nothing but a choice to make. You don't actually need to satisfy tons of prerequisites to step up to a new financial level. But if you've already locked those prerequisites into your mind, then you will have to work through them in some fashion. Sometimes it's easier to satisfy the beliefs you've already installed as opposed to uprooting and replacing them. It's up to you to decide which beliefs are helping to sculpt you into a better person, and which ones are merely getting in your way and holding you back.

DROP THE SOCIAL DEAD WEIGHT

You probably have people in your life who've become rather attached to your financial status quo. This doesn't mean they're financially dependent on you. It just means they've gotten comfortable with where you are now—and they'd become uncomfortable if you were to make some big changes.

If you boost your finances, other people in your life may feel they're being left behind. Be prepared for this. It happens.

Can you identify anyone in your life right now who'd have a problem if you doubled or tripled your income? If so, you'd better deal with that up front. Either talk it through, or decide to part ways. Otherwise this person may (perhaps inadvertently) try to sabotage your financial increase, often by making negative comments that make you feel bad for earning more money.

I assure you there are plenty of people on the other side who will be happy and excited to see you improving your finances. This is especially true among entrepreneurs, but it really depends on the field you're in. I have some friends that are very encouraging when I talk about boosting my income, but I have other friends that would feel threatened or intimidated. The difference has little to do with how much money these people are making—it has to do with their attitude toward financial increase in their own lives. Those who are encouraging invariably have a positive outlook for the future. Those who are discouraging are dissatisfied with their own financial situation.

One of the best things you can do is to make friends with people who have a positive financial outlook. It doesn't matter how much they're earning right now. It could be 10x more or less than you. Look for people who assume 100% responsibility for their finances—people who don't blame others for their setbacks. Such people make good long-term friends because they won't freak out every time you boost your income.

Again, entrepreneurs are generally a good bet here. Commissioned salespeople are another good choice. And investors (any kind) are good too. Long-term employees (salaried or hourly) usually don't have anywhere near the same level of financial enthusiasm as these other groups. That's why they're willing to trade hours for dollars and donate most of the results they generate to someone else, such as an entrepreneur, salesperson, or investor. Employees are certainly generous, but usually dumb as stumps (http://www.stevepavlina.com/blog/2006/07/10-reasons-you-should-never-get-a-job/) with their financial lives. :)

INCREASE YOUR SERVICE

Money is a medium for exchanging value. If you want more money, you can create more value and/or deliver your value to more people.

One of the best ways to improve your service is by putting it into a permanent form. This way you can provide value even when you aren't physically present.

For example, if you recite a poem to a group of 20 people, you may deliver some value to those 20 people. But that's a one-time event. Every day you're starting over from scratch. This is the approach that most employees use. They don't build anything that they retain ownership of. Instead, they merely trade hours for dollars, so someone else ends up owning what they helped to build—and thereby reaps all the long-term benefits of ownership. Again, this is very generous of employees, but very unwise if you wish to get ahead financially.

Historically speaking, wealthy people have done a pretty good job convincing the masses that getting a job is the way to go. This is nothing but brainwashing though. If you get a job, you can't complain about the wealthy growing wealthier because you're helping them do it. You're doing the work of building and running systems that someone else owns and controls. How does that help you in the long run? All you're doing is tending to your master's plantation. If you dread going to work each day and have a hard time motivating yourself, perhaps you should stop volunteering for slave labor.

Whenever I make statements like this, somebody will say, "But we have to have jobs and employees. Otherwise who would pick up the garbage?" That's the same thing as saying, "But we need to have slaves. Otherwise who will harvest the tobacco?" Is that reason enough to serve as a slave? Perhaps we can come up with better solutions if people stop submitting to slavery. Maybe we don't need to generate so much garbage (and tobacco) in the first place. Personally I would rather trade value with free people than with employees/slaves.

Going back to the poetry example, now consider the poet who puts his/her poem down in writing and then publishes it, perhaps on a website somewhere. Now the poem can provide value even in the absence of the poet. The poem may be enjoyed by thousands instead of just the original 20. This is how an intelligent entrepreneur thinks. Instead of trading hours for dollars, the idea is to invest your time building something that will provide enduring value, even when you aren't physically present.

If you can provide passive value, you can generate passive income. For example, the poet could sell a collection of poetry, license his poems to a greeting card company in exchange for royalties, or set up a "poem of the day" subscription service and sell advertising.

If you're currently an employee, the word "entrepreneur" may sound complicated and scary. But it's really not a big deal to generate income from self-employment if you give yourself permission. Even high school students are generating income this way.

I recommend that you don't start out by thinking about passive income. That's putting the cart before the horse. Focus on creating and delivering passive value first. Create something, put it into a permanent form, and get it into people's hands. Start small. Write an article. Write a recipe. Compose a song. Then share it as widely as you can. Then repeat over and over.

I began to understand the benefit of providing passive value when I was in high school. During my junior and senior years, I started writing some computer programs in BASIC and Turbo Pascal to explore what I was learning in my math classes—probabilities, synthetic division, polar graphs, etc. I also wrote programs for the Casio FX-7000G and FX-8000G programmable calculators, which many students in my school owned at the time. Most of these were very short programs, usually less than 20 lines of code. (Incidentally, I still have my FX-8000G today, and I occasionally write quick programs for it. Even 20 years later, it still runs great. One of Casio's best products ever.)

To help other students with their math homework, I began making copies of these programs and passing them out at the math club. Then I noticed people outside the math club had gotten copies. I wrote a few simple games and shared those as well. Eventually one of my programs was published in the school newspaper.

How did this help me? Well, it gave me a very positive reputation in my school, among both teachers and students. I went to a Jesuit high school where academic aptitude was well-respected. When it came time for me to seek letters of recommendation for my college applications, I had a very easy time of it. I stood out from the crowd because I did something way beyond what most students did. Consequently, I got acceptance letters from some competitive schools like UCLA, UC Berkeley, Carnegie Mellon, and Cal Tech. But the truth is that I wrote those programs just because I enjoyed creating and sharing them, not because I was trying to get something out of it. Focus on the giving side, and the getting takes care of itself.

If you're currently struggling with your finances, I know you'll be tempted to focus on the money side first, but I implore you not to do that. Put your attention on the side of creating and sharing. You must give before you get.

Share something you enjoy creating. Put it onto some kind of tangible media, and pass it around.

I know of many successful software businesses that started because some guy wrote a cool program and shared it with his friends. Then his friends shared it with others. Pretty soon, he started getting support requests from total strangers and had to start charging for the program. This is basically how shareware was born. Put something out there for free, and see how far it goes. If people like it, they'll share it.

People have opened restaurants the same way. They started sharing their recipes with friends, and eventually they're encouraged to open a restaurant and share their food with a lot more people.

It really is this simple. Don't overcomplicate it.

I like writing articles, so that's something I choose to share. When I started this website about 4-1/2 years ago, I only earned $167 total during the first six months. Why? I was focused on sharing value, not on making money. Eventually people started giving me all sorts of ideas to monetize my work. I also reached the point where I had to turn it into a viable business because it was taking up more time and energy and becoming more popular. Eighteen months later, the site was earning more than $40,000 in a month. So again, don't worry about the income side. If you get the value side right, the income side will typically take care of itself. It's really not that difficult to generate a decent income if you can provide a lot of value at low cost. So focus, focus, focus on the value side. The simple truth is that most people who are struggling financially just aren't creating and delivering much value. Maybe you can convince people to pay you for nothing, but that isn't an approach I feel good about.

Putting your work into a permanent form is very important. If you don't do this, you'll have to keep recreating your value over and over.

That takes you back to the employee mindset. Even if you're technically self-employed, you'll merely be creating a job for yourself.

BUILD YOUR OWN DISTRIBUTION NETWORK

Some of my friends who are pro speakers earn a lot for every speech they give, but they have to constantly market themselves, travel, and customize presentations for different audiences. Many of them love speaking, but being on the road 150-200 days per year takes its toll after a while.

I work in the same general field as many of these speakers do, but instead of giving a speech to a limited number of people, I put my work online, so it's always accessible. Even my friends who have products to sell will see their income drop when they aren't speaking frequently, but I can maintain my income pretty well on just a few hours per week—no travel required.

Note that these friends do have products to sell. They record their speeches and workshops and create CDs and DVDs. The problem is that they never took the time to build a network to sell a decent volume of products when they aren't speaking. Most of them have websites with low traffic and newsletters with few subscribers. So they have to keep pounding the pavement to stay afloat—if they stop speaking, they start hurting financially.

If you want to escape the rat race, it's a good idea to build your own distribution network. My favorite way to do this is to give away value for free. People love free—if it's good quality free.

Building a good distribution network isn't that hard these days. I think the best way to do it is by building a website because online solutions are very cheap compared to the alternatives. My speaker friends have to fly all around the world to distribute their value. I just click "Publish."

SHIFT YOUR MINDSET

In order to move beyond living paycheck to paycheck, you have to shift your mindset first. If you get your mind right, the right actions will follow. If you remain stuck in the wrong mindset, it doesn't matter how hard you try to escape—you'll just stay locked in the same cage. You might even make things worse.

What helped me most was realizing that I'm not doing anyone much good by holding myself back financially. How does limiting my income actually help anyone? All it does is make it harder for me to create and share value. It kills my ability to serve others. I'm certainly able to help a lot more people today than I did when I was just scraping by. I can share from a place of abundance instead of scarcity.

Kahlil Gibran wrote, "If you grudge the crushing of the grapes, your grudge distills a poison in the wine."

If you resent the work you're doing or the situation you're in, you're poisoning the outcome. You may actually be doing more harm than good. If you're just scraping by and feeling poorly about it, you're probably not doing the noblest of work anyway. It's not like the world needs you to be broke.

The only person who can step it up is you. Do you want to keep living at your current level, or are you ready to level up?

4.
Mental Blocks to Making Money

The essence of successful income generation is value creation. If you want to earn income, you must provide something that matters enough to someone else that they'll pay you for it. The act of providing value may be direct, such as selling a useful product or service, or it may be indirect, such as providing a free service and monetizing it via other means. But in either case the core activity is to create and deliver value to others.

The notion that you generate income by trading value is a simple concept, but it's amazing how many people still don't get it. Here are a couple examples of incorrect thinking about income generation that seem to trip up a lot of people:

MISTAKE #1: MEDITATING AS AN ATTEMPT TO GENERATE INCOME

Every week I receive emails like the following:

"I don't understand it. Every day I am meditating, writing down my goals, visualizing what I want, and focusing on attracting abundance. But I'm still not making enough money to cover my expenses. In fact, I'm sinking deeper into debt each month. I write in my journal. I pray. I read. But nothing is working. I'm at my wits' end. What am I doing wrong?"

It's great to be working through your inner blocks. I don't want to suggest that kind of work isn't important. But inner work by itself is NOT an income-generating activity. How are those actions providing value to others such that they'll gladly pay you in exchange? Journaling and meditation may have tremendous value for you personally, and I highly recommend you do them, but understand that they do virtually nothing for others. Don't expect to receive a paycheck for meditating.

You may have done a great job of energetic house-cleaning, but if you want to generate income, that energy needs to flow into some form of value creation and delivery. No value, no money.

It's like you're looking at a fire (a metaphor for your financial problems), and you're running around scrubbing the fire hoses, polishing the nozzles, and setting up a reverse-osmosis filter for the water supply. Meanwhile the fire is continuing to burn, seemingly unimpressed by your elegant fire-suppression system.

Turn on the freakin' water!

Stop cleansing, balancing, and saging your aura, and start directing your energy into the physical reality all around you. If you do this correctly, your physical body will move—a lot! You'll be taking lots and lots of action. You are a part of this world, and it's time to recognize that your physical body is the primary mechanism through which financial abundance will manifest. This is a key block you must still address. Like it or not, if you want a physical result like cash in the bank, you'll have to use physical mechanisms like your voice and your body to get things done. I know it sucks compared to how things work in the astral realms. Such are the vicissitudes of life in the physical plane.

Ultimately, physical abundance will manifest as the reflection of your physical contribution. If you stay home all day playing with your chakras, you won't be contributing much to physical reality. Hence, you'll go broke.

Energetically there are a lot of different "manifestation frequencies" at play here. Some, like those that can cause amazing synchronicities, tend to work in subtle ways and can take a long time to weave their way through the physical plane. You'll probably feel them working long before you see them working. However, here in the physical universe, the fastest and most direct manifestation frequency is plain old physical action. I encourage you to continue experimenting with other frequencies via the Law of Attraction, but if you resist embracing the frequency of physical action (which is the primary, dominant manifestation frequency in the physical realm), you're in for a very long wait to get what you want.

Direct physical action is not the only frequency available to you, just as a car isn't your only choice of transportation. However, there are abundant situations where physical action is the fastest and most direct way to get what you want, just as driving a car is often the fastest and most direct way to get where you want to go. Direct action needn't be the only tool in your bag, but overall it's a pretty darned important one, equivalent to a hammer in a world filled with nails.

A clean aura is certainly helpful, but unfortunately it won't pay your bills.

MISTAKE #2: FOCUSING ON GETTING MONEY INSTEAD OF PROVIDING VALUE

These emails take a variety of different forms, but the basic idea is that the person is trying to create an income stream without much, if any, concern for other human beings. Here's an example of the kind I often receive from fellow bloggers:

"I've put a ton of effort into trying to make money online, but something isn't working. I've posted hundreds of articles on my blog, and I keep adding stuff every week. I've been using good headlines, stuffing articles with intelligent keywords, writing top 10 lists, and more. I've experimented with Adsense ads, text link ads, affiliate programs, and other ways to make money. At first my traffic started growing, but then I hit a plateau. I've really tried to build a following, but I'm barely making any money from it. What am I doing wrong?"

Your problem is simply this: Who the hell cares?

It may not look like it at first glance, but this is essentially the same problem as Mistake #1. You're too wrapped up in your own little world of me, me, me. Where's the value? Articles, content, ads, and affiliate programs are not value. Building a following is not value. These are simply the means—the shell—for providing value.

Too often that shell remains hollow, containing nothing but recycled and rehashed ideas that can readily be found elsewhere. There's no innovation or risk-taking. Hundreds of others are already doing a better job performing essentially the same service you're trying to perform. Your service is comparatively useless. It just isn't needed. You're trying to milk a system instead of using that system to provide real substance.

Recognize that if someone else created what you've created, you'd never patronize them. You don't care about the service you provide any more than your would-be visitors do.

By focusing on trying to get money, you're missing the point. The point is to provide value to others. This means serving people in a way they aren't already being served, in a manner that aligns with your unique creative self-expression. Share what only you can share. Express what only you can express in the way that only you can express it.

Even if your shell game business becomes financially successful for a while, it won't last. If you somehow find a way to make money providing little or no value, you can bet your market will soon be flooded with me-too wannabes. The field will be sliced into tiny little pieces. Meanwhile your spirit will be screaming at you to stop doing what you're doing because it's mind-numbingly boring, regardless of how much money you're able to make from it.

On some level you already sense where this focus will take you. In the long run, trying to get money is a business model from hell. It's ironically more fun to fail at such an attempt than it is to succeed, and failure in this case is a lot healthier for your spirit.

Try to look past your own needs and recognize there's a pretty interesting world around you. Through your actions you can have an impact on it, for better or worse. Think about how you can provide something that people want or need in a way they aren't already being served, something that will make a positive difference. Then act on it.

There are many more mental blocks of course, but these are the two most common I've been seeing in my inbox lately. In both cases the solution is to get out of your head and focus on creating something of value for other people. With a value-driven mindset, you'll be properly centered on the very thoughts and actions that will produce a sustainable income stream.

5.
Money and the Law of Attraction

How much money is a large sum? It was really interesting to see the full spectrum of reactions in offering formal coaching and consultations services. I expected this would be a polarizing topic for some people, so the reactions weren't surprising.

The essence of that article was that if I move forward with coaching and consulting, I intend to start at $500 per hour with a one hour minimum. On the one hand, some people said it was a mistake to charge $500 per hour because that price was way too high and would make it impossible for most people to afford, so it was an elitist and/or greedy price point.

On the other hand, several people cautioned me that it was a mistake to charge $500 per hour because I'd be quickly overwhelmed. They questioned my reasons for going so low. A few said they were eager to take advantage of such a bargain and that they knew others who'd be interested too. However, the undertone was that this wouldn't be a practical price point in the long run and that for my own good, I'd have to raise the price quickly.

The first form of feedback came mainly via the forums; the second was mostly via my private contact form. This didn't surprise me. The forums tend to attract a younger audience (since younger people are more comfortable using forums and tend to have more time for them), and younger people are more likely to fall into the "$500 is a huge sum" group.

What's interesting is that this feedback has little to do with the actual price. I'd have gotten the same feedback if I'd said the price was $50 or $1500. The volume of feedback on each side would shift, but there'd still be people on both sides.

Is $500 a large or small amount? It depends on your perspective. If you're in a scarcity mindset, it might seem like a huge sum. If you have a wealthy mindset, it may be a tiny amount. That may be hard to believe, but it's true.

I used to think $500 was a lot of money. It certainly seemed so when I would end a month with less than $100 total. If I gained or lost an extra $500, it could make a difference in my finances for months to come. An extra $500 was a significant amount of money.

But after shifting my mindset about money to invite more abundance into my life, $500 began to seem like a tiny amount. Five hundred dollars represents the cash I might carry in my wallet. If I gain or lose $500, it makes no real difference in my finances. Five hundred dollars is a fairly insignificant amount.

Once I got my mindset to this point (which I did mostly by imagining what it would feel like to be there in reality), it wasn't long before my reality began to reflect it. I became a "vibrational match" for earning larger sums. At one point having more than $100,000 in the bank would have seemed rich or wealthy. But now it just feels normal, *like duh, I'm supposed to have that much cash all the time.*

SOME EXAMPLES OF FINANCIAL RELATIVITY

Here are some examples to help shed more light on the concept of financial relativity.

A REALTOR THINKS HAVING $50,000 CASH IS NORMAL

Shortly after Erin and I first moved to Las Vegas in 2004, we were chatting with a local realtor who said she liked to keep at least $50,000 cash on hand at all times (not for investment, just for her personal money). Erin and I gave each other a quizzical look. We thought she must be very snooty or elitist to feel that way. Why would anyone need that much cash?

Eventually we realized that our reaction to her statement was precisely why we could never save up $50,000 in cash. We were pushing it away from us by assuming it was too much money to hold onto. Having $5,000 cash was about normal for us; $10,000 meant we were doing incredibly well.

I realized these figures were arbitrary as far as the universe is concerned, so we should be able to raise them at will. I began imagining having $50,000 cash AND considering it normal to have that much. The second part is really critical. In order to become the kind of person who could have $50,000 cash in the bank, it had to feel just plain normal to me, not fantastic or incredible. So I actually visualized seeing this sum on my bank statement and reacting with a ho hum, excitement-free response.

This might sound counter-intuitive at first, but it worked. We were able to have $50,000 cash only when we began to see it as a normal amount to have in the bank instead of a windfall.

Today if I were to have *only* $50,000 cash on hand, I'd feel some financial pressure to raise it back up again.

Now if your reaction to my saying this is similar to how Erin and I initially reacted to that realtor (something like, "Steve, you've become a greedy, elitist bastard!"), it's safe to say you're keeping yourself out of resonance to having such sums of money yourself. The big question is: Why are you doing this to yourself? Why not invite larger sums into your life instead of pushing them away? Are you suffering from low self-esteem or something?

Keep in mind that other people may be equally shocked by *your* opulent lifestyle even if you think it's a normal (not wealthy or excessive) place to be. There's a good chance you're a lot wealthier than most people on this planet. What may feel normal to you could be a windfall for someone else. Who are you to be able to eat whenever you're hungry or to have access to medical care when you need it? Do the expectations of others make you want to live below your potential to satisfy them? Or would you rather help those people raise their standard of living to at least the level you consider normal?

A POKER PLAYER THINKS $60,000 CASH IS NOTHING

A few years ago when I was studying poker (just for fun), I watched a poker tournament on TV where Daniel Negreanu (one of the "winningest" players on earth) got knocked out of the final table. His prize money was $60,000. The top prize for first place was probably around $1 million. In the exit interview, he was asked what he was going to do with all the money he won. He chuckled with surprise, as if to say, "Money? What money? I lost the tournament." Then he said something like, "I dunno. $60,000? What can I do with that? Buy a car maybe?

[sigh]." He clearly had the attitude that $60,000 was a small, almost negligible amount of money. It wasn't a serious sum.

It was as if the interviewer had said, "Daniel, you just won a dollar! What are you going to do with it?" And Daniel replied jokingly, "I dunno... buy a soda maybe? [sigh]."

While some people might see Negreanu's attitude as haughty, arrogant, or elitist, I think it's a reflection of a wealthy mindset. This may help explain why his tournament poker winnings exceed $10 million to date. Since $60K represents a small amount to him, he's a vibrational match for earning and holding much larger sums. If $60K was a lot of money to him, he probably wouldn't be able to win even that much, and even if he did win it, he'd have a hard time holding onto it.

Incidentally, Negreanu lives in Las Vegas and has been vegan since 2003. Just had to throw that in.

A BUSINESSMAN THINKS $24,000 IS A FAIR PRICE FOR AN HOUR OF HIS TIME

Earlier this year I spent a few hours talking with a businessman who consults for $24,000 per hour. And yes, people actually pay him that amount. In a short period of time, he can help his clients optimize their businesses in such a way that this is a profitable exchange for them.

If I tell him I'm charging $500 per hour for a consultation, there's a good chance he'll laugh at me, as if I'm suffering from low self-esteem or something.

Is a 30-minute consultation with this man really worth as much as 24 hours of consulting with me? Does he have 48x as much business knowledge, experience, and insight as I do? Of course not. He gets paid this amount because he's a match for receiving it. To him this is normal. For me it would still seem amazing or incredible.

BECOMING A MATCH FOR A MILLION-DOLLAR HOME

Many years ago, Erin and I were on vacation in San Diego. At the time we were basically broke and deep in debt. We were driving around Rancho Santa Fe, a wealthy neighborhood with homes that cost a few million dollars each. As we drove past a real estate office, an idea struck me, and I asked Erin if she wanted to have some fun. She consented.

I walked into the realtor's office and confidently proclaimed that Erin and I were interested in buying a house in Rancho Santa Fe, something in the $2-4 million range. (I knew that was a reasonable price range because Erin and I had checked out the listings taped to the office window before we walked in.) I was probably 25 years old.

A realtor welcomed us and asked us a few questions. I answered honestly that I ran a software company in Los Angeles. Next thing I knew, the realtor was driving us around in her Jaguar, shuttling me and Erin to various homes for sale in the area. Erin and I had a fun time pretending we could actually afford them while trying not to look like total idiots. "Hmmm…that tennis court looks like it will need repaving soon."

At the time I thought this exercise would help us adopt a wealthier mindset. We'd be inspired by all the wealthy homes. But it didn't work at all. We just weren't a match for those kinds of homes. They were too exciting to us. We couldn't imagine living there and having it feel normal. It was too big a leap, too impossible.

Fast forward about 12 years to 2007. Erin and I went shopping for a new house in Las Vegas, this time for real. Our price range was $1-2 million. We paid a little over $300,000 for our previous home, so this was a big step up. But this time when the realtor took us around, it was totally different than when we were looking at homes in Rancho Santa Fe. This time we could actually imagine living there and having it feel normal to us. We were mildly excited but not overwhelmingly so. We looked at many different homes and ended up buying our first choice.

Years ago this house would have seemed amazing or extravagant to us. But now it just feels normal to live here. It actually surprises me when people visit and seem overwhelmed or amazed by it. We certainly enjoy living here, but it isn't amazing or overwhelming to us.

Do you ever buy things for yourself that seem like normal purchases but which other people might consider an extravagant or wasteful luxury? Have you ever bought a cup of coffee or a bottled water? If you buy such items regularly, you probably don't consider them luxuries. They're just normal purchases. But many people would disagree and say you're being incredibly selfish and wasteful. You don't need coffee, and you could just as easily drink tap water. You elitist pig!

My point is to demonstrate that if you think something is out of reach for you, it is. If you think it's normal or expected, it becomes so. Realize that your comfort zone is totally arbitrary though. To many people on earth, getting adequate nutrition is a luxury. To some people, a million-dollar home would be slumming it. You define your own comfort zone.

Imagine having 10x as much cash and income as you have now. Would it make you uncomfortable, at least initially, if you suddenly found yourself there—not in fantasy but in reality? Would you feel awkward, uncertain, unworthy, or anxious? What would it take for you to embrace the mindset that this higher level of abundance is perfectly normal for you?

Just because you've been conditioned to believe a certain level of wealth is normal for you doesn't mean that standard is objectively meaningful. You needn't spend the rest of your life remaining loyal to arbitrary inherited beliefs.

MONEY AND THE LAW OF ATTRACTION

I know it may seem counterintuitive to aim to feel normal instead of excited when it comes to earning more money. The truth is that too much excitement will actually block you from receiving larger sums because that probably isn't how you'd feel if you were actually there.

If you think $X is a large sum, and the amount makes you anxious or excited, you simply won't be able to attract and hold $X. If you really had $X and could hold onto it easily, how would you feel about it? It would seem as normal to you as your current financial equilibrium.

In this case the proper application of the Law of Attraction is actually to dampen—not to magnify—your emotions, such that the new level you want to reach begins to feel normal, expected, and believable. Otherwise you're holding yourself in a state of disbelief. If reaching your goal seems like a miracle or a monstrous windfall, you're actually pushing it away from you. This is true not just with money but with anything else you might wish to attract, including new relationships, career advancement, spiritual development, health gains, etc.

General enthusiasm about your goals is fine, but if you're holding yourself in a state of awe and amazement when you think about them, it's a safe bet you'll never get there.

If you want to enjoy more financial abundance, you must learn to become comfortable with the kinds of changes that currently make you feel uncomfortable.

6.
Making a Financial Turnaround

Have you ever found yourself in a negative financial situation, either broke or deep in debt? Maybe you're in the midst of such a situation right now. In this chapter, I'll share with you some insights on how to successfully recover from a negative financial situation.

ACCEPTANCE

The first step in recovering from a negative financial situation is to fully accept where you are. You'll never solve your problem while in a state of denial. This acceptance process comes in three parts:

First, accept that you're not going to magically transform your financial situation from scarcity to abundance overnight. If you want to solve this problem, the first thing you have to do is respect the magnitude of the challenge, which is on the order of overcoming a major addiction. Maybe it will in fact take you years to recover, so you may as well surrender to that idea now.

Secondly, accept the reality of your present financial situation. I don't think it's necessary to calculate your net worth to the dollar, but at least do a halfway decent assessment of where you stand in terms of income, expenses, assets, and liabilities (debt). Consider what will happen if your situation continues into the future. Is it sustainable, or are you headed towards a crash? If it's the latter, then accept and acknowledge that one way or the other, something must change, either by choice or by force.

Thirdly, accept and acknowledge how you honestly feel about your financial situation. When you're broke or in debt, you know something isn't right. That sinking feeling you get whenever a bill arrives in the mail isn't healthy. When your finances are strong, a bill is nothing but a piece of paper that takes two minutes to process. But when your finances are weak, a bill can be a stressful burden. It's easy to fall into the trap of denying these negative feelings and going into escapist mode. Those feelings of stress and worry are there to tell you it's time to make a change. You need to do something to correct this situation. The way out is through action, not avoidance.

Acceptance basically comes down to admitting to yourself, "This is a bad situation I've gotten myself into, and I accept that it's going to take some serious effort and commitment on my part to turn things around. It won't be easy, but it will be worth it."

GOALS

The next step is to set some goals or intentions for how you'd like to improve your financial situation. Don't worry about the how at this point—just focus on the *what* and the *why*.

I don't think it's realistic for most people to set a goal of going from total scarcity to total abundance. It's too hard to believe, so the intention will just be overridden by fear and self-doubt. Start with a realistic goal such as stabilizing your financial situation at a certain level you feel is reasonably attainable. As your financial situation improves, you can always set new incremental goals.

When I was broke and in debt, I wrote down all kinds of abundance goals. I focused on my ideal financial situation. Very little changed because I couldn't see how it was possible to get there, at least not anytime soon. So I stepped back and set much more reasonable goals, ones I could believe were possible from my current starting point. That was very effective. Big goals are great, but if you can't see how they're even possible, step back and define a milestone that's a little closer to you. This will allow you to use the process of Creative Observation (http://www.stevepavlina.com/blog/2006/08/creative-observation/) to begin seeing your goal as real.

I highly recommend posting your monthly income goal in a place where you'll see it often. Many years ago Erin and I wrote our income goals on pieces of paper and taped them to our apartment walls. By keeping the goals in front of us at all times, we stayed focused on doing what needed to be done.

For some tips on how to set realistic goals, read *The Power of Clarity* (http://www.stevepavlina.com/articles/power-of-clarity.htm).

PLANS

Before you jump into the planning phase, let your goal/intention incubate for a few days. This is especially important if you're not sure how you'll achieve your goal. Goals and intentions can be very powerful, but most likely you'll be the primary vehicle for them to manifest, so be prepared to put in some effort. Allow your goals to manifest through you. Often within a couple days after setting a goal, you'll begin getting ideas for how to make it work. You may also attract some helpful synchronicities to speed you along your path.

Once you've allowed your goal to incubate and have generated some ideas, develop a plan of action. How much planning you need to do depends on you. Some people require a detailed step-by-step plan to get moving. Others only need the general idea, and they're off and running. Just make sure that no element of your plan requires a mystery step equivalent to, "Magic happens." Good plans have an aura of inevitability to them: If I work the plan, I'll eventually reach my goal.

What if you're too deep in debt, the bills are piling up, you don't have the skills to generate sufficient income to cover your minimum payments, and your creditors aren't willing to wait? If you're forced to conclude that bankruptcy is inevitable, then bankruptcy needs to be part of your plan. If you can't avoid it, then plan through it. Despite the social stigma, bankruptcy is intended to be a financial recovery tool. Bankruptcy laws help people who've made financial mistakes avoid lifetime financial ruin and get back on their feet with a fresh start. Restoring people to productive capacity is to the benefit of all. Over a million Americans file for bankruptcy each year. Bankruptcy filers include Donald Trump, Abraham Lincoln, Walt Disney, Francis Ford Coppola, Richard Harris, Larry King, Stan Lee, Jerry Lewis, Willie Nelson, Mickey Rooney, and Samuel Clemens. Of course you want to avoid this situation if at all possible, but if you do find yourself filing for bankruptcy, visit the non-profit *After Bankruptcy Foundation* and read every issue of their free newsletter—with their help you can be fully recovered in two years or less. I know that many countries don't have bankruptcy laws as liberal as the USA (even after the US laws were recently tightened), but do your homework and see if there's a bankruptcy recovery process in place that you can use. It might be a difficult path, but there's usually a light at the end of the tunnel. For some people, bankruptcy is a very positive step in the turnaround process.

Sometimes when you're making plans, you have to consider what sacrifices you're willing to make. What costs will you cut to reduce your expenses—cable TV, newspaper and magazine subscriptions, coffee, going out to dinner, etc? But cost cutting will only get you so far because you have a hard limit on how low you can go. While cutting costs can make things easier in the short-term, it's usually much more productive to focus on boosting your income, so unless your expenses are irresponsibly high, I suggest you invest most of your planning attention on the income side.

COMMITMENT

Once you have a reasonable plan, you must commit to it. If you won't commit to your plan, you're just wasting your time.

Saying to yourself, "OK, I'm committing to this," is *Commitment for Dummies*. That's like saying, "OK, we're married," as your entire wedding ceremony. If you want to succeed in your financial recovery plans, you need to marry them in a big way. Similar to getting married or moving in with someone, committing to a goal is a process in itself.

There are a couple articles that can help you with that process: *Cultivating Burning Desire* (http://www.stevepavlina.com/articles/cultivating-burning-desire.htm) and *Overwhelming Force* (http://www.stevepavlina.com/blog/2005/09/overwhelming-force/). Read those articles to learn how to really commit to a goal.

If you want an honest assessment of your commitment level—and if you're brave enough to hear the answer—tell a friend or family member about your recovery plan, and ask him/her if you seem 100% committed to it. Then bite your tongue while you listen. It's important that you uncover anything that might hold you back from sticking to your plan. If something comes up, modify your plan to account for it. For example, if your friend says you don't have the discipline to follow your plan, and you think there's some truth to that, then integrate building self-discipline into your plan.

You know you're committed when you can ask yourself, "Is this a done deal?" and answer yes without hesitation. It's extremely unlikely you'll be able to do that right off the bat. To be certain your goal will be achieved means you need to have sustainable motivation and self-discipline to follow through. *Sustainable* is the hard part. You need to reach the point of being in a committed relationship with your goal, so you don't jump ship when the water gets a little choppy.

Just as it takes time to plan a wedding, it takes time to establish a true commitment to your goal. In many ways it does resemble a marriage. You're about to embark on a new life, leaving behind your bachelorhood period of financial scarcity. Respect that the process of commitment can take days, weeks, or even longer—it all depends on how badly you cling to your current situation and resist leaving your comfort zone. You'll know you're ready when you can finally say, "I do," and mean it.

ACTION

Work the plan you've established, and never give up. Perform some action from your financial recovery plan every day, even if it's just balancing your checkbook to keep your finances in order. This will build positive momentum. You won't always have the awareness to think about your plan consciously, so it's important to habitualize the routine actions, so you learn to do them automatically. In the long run, your financial habits will largely determine your results.

One of the best ways to get started on your new plan is to kick it off with a 30-Day Challenge (http://www.stevepavlina.com/blog/2005/04/30-days-to-success/). Use the first 30 days to establish the new habits you'll need, and break the old habits that no longer serve you. If you view your plan as something you only need to maintain for 30 days, you'll find it easier to commit to it. By the end of the 30 days, you'll be able to see some results coming in, which will make it easier for you to commit for the long term.

WEALTH CONSCIOUSNESS

Recovering from a negative financial situation is one of the most fascinating challenges of the game of life, and an amazing growth experience. Even though you may feel very down when you're stuck in debt and can't pay your bills, the long-term process of improving your financial situation can be extremely rewarding. The best part is that once you figure out how to achieve financial abundance for yourself, you can turn around and share your lessons with others who are still struggling. So you aren't just solving this problem for yourself—you're solving it for all the people whose lives you'll touch. If you fail to overcome this challenge, you're letting down a lot of people you could have otherwise helped.

Moving from financial scarcity to financial abundance is a process of getting past our limited egos. Financial scarcity is what you attract when you focus on me, me, me—my needs, my problems, my wants. Financial abundance is what you attract when you focus on we, we, we—our needs, our challenges, our potential. The ego is too small of a container for wealth. If you want to attract financial abundance, you need a container worthy of it, like contribution or service.

I remember the moment when my financial situation began to turn around for the better. I can trace everything back to a specific shift in my mindset that happened in late 1998. Up until that point, my focus was largely on ego-driven goals, and no matter how hard I worked, my financial situation kept getting worse. Eventually I was so fed up that I abandoned that mindset and replaced it with a new one. I said to myself, "Living just for myself is getting me nowhere. I'm going to concentrate on making a contribution instead. If I go broke, then at least I'll go broke doing something worthwhile." Unbeknownst to me at the time, that shift in consciousness would have the long-term effect of turning my financial situation completely around. The problems weren't corrected overnight, but it became clear after a short time that this was the right path. Now Erin and I earn more income each month than we used to earn in a year. What a difference a seemingly subtle shift in mindset can make.

Overcoming problems merely for your own satisfaction is very weak motivation. Doing something you know will benefit a lot of people is much more sustainably motivating. The more you fall into your ego, turning your personal problems into your whole world, the more you lower your consciousness, shrink your options, and attract scarcity. The more you focus on serving others, even in the midst of financial crisis, the more you raise your consciousness, expand your options, and attract abundance.

This mindset shift is the real solution to financial scarcity. The goal-setting, planning, and action steps are just a facilitator. The reason those steps help is that they shift your consciousness away from fear. When you set goals and make plans, you build certainty that you're about to move in a more positive direction. This reduces your anxiety and summons courage. And in turn this helps shift your focus away from your ego (which is fear-centered) and towards contribution (which is love-centered).

7.
How to Become Financially Successful

How do you feel about people who are very successful? What's your attitude toward the movers and shakers in your field?

Do you admire and respect them? Do you speak highly of them?

Or are you suspicious of them? Do you criticize or attack them?

What's the true role of these people in your life? What do they represent?

Subjectively speaking, your relationship with the most successful people in your reality represents your relationship to success itself. Those people represent your potential and how you feel about it.

I use the term "relationship" to mean your general attitude toward people who are ultra-successful. It doesn't matter if you know them personally because your relationships are all in your mind anyway.

If you don't know any very successful people personally, but you still hold strong opinions, that indicates that you don't have a close personal relationship with your own success potential.

On the other hand, it's equally suggestive if you count highly successful people among your closest and dearest friends and family. It suggests that you have a close personal connection to your own success potential.

BIRDS OF A FEATHER

Objectively speaking, successful people flock together. You really don't see highly successful people all by themselves, surrounded by those who have a negative attitude towards success. The movers and shakers in any field tend to be friends and often hang out together.

Similarly, people who have a negative attitude toward success flock together as well.

If you want to get a better picture of your own relationship to success, look to the people you hang out with. Do you befriend a lot of successful people? Or do you hang out with those who resent them or who are envious of them? This will give you a good picture of your relationship to success itself.

It's all too easy to say that you have a successful attitude, but if you keep company with those who shun success, you're incongruent.

Successful and unsuccessful people tend to repel each other, at least in terms of forming close friendships. One reason is that unsuccessful people are constantly complaining. They're veritable fountains of grievances. They do it dozens of times per day, usually without being aware of it. If you ask them what they think of any random celebrity, it's a virtual guarantee they'll focus mainly on what they don't like about that person.

Successful people, on the other hand, are constantly talking about their dreams, goals, and projects. This doesn't mean they're blindly optimistic about everything. They simply have a strong tendency to focus on what they want. They inspire and motivate themselves, and they inspire and motivate each other.

When you put the two different types of people together, you have the unsuccessful person talking about their grievances, which annoys and disturbs the highly successful people if overdone. Initially a successful person may try to help out by offering advice or mentoring. But when he observes that the unsuccessful person applies none of it and comes up with excuses to maintain the status quo, it's an immediate turnoff. The successful person will usually bow out and go where his talents and skills are appreciated.

Similarly, you have the successful people constantly yabbering on about their goals and dreams. This annoys the unsuccessful people to no end. They can't stand it. They'll often try to "help" the successful people by cautioning them about negative outcomes. But successful people aren't phased and continue to press on anyway. The unsuccessful person can't keep up and ducks out.

ATTITUDE

Being successful or unsuccessful isn't about how much money or status you've achieved. It's an internal quality. It's your attitude.

I've met people who have a lot of money, but their attitude toward successful people is so negative, they repel such people everywhere they go. I've also met people who are dead broke, but they easily attract highly successful mentors to help them out, and it isn't long before their external world begins to reflect their inner truth.

When you harbor negative feelings toward successful people, you push success away. When you harbor positive feelings toward them, your own success draws nearer.

I've seen a very basic form of this advice in many books on wealth and success. You've probably encountered it as well. It goes something like, "If you hate wealthy and successful people, you'll never be one of them because you won't allow yourself to become something you hate."

There's some truth to that, but I think it's easier to see why it works when you view it through the lens of subjective reality (http://www.stevepavlina.com/blog/2007/09/subjective-reality-simplified/). Since your relationships are all in your mind, your relationship towards any particular class of people is a reflection of your relationship with whatever those people represent to you.

This means that you can understand your relationship to success by exploring your relationships with the most successful people in your reality.

Are the most successful people in your life close to you? Do you count them among your dearest friends? Or are they way off in the distance somewhere?

Do you love successful people? Do you speak highly of them? Do you feel loved and appreciated by them? Or do you shun them? Do they shun you? Do you move in totally different circles?

Who do you think is responsible for that?

A SIMPLE EXERCISE

Select a person you regard as very successful. It doesn't matter if you've actually met the person.

Take a few minutes to write down your thoughts about this person, including what you like and don't like. Then read back what you wrote as if you've been writing about your own relationship to success.

I think you'll find this exercise very insightful.

What if you've never even met the other person? How can you possibly know what they're like? Where is your attitude really coming from? Your own beliefs about success are filtering it.

SEEING IT FROM THE OTHER SIDE

Have you ever been told that someone you've never met holds a certain attitude toward you. "Joe absolutely adores you; he talks about you all the time." "Mary thinks you're a loser; she talks about you behind your back."

Does it strike you as odd that people could form such strong opinions about you without actually meeting you?

I get this all the time as a blogger. Lots of people hold strong opinions about me, but the ones with the strongest opinions have never even met me. To back up their opinions, they select a few clips to support their opinion from the nearly 2 million words I've written. Of course they're really selecting to match their beliefs about whatever I represent to them, perhaps their own relationship to personal growth since that's what I write about.

I've noticed that people who hold a low opinion of personal development will invariably hold similar thoughts toward me. I'm lame or stupid because of what I represent to them. Those who love personal development and have a strong relationship with their own growth tend to feel good about me. I'm helpful or brilliant because of what I represent.

I'm just using this as a general example. To a lot of people I represent growth and change because that's what I write about, so this is the role people assign me in their reality. But of course it could be something entirely different. It's your reality, so you assign the roles.

What do I represent in your reality? Can you see how your attitude toward me is a reflection of your attitude toward whatever I represent? Is it possible you're assigning qualities to me that may be inaccurate and that your opinion might shift if we had a face-to-face conversation?

HOW TO BECOME MORE SUCCESSFUL

If you wish to become more successful, then work on improving your relationship with the most successful people in your life.

Forgive them. Befriend them. Love them. Do whatever it takes.

Forgive, love, and befriend the part of yourself that wants to have a positive connection to success.

This doesn't mean hanging out with people whose values and morals disgust you. Just loosen your grip on some of your criticisms. Realize that successful people are human. Notice what blocks come up. What is it about highly successful people that bugs you?

For example, if you get caught up in thinking about their character and personality flaws, what does that say about you? Does it mean that in order for you to have a close relationship with success, you must be perfect? Is that realistic? Can you see that you're always going to repel success with that attitude because you'll never be perfect?

I've seen this happen with some of my long-term readers. I write hundreds of articles they love, but as soon as I write about that one hot-button issue where we have a difference of opinion, they send me a nasty email and tell me I've lost them forever, despite numerous breakthroughs they previously thanked me profusely for helping them achieve. This often happens when they're getting close to success in their own lives, but they aren't ready for it.

Do you expect every teacher or mentor to be perfect? Do you expect to see eye-to-eye in every situation? Will you run away forever if someone challenges you in a way you don't like?

Is this how you'd like to see other people deal with your success? Do you want them to put you on a pedestal, to analyze your every action, to expect perfection from you at all times?

Or would you prefer to be treated like a human being, accepted and loved as you are? Is this how you relate to the successful people in your life?

What if you believe that successful people are greedy? Do you ever complain that they should donate more to charity? What does that say about you? Are you more greedy than you realize but secretly resentful of your own selfishness? Do you feel you should be donating more than you are?

What do you think about enjoying the rewards of success? Can you feel good when some celebrity rewards themselves? Do you feel guilty about rewarding yourself with a treat now and then? Or do you feel good about it, knowing that rewarding yourself helps motivate you to create even more value for others?

BECOMING CONGRUENT WITH SUCCESS

We all have blocks that keep us out of harmony with our great potential. The people in our lives are always reflecting that inner attitude back to us.

To fix the inner attitude problem, you must at some point admit that you were wrong and forgive yourself for it.

"I was wrong about so-and-so. Perhaps he isn't such a bad guy after all. Maybe he's just human. I will do my best to love and accept him as he is."

You can extend what I've said about success to any quality or character trait. Your feelings toward sexy people reflect your relationship with your own sexiness. Your feelings toward healthy people reflect your relationship with health. Your feelings toward rich people reflect your relationship with wealth. Your feelings toward creative people reflect your relationship with your own creativity. Your feelings toward highly productive people reflect your relationship with productivity. Your feelings toward highly spiritual people reflect your relationship with spirituality.

How do you feel about psychics? Are you skeptical? Do you feel they're all frauds and charlatans? Do you harbor serious doubts about their so-called gifts? If so, does it surprise you that your own psychic senses are virtually nonexistent? Do you wonder why your intuition is so cloudy that you can never trust it?

On the other hand, do you feel that psychics are loving people with a special gift to share? Do you accept their guidance with gratitude? Is it any wonder that you're also able to gain much value from your own intuitive and psychic senses? Do other people comment on how gifted you are?

If you hate or distrust certain people, you're pushing away that part of yourself. If you love and accept certain people, you're in harmony with that part of yourself.

You can massively accelerate your personal growth by tweaking these relationships consciously and deliberately. It's all in your mind anyway.

AS WITHIN, SO WITHOUT

When you make the inner adjustment, your external world will shift to reflect the inner change. Recently I did some inner work on my attitude towards certain people. My block had to do with people who spend money on nonessentials, sometimes as a way of rewarding themselves. Spending money on nonessential items would usually make me feel uncomfortable, even if I could easily afford it.

Erin and I had a 13-year old couch in our home that was ripped in a couple places and pretty ratty looking. One of the built-in recliners was broken. She'd been talking about getting a new couch for at least a couple years, probably longer, but I always blocked her. "This couch is fine. We don't need to spend money on a new one." We had plenty of money though, and a new couch wouldn't make a serious dent in our finances. She tried to get us to go couch shopping a few times, but I rejected her choices. There was always something wrong with them.

After doing some inner work on my attitude toward spending money and enjoying the rewards of success, I was able to get past this block. We went couch shopping and were helped by an exceedingly gregarious and non-pushy salesman. We shopped with an attitude of positive expectancy and soon found the perfect couch for our space. We also found some great recliner chairs and small tables for one of our upstairs rooms, and we bought those too.

When we got home, Erin posted an ad on Craigslist to offer our old couch for free to anyone who was willing to pick it up. We would have donated it to charity, but most charities wouldn't take it. Erin received about 40 replies to her ad in 24 hours, and we gave the old couch to some people who were grateful to squeeze more life out of it.

I'm very much enjoying the new couch and chairs. In retrospect it seems like such a silly block to have. The solution was that I had to reassess my attitude toward people who use their money to reward themselves. I went from "What a waste of money; do they really need a new X?" to "Great to see people enjoying the rewards of success; they certainly deserve it!" Once I shifted my attitude toward others, my inner relationship with that aspect of abundance also changed. And soon my external reality came into harmony with the new attitude.

Even working through small blocks can bring more success into your life, sometimes in unexpected ways. Around the same time I was working through this block, some new interview requests came in. Later this month Deepak Chopra will be interviewing me for his radio show, and next month Jack Canfield is scheduled to interview me as well. Did they appear on my radar as a result of my inner shift?

Who are the people you hate most in your life? Who are the people you love most? Can you admit that your attitude toward those people is going to have to change if you want to change your relationship with what they represent?

Can you see that if you harbor ill feelings toward the top performers in your field, you'll never become a top performer yourself?

Before posting this article, I asked Erin to give it a quick read. When she was done, she asked me, "How do you feel about people who have decent patio furniture?"

What, those losers???

Part II: Creating a Healthy Relationship with Money

8.
Is Spirituality and Wealth Mutually Exclusive?

Usually your spiritual journey, or personal growth quest, doesn't begin until you've experienced some form of suffering in your life. In this case, you've probably experienced, or currently are experiencing, a degree of financial lack. And because of the financial lack and consistent suffering, spirituality has been your escape goat. You have "crossed to the other shore", maybe only for a glimpse, and have felt the presence that underlies all form—Big Mind.

It's so much nicer over here, at this "other shore." The suffering you have endured day in and day out is either gone, or rarely shows its face. Your financial situation doesn't matter, you don't care to accumulate possessions, and it doesn't matter what type of person you become. Freeing, isn't it? To not give-a-shit of the relative consequences or what happens in the world.

This is exactly how I felt when I was in financial ruins from a bankrupt real estate business; I noticed the gap of nothingness between my thoughts. I saw form in its true essence, without labels, judgments, or any preconceived ideas. My initial time spent over at the "other shore" was short, maybe a few minutes. But I made frequent voyages between the main land that billions of people know and the small populated "other shore," which I call Big Mind. I found my row boat to the "other shore" by asking a simple question, "Who am I?" Rather than thinking about the type of person I was, what I went to school for, and the possessions I thought I had, my mind drew blank, as if all the clouds in the sky disappeared, and I swam in an infinite sea of blue.

I admit for being a ripe candidate from the amount of financial suffering I endured. I inserted the key of "who am I" into the proper door. But what I found behind that door was the vehicle—the boat—to get to the "other shore." For the next three years I explored the shore of Big Mind, and made infrequent trips back to main land. It wasn't like I dropped off body and mind to a complete useless human being; I still took care of myself, socialized, and worked for money. The difference was the *knowing* that I possessed—all life is suffering, and there's nothing I can do about it; therefore, I stopped desiring, stopped grasping, and didn't care to attach to things.

Eventually I began to stink. No, not physically stink; modern showers are available at the "other shore." I stunk of Zen. In other words, I appropriated the Big Mind experience and developed a spiritual ego. I turned Big Mind into a graspable object and identified as being spiritual—one with everything who is beyond thought and all suffering. I judged others who didn't have a spiritual practice. And I criticized people for being stuck in their ego—*if only he would stop wanting more money he would be free.*

I tried the money game and failed. When I had money, I wasn't happy. I continually felt that I needed more and had to protect the money I did have. It was exhausting, and I was tired of making my entire life about money. Then, when I didn't have any money, I felt worthless and afraid. My solution to that dilemma was to become spiritual and conclude that spirituality and wealth are mutually exclusive. If I wanted to be happy and free, then I needed to abandon the game of money and not care about it except for basic needs.

What a dummy I was, that approach didn't work either. From a distance I was happy and blissful practicing spirituality and clearing my emotional blocks, but my exterior life descended deeper into dysfunction. I ignored debt, and that consequence kept pulling in and out of fear. I lacked money and mooched from others to eat, have shelter, turn on the lights, and to heat my home. What's more, desire crept in. I wanted to help people alleviate their suffering; I wanted to make a difference, pay the rent, travel, and do fun things that cost money. I wanted to take responsibility for my life and enjoy the fruits that life had to offer.

But I was conflicted: *How can I be happy and free, and have money at the same time?* It didn't work before. Why should I get into that mess again?

You may have a similar dilemma going on right now. You know that money isn't everything. You want to tap into your true power and creatively express yourself. But you feel the two do not go together—creative expression and earning money. I bet this is how starving artist feel. They never want to toss in the towel and quit their creative work to get a job. He would rather die, than trade in his paint brush for a key card.

You can have both, however—that is, creatively express yourself and reap the rewards of money. It took me awhile to get it, but the starting point is to consider that spirituality and wealth are interdependent. Your spiritual realization, or another way of putting it is realizing your highest Self, needs support from wealth—the relative world. Without playing in the world, grasping to things, and making a livelihood, you could not *know* Big Mind, nor would life be fun. Likewise, the relative world needs support from your spiritual realization to function resourcefully. Without Big Mind grounding into your experience, the human ego dominates life.

Once I considered that perspective, a nugget of insight hit me like a meteorite falling from the sky. And that moment of clarity came after I read this stanza from the *Genjo Koan*:

> *Gaining enlightenment is like the moon reflecting in the water. The moon does not get wet, nor is the water disturbed. Although its light is extensive and great, the moon is reflected in a puddle an inch across.*
>
> *The whole moon and the whole sky are reflected in a dew-drop in the grass, in one drop of water.*
>
> *Enlightenment does not disturb the person, just as the moon does not disturb the water.*
>
> *A person does not hinder enlightenment, just as a dew-drop does not hinder the moon in the sky.*

What does this mean? It means a lot of things; but in context of this chapter it means that everything in the universe is connected, one, and interdependent of each other. You cannot have form unless the formless is present. Likewise, you cannot realize the formless unless the impermanence of form is present. Everything is interdependent, just like we need the Sun to burn at an exact temperature, from an exact distance away from the earth, for life to exist. Alter the Sun's conditions and qualities, and you alter life on this planet. But the Sun needs you, too. If you are not here to observe the Sun and use its resources, does the Sun exist?

The same goes with spirituality and money: money is spiritual because its essence *is* the formless; therefore, having any amount of money is not judged. It's all good. You could have millions, and that's spiritual. You could have zero dollars, and that's spiritual, too. In the eyes of Big Mind the amount or its use doesn't matter. Money is Big Mind and Big Mind is money—no difference. *The whole moon and the whole sky are reflected in a dew-drop in the grass, in one drop of water.*

The problem to why you feel that spirituality and wealth are mutually exclusive is because you're stuck in the dualistic mind. The dualistic mind thinks that money is not spiritual. The dualistic mind thinks more is better, or money brings happiness, or money is evil. It also juggles between right and wrong, and piles things into black and white containers. The key word here is *think*. When thinking is involved, you are identifying to a concept. This is completely healthy. In order for you to make any decision, you need to grasp a concept or idea and then make it happen. But you are conditioned to think "this" way and not "that" way. For example, if you're parents grew up thinking that the only way to earn money is to trade dollars for hours as an employee, then you will mostly like think and behave in the same manner.

Let the dualistic mind be the dualistic mind, don't try to get rid of it to become spiritual or creative or think positive to fix your Self. Rather, embrace the dualistic mind for what it is, and insert the absolute into the relative. This means you are fully aware of your essence, of Big Mind, but you also have one foot firmly planted on the main land. In other words, you bring your Big-Mind-Awareness into who you are and what you do.

WHAT DOES THIS HAVE TO DO WITH EARNING MONEY?

It has nothing to do with earning money—that part is easy. Go out on the street and within minutes you'll find some coins. Get a job, and you'll earn money. Help someone solve a problem with the guarantee of money for your help, and you've earned money. Earning money is not the point; lack of money is not the problem either. Your financial life reflects the relationship you have with your Self and with money. The relationship is always showing you which qualities of your Self are healthy and which qualities are disowned. If your relationship with money is unhealthy, it's likely that you are disowning qualities of your Self that are needed for your growth.

I used to believe that *more is better*. The more money I have the happier and better off I am. That didn't work, however, because no matter how much money I accumulated I was unhappy. The pursuit of money consumed my life, along with its insecurities. Then I considered the *less is better* approach. Guess what? That didn't work either—I was still unhappy. Finally I realized that I was trapped in my dualistic mind and *that* was the cause of my unhappiness, not *more is better* or *less is better*. I needed to own and embody both sides of the coin for my growth—dualism and Big Mind.

When I stopped clinging to both preferences, and fully owned the qualities of dualism and Big Mind, the amount of money was irrelevant. It was only important during its medium of exchange. I was free because my Self was free from clinging to the idea of money and its false power. Ironically, when I reclaimed my power back from money, the flow of money couldn't help itself and hasn't stopped finding me.

Insert Big Mind into what you do and the lack of money is removed. You free the flow of money to you because you have freed your Self from its small mindedness: *I'm not worthy, I don't deserve it, mistakes and failures are bad, and more is better*—all dualistic qualities. A free Self is a healthy Self. And a healthy relationship with your Self is a health relationship with money. I believe the greatest value money has is to show where you are stuck. As soon as you're able to see where you are stuck, you can jump out. Here are some questions for you to consider:

What are you clinging to? Do you need it for your survival? Do you need it to *be* somebody? How do you react when you don't have enough money? How do you react when you have plenty of money to get by?

What beliefs are you identified with? Do you feel worthless without money? Do you need to work hard for it? Do you deserve money? Answer this: Money is…

What aspects of your Self are you unwilling to look at and to make peace with? Are you a perfectionist? Do you procrastinate? Do you lack courage? Are you too passive? Honor those qualities and embrace them like a friend.

What type of character are you? If you already had the money you desire, what type of person would you be? How can you be that person now regardless of money?

The next chapter shows you how to merge with the presence of money and uncover its truth in your life.

IT STARTS WITH BIG MIND

Have you crossed to the "other shore" yet? Sometimes you think have, but are unsure to what it's supposed to be like. Big Mind isn't something you do or a goal you can achieve because you already are Big Mind. Trying to become Big Mind is like trying to see the back of your eyeballs, the inside of your nose, or the white on your teeth—you cannot do it. And the harder you try the more frustrated and distant you are from really knowing it. What you can do is become accident prone so Big Mind *just is* in your life. You do this with pointers to Big Mind, like how a mirror points or shows you the white on your teeth and the inside of your nose. Unfortunately, no amount of time using a mirror will make you accident prone to one day seeing the white on your teeth. Sorry. But enough practice with Big Mind pointers will eventually integrate the realization of Big Mind.

One pointer is meditation. You can sit on a zafu and count your breath until it drops off into nothingness. Or, you can sit on a zafu and hold the ever present awareness of Big Mind. I'm not going to there, however. I want to focus on this pointer: "How big is my mind?" Earnestly try to find Big Mind. Point to it. Show me how big your mind is. I want you to seek Big Mind until you are exhausted and find it hopeless to know what Big Mind is. Any time you get an answer to *how big is my mind?* know that it's not the right answer. Keep the question, *how big is my mind*, in the forefront at all times. At some moment, in an instance, the stream of thought will stop and the answer is revealed: *I don't know*. The answer is not a thought of *I don't know*, but rather it's an unshakeable presence and peace with *not knowing*. You are comfortable with uncertainty and look forward to it. The answer is an unexplained beauty and the appreciation for life as it is.

INSERTING BIG MIND INTO WHAT YOU DO

It's all about awareness. If you can become aware of how you do your financial life—that is, how you feel while interacting with money, the meanings you are giving in the moment, and the thoughts you're identifying with in the area of money—then you cannot continue to create a dysfunctional relationship with money. This is why it's important to know Big Mind firsthand. You need to watch, like a watchman from a light tower, the thoughts, feelings, and meanings zooming by without attaching to them. This means rather than acting unconsciously to conditioned habits and behaviors, you have choice, and you can discern with wisdom and compassion to what's appropriate for the moment.

Imagine becoming aware of beliefs such as "I'm not good enough, I'm not important, and I don't deserve it" in the moment they are happening? How do you think that will impact your financial life? Especially if you're trying to create a healthy relationship with money? You won't be able to act out that dysfunction because the rule of thumb is whatever you are consciously aware of, you cannot do anything dysfunctional to yourself, others, and the situation at hand. It's impossible because you are hard-wired for full function.

You *really* don't gain awareness because it's inseparable from the complete you. There's nothing to gain, nowhere to go, and nothing to get, however, the layers of the ego have covered up the bright light of awareness. With practice, you can peel back the layers and allow the light of awareness to shine.

THE PRACTICE

FIRST THING

Your feelings are pointers to the meaning you are giving in the moment and the beliefs you are identifying with. As you go about interacting with money, pay close attention to how you feel in that moment. Are your feelings positively charged? Neutral? Or negatively charged? It doesn't matter what kind of charge they have, all you need to do is notice how you feel in that moment. No need to do anything about the feelings, only allow its presence.

For example, you grabbed your laptop and are logging-in to your online banking website to check your balance. You feel nervous and anxious. You fear of not having enough money. You don't want to be pathetic and ask to borrow money. Then, you see your checking account balance. Are you relieved? Did your stomach get sick? Are you panicking? It doesn't matter because you're depending upon circumstance for your happiness. You have limited yourself to one choice: suffering. The unconscious person continually recreates this suffering each time he checks his banking balance. He also tries to avoid the suffering, too, by working hard and stressing out.

What I want you to do *is* stop recreating suffering. The thoughts and feelings you are identified with determine how you behave. Becoming conscious of your thoughts and feelings stops the suffering on a mental, emotional, and physical plane of existence. You remember the rule, don't you? *Whatever you are consciously aware of, you cannot do anything dysfunctional to yourself, others, and the situation at hand.*

Next time you interact in your financial life, and this means anytime where money has a presence, pay attention to the feelings and state of your body. How do you feel? What's the emotion? What does it feel like in your body? Where in your body is the feeling strongest? If you're anxious and feel fear, let that be okay. Pay attention. Be alert. Allow any feeling its presence. Never try to push the feeling away. Avoiding and pushing away what's present, and in this case negative feelings, disowns qualities needed for a healthy Self. It's magnifying the dualistic mind and playing an intense game of black and white in which white must win.

Practice watching your feelings anytime you interact with money for seven days. Pay close to attention to the negative feelings. And if you want to hold yourself accountable and accelerate the process, carry a 3 x 5 note card with you and place a "check" on that note card anytime you have a negative feeling when dealing with money.

SECOND THING

By now you are getting good at watching your feelings. Noticing and allowing any feeling its presence makes you conscious and gives you choice to how you want to act (which may mean no-action) according to the present moment. Let's take it a step further, and go deeper into Big Mind.

When you notice a negative feeling while interacting with money, silently ask yourself, "Who am I?" and watch the situation with awareness. No need to judge or think about it, keep doing what you are doing, but bring that awareness into what you do. The moment you ask, "Who am I?" you have dropped your fixed perspective to the situation and are open to other possibilities. Again, when many possibilities are available, you have choice. Choice to do what? Well, you have choice to accept the situation, to drop limiting beliefs, to allow a deeper intelligence guide your actions, to choose no action, and many other choices when the moment arises.

For example, you are checking your online bank account. At some point during the process, you notice a negative feeling and an interesting thought, "I don't have enough." Notice, with awareness, the thought and feeling you are having. Allow its presence. Then, silently ask "Who am I?" Keep watching. Eventually the negative feeling will dissolve and you'll feel okay with the situation. The point isn't to get rid of the negative feeling or limiting thought, the point is to bring presence to the thought and feeling so it matures and functions for you in a resourceful way.

All feelings and all thoughts have their purpose to serve you in a functioning way. They become dysfunctional, however, because *you* disown them by separating some feelings into a "good" pile and other feelings into a "bad" pile—that's the game of black and white. The bad pile of feelings is like the bad children in the family. They run amok, give you headaches, sabotage your efforts, and create clutter throughout your house. The more you yell and punish the bad children, the more problematic they become. Have you ever considered what the "bad" children want? They want your love, and for you to embrace them and respect their uniqueness. The same goes with your "bad" feelings. They're not *really* bad because you're the one that gave the "bad" label. Any and all thoughts and feelings want your love and presence. If you can give them that, the feeling or thought will help you in a resourceful way when the time comes.

For example, most people see fear as a bad thing. They will do anything to avoid fear. So they avoid taking risks, conflict, dealing with difficult people, and ignore their true desires. The irony is that the fear never goes away. As much as this person tries, he cannot avoid conflict, dangerous situations, and even imaginary fear. *What was that sound? Did you hear something in the basement? Will I have enough money to pay the bills?* You can never get rid of something; you can only embrace it or disown it. Now, if this person allows his fear presence, and watches it with awareness, he will see that fear has no power over him whatsoever. In fact, he will recognize that fear is a resourceful and functioning quality for the appropriate moment.

Fear is good. If someone is pointing a gun at you, are you going to try to get rid of fear? No, and why should you. Please fear for your life. Get out of there if you can. But if your fear was disowned, you may not know the appropriate action to take. When you should have run, you let pride stand in the way and you got killed. Or, when you should have stayed and fight, you let fear cripple you, and you sank to the ground crying. Dead.

Embrace everything and your problems go away. Problems are mind-made anyway; there are only situations to be dealt with.

THIRD THING

As you lie in bed at night, and before you go to sleep, think of one negative event that happened to you today. Replay that situation in your imagination. Make it as real as possible. During the visualization, go into that negative feeling.

Now, wonder what meaning you gave to that event. How did you do that feeling? What you're looking for are the string of thoughts, the labels, or the beliefs that created the negative feelings. What did you notice?

I did this exercise the other day while lying in bed. Earlier in the day, I had an idea for a book, and while I was thinking about the book, a bunch of negative feelings overwhelmed me. I replayed the event in my imagination and made it as vivid as possible. Then, I asked, "How did I do this feeling? What meaning did I give to that event?" I noticed that I thought "I'm not good enough." It was an interesting realization because the next day I went into "idea mode" for a new home study course, I noticed, with awareness, the belief of "I'm not good enough" pop into my consciousness. This time, however, I wasn't identified with the belief anymore. It was a passing thought that didn't cripple my state of being. I was free and able to act resourcefully, which is the book you're reading right now. If I never realized the limiting belief of *I'm not good enough* towards the ideas I have, I would have a difficult time creating what I want in the world.

Practice this exercise for another seven days. Essentially, this exercise is practice for catching limiting thoughts, feelings, and beliefs in the moment so you can drop the unresourceful ones and act with wisdom and compassion. It's like practicing your baseball swing: there's a time to practice the mechanics of your swing, but then it's game time, and you unconsciously bring your practice into realization.

Awareness or Big Mind are not magical pills to fix your life. Freedom from the tyranny of your thoughts and feelings happen in an instance, but integration as a *way of life* takes time. It's much like the dating process from first date to marriage. When you meet someone with common interests and have an attraction to her, you typically do not get married after the first date. It takes days, months, or years to build a relationship with that person, and to mold the relationship the way you both desire for each other's happiness. The dating to marriage process also applies to creating a health relationship with your Self and with money. You will need intimacy, courage, sovereignty, patience and love to make the relationship work.

Most of us are really good at *doing* something to earn money. We are also good at craving and desiring new experiences and levels to the game of money. It's easy to over look the spiritual alignment and relationship aspect to money. However, it's possible that neglecting the relationship with money is the reason why you struggle so much. I know it was for me. I use to treat money like how I treated my relationship with women in college; I only did things for them so they would like me. My relationships with women were superficial and shallow. I felt empty and alone. It didn't matter how sexy, nice, or caring that person was, every relationship was the same shallow pit. It wasn't their fault. It was my issue with intimacy. I feared having a true, heartfelt relationship with another person. My dualistic mind and ego were too strong. I lacked love.

Inserting Big Mind into what you do is opening the conduit that you are for wisdom and compassion to come into your relationship with money. You need to go beyond the dualistic mind to see your true needs and the intimacy your relationship with money is crying for. Spirituality and wealth are not mutually exclusive. They only *seem* that way because you are judging yourself; you're attaching to concepts and ideas and then placing them into piles of black and white. You are looking through the lens of the Self and seeing two apparently opposite things: spirituality and wealth. If you look through the lens of Big Mind, spirituality and wealth are one. When you realize this "oneness," fear is removed and you're free to pursue and have an intimate, healthy relationship with money.

9.

It's Not About Value, It's The Relationship That Counts

Every summer my fiancé's parents plant a tomato garden. I love fresh, locally grown tomatoes. They're so damn succulent and nice to look at. A home-grown tomato beats the pants off anything available at the grocery store.

Her parents do such a nice job of growing the tomatoes, too. They care for the soil, nurture the seed, give plenty of water and sunlight, and use wooden stakes to support the tomato plant for its healthy growth. A few weeks later, the tomatoes are ready for picking. Each tomato is unique in shape and size—I remember receiving one that was as long as a hot dog. The tomatoes are lush red with the perfect amount of firmness—not-too-soft and not-too-firm. And every bite gushes with flavor.

Growing the perfect tomato is much like how to have a healthy relationship with money. When you want succulent, lush red tomatoes that explode with flavor in your mouth, you invest eighty percent of your efforts into caring for the plant. You prepare the soil, give plenty of water, feed the plant nutrients, remove the weeds, and possibly even sing or play music. You're focused on giving love to the plant so it can grow and mature into a healthy state.

What you're not doing is stressing over the crop that you are about to receive. You may anticipate the reward of beautiful tomatoes, but hoarding the whole garden is not your one-hundred percent concern. Much of the reward to producing a healthy tomato plant is enjoying the labor, seeing the beauty in your garden, and sharing it with friends. You go about your business doing the best job you can to have a prosperous tomato plant.

The other twenty percent of your efforts is caring for the tomato once it has sprout. You water and clean the tomato; and you use organic, all natural chemicals to keep the tomato from rotting or having a bug infestation. Imagine that all you did, however, was care for the tomato. Forget about the entire plant, you have a succulent fruit that needs tending to. So you neglect caring for the soil, or watering the roots, or supporting the plant with wooden stakes. Do you really think you'll have juicy red tomatoes to enjoy? Nope. You'll have minimal growth and the crop will probably die.

The question I have for you: are you focusing on the eighty percent or the twenty percent part of the relationship?

THE TWENTY PERCENT

The twenty percent part of the relationship with money is important, but it's not the life blood that grows and evolves your relationship with money. It's more about "money maintenance," in which you steward your income and expenses with respect and value. Most people earn money and immediately spend it on their usual expenses. They misallocate their income, and then buy things that they do not even value. The money comes in, and the money goes out. There's no appreciation or intimacy with the cash. At the end of the month, when they look at their bank balance, they get upset and wonder *where did all the money go?*

Allocating your money into what you value takes care of the twenty percent. The chapter titled "Pay Yourself First" goes into great detail about allocating and taking care of your money. What I want to focus on here is bringing truth to your expenses.

We are creatures of habit. It's too easy to keep spending our income on things that we don't value. The reason why you feel as if you don't have enough money at the end of the month is because you're spending money on things you do not value. If you spent every penny that you own on something you want and value, it feels good. Money is meant to be exchanged for things that you want. Holding onto your money or hoarding it does not have any value whatsoever. If that's what you do, what's the point of working for it? This doesn't mean you need to liquate your savings, I think it's wise to have six months of cash on hand that matches six months of your expenses.

Unfortunately, the free market is not so "free" now-a-days. It's diseased with government spending and the monopoly over the legal tender of debt. And because of that consequence, you're going to spend money on things that you don't value—taxes, inflation, the post system, and utility companies that have a monopoly. But you can focus on the direct expenditures you incur.

I recommend keeping a detailed list of your expenditures for a month. You know those transaction record booklets that you get with your check books? Use those to keep track of your expenses. When you buy something, write the date, the name of the business, and the price of the expense. Do this every time you buy something, even if it's a twenty-five cent gum ball. This takes discipline, but your efforts will be well worth it.

At the end of the month, go line-by-line and ask this question: "Was this expenditure aligned with my purpose and values?" If you said *yes*, put an asterisk next to the expense. If you said *no*, put a dash next to the expense. If the expense felt neutral, put a zero next to the expense. Tally up the number of asterisks; then tally up the number of dashes; finally, tally up the number of zeros. What's the ratio? Is it something like 10-25-4 (purchases you value-purchases you don't value-purchases that are neutral). What can you do to eliminate more negative expenses and align your expenses with more things that you value?

When I did this exercise, my ratio was roughly 45-15-7. Not bad, but I knew that I could do better. I noticed that I bought a cup of coffee everyday for $2.25. That's roughly $67 in coffee for the month! I realized that I didn't value spending $67 for my coffee habit. I could have saved that money, or bought two educational programs, or bought swing dance classes—all things that I value—instead of wasting my money. So I cut that expense by 75% and saved $50 per month. I even cut my cable bill in half and basically pay for internet only. I don't value watching TV, and the three shows that I do like are either on Hulu or the ten channels I get. Why pay for something that I do not value? If you're wondering what shows I watch, they are *Castle, Being Human, and Fox News*. I watch Fox News fifteen minutes per day, and the other two shows combined take up 90 minutes of my time per week. It's a good 90 minutes, however, because I get to snuggle with my fiancé.

Tracking my expenses for that month trimmed $200 of expenses that I didn't value. I'm a much happier guy because I'm allocating my income into resources that make me feel good. There will be months when every cent that I spend feels amazing. Tracking my expenses (I also track my income) has helped so much that I do it every month. I have streamlined the process and use a convenient app on my iphone called, "iXpenseIt."

THE EIGHTY PERCENT

The eighty percent of your relationship with money is the life blood. Focusing your attention in this area will renew and recycle the flow of money in and out of your life. This area also gives you a healthy relationship with money. Eighty percent of this book focuses on the eighty percent that gives you a healthy relationship with money. By reading and re-reading this book many times you will naturally develop the relationship you desire—though, doing the exercises and taking action is necessary.

The key to your success in creating a healthy relationship with money is to focus on Truth, Love, and Power. Imagine that these three qualities represent spokes on a wheel. To keep the wheel healthy and full functioning the spokes need to be intact at all times. If one spoke is weak or broken, it could comprise the entire wheel. Each quality—Truth, Love, and Power—need your on-going attention for a prosperous relationship with money, or with any area of your life.

TRUTH

When you think of Truth, most people conclude that means to be honest, sincere, or raw. For the most part that's true. When you get down to the bare bone, or when you shine the bright light of Truth on the situation, you see the situation as-is. That means knowing the situation without the fluff-n-stuff.

Truth is helpful for your relationship with money because it assesses your level of health and maturity with money. You are able to see where you're at with the relationship on an emotional, spiritual, and physical scale. For example, you're at the doctor's office because you hurt your arm. You think that it's broken, therefore, you immediately tell the nurse to get you ready for surgery. She's going to decline your request, however. They haven't taken any x-rays, nor has the doctor examined the situation yet. The medical staff is unclear to what's going on with your arm. When they discover the Truth to your situation, they'll assign the necessary prognosis.

Once you've diagnosed the problem to your relationship with money, you're able to ingest medicine to make the relationship healthier. This medicine maybe a change in mindset, eliminating limiting beliefs, embodying qualities, cutting social baggage, limiting expenses, starting a business, being more intimate, or taking direct action to exercise your power. You won't know *what to do* unless you are clear about the maturity of your relationship with money.

LOVE

You can say that Love is the glue that holds the relationship with money together. Love is the intimacy that every relationship yearns for—yes, that includes objects such as money. When you fully embody Love, you know in your heart that separate things do not exist. Everything in this Universe is connected, interdependent, and originates from the same source.

The way I like to prove this Truth of *oneness*, which is a quality from Love, is to think about how *I* was made possible. *Me* having this life wasn't only dependent upon my parents birthing me; many other factors had to be in place. In order for my parents to birth me, they needed to have parents; and my parents parents needed to have parents; then my parents parents parents needed to have parents; and the list goes on forever until the first human being. At that point, did the first human being magically appear on earth? If you believe that, then the first human being came from God, and what is God? Better yet—what comes before God? If you believe that human beings evolved from an animal species, then where did that species come from? What other miracles had to happen for that species to exist so it can one day evolve to become *me*?

If you try to wrap your head around this thought, eventually your thinking mind will seize and you'll see the Truth and feel the Love. Your heart will open, and a new founded compassion will integrate throughout your life. You will walk about life seeing everything as a relationship, not an object to obtain. And since everything *is* a relationship, you'll nurture, be intimate, and care for the relationship.

The foundation of prosperity is Love. The tomato plant growing from its seed and into a healthy, fruit bearing plant is an act of Love. In order for the tomato plant to be healthy and mature you need to be intimate with it. The same goes with money. You need to bring intimacy and oneness to your relationship with money. It's not an object to obtain, but a relationship that's continually giving feedback about how much love is pouring into your life. If you are experiencing lack in some areas of your life, it's most likely there's a lack of Love in that relationship. Where's the love in this moment?

POWER

Power embraces Truth and Love and is the force that manifests those qualities into your life. Power takes you from where you are (Truth) to where you want to go (Truth and Love). When you think about someone that has a lot of Power, what you're referring to is that person uses his energy in a way to get what he wants in life. Sometimes Power is disowned, and used to manifest one's desires without the quality of Love. When this happens, the qualities of greed, rage, and control feed your desires. This is why you need to nurture all the spokes—Truth, Love, and Power—on the wheel of life, so the exertion of your Power comes from a mature and healthy place.

Without Power your desires are left in the unmanifested; at best they are thought forms. Power buddies itself with courage so the thought forms of what you want manifest in your life. Many law of attraction enthusiast disown the quality of Power. They fall into the trap of *ask, believe, and receive* thinking that his desires will magically manifest. For example, if you desire more money, but all you do is sit on your duff and visualize swimming in cash, not much is going to happen—except that you'll go broke. The only purpose visualization serves is to train your mind to notice opportunities that align with your vision. You must exert your Power to capitalize on that opportunity.

Power is a tricky quality to fully own and embody for spiritual people. Power resides at the apex on the wheel of life; therefore, Power embraces and transcends Love and Truth. Power includes Love and its oneness, but is not complete oneness. It's as if Power individualizes itself so Power can live and operate in the relative world. Power is tricky for spiritual people because we often get stuck in Big Mind, which is oneness. Spiritual people have a hard time making the jump from oneness to Power. The fear is that we will lose our connection to oneness and suffer. What we cannot see, however, because we are stuck in oneness, is that being stuck in oneness *is* suffering. You are a human being that must face relative consequences. When you're stuck in oneness, Karma continues to build and it will manifest itself in an ugly way.

My favorite way to own and embody power is to set goals and do everything I can to achieve them. Of course, I do not neglect Truth and Love in my life because that would cause me to misuse my Power. Plus, it's a lot healthier and enjoyable to have wisdom and compassion run in and through you. But I set an intention and do what I can to achieve that intention based on my position, the time, and the place. As I'm exerting my Power, I pay close attention to the thoughts and feelings that weaken my Power. Often times I'll discover limiting beliefs such as, *I'm not good enough or I have to value myself more.* That type of thinking weakens my ability to achieve my desires. I take care of those limiting beliefs and act in spite of them.

There's the overview of the importance for Truth, Love, and Power. The rest of this book will show you how to embody Truth, Love, and Power so you can have a healthy relationship with money.

YOU CAN'T VALUE YOURSELF MORE

The practicality of money is simple: create something that somebody wants and is willing to trade money for, and deliver that "something" to that person. For example, this book you're reading has a certain level of value for you; therefore, you traded money to consume the value, and I delivered it to you. You are happy because the value received is useful; in some way the value has increased your standards of living. I'm happy because I received money for creating and delivering the value, which I thoroughly enjoyed doing. If that was too simple, here's a more complex version. Your ability to get paid depends on three factors:

1. The perceived value of what you're giving.

2. Actual usefulness of the value.

3. Your ability to successfully deliver that value.

If you can take care of those three factors, you'll have no problem earning money. And if you want to increase your income, you must either increase the quality of your value, or deliver your value to a wider audience, or do both.

If it's that simple to earn money, where do most of us get hung up? Why is it difficult to earn money? I believe the biggest "hang up" is that you try to value yourself too much. Yes, you do need to create and deliver value to receive money. But the problem with valuing yourself more is that *value* can be judged.

Have you ever created a piece of art or music? Maybe you have written a book or created a product? Afterward, did you ever wonder if your work was good enough, or questioned whether you deserve money for the value created? I was stuck on this wheel for a long time. I created info product after info product about some good stuff, such as how to attract your desired relationship, how to earn money, how to awaken to your presence, and so on, but I never released a product. I even wrote a book in 2009 that I never delivered. When I completed each product or book, I thought they weren't useful anymore, and questioned whether anyone would buy my work. I would create my product from start to finish, give one final review, and concluded that I needed to do better. Call me a perfectionist, but I continually questioned whether my created value was good enough to make a difference for someone.

The problem I had was judging myself: *what if someone hates the product and wants a refund? What if my value isn't good enough and it doesn't help? What if no one buys?* Crazy, right?

To give you another short example, imagine that you're in a relationship with an attractive woman. You like this girl, and want to be with her, but you're only in it for the sex. You don't invest the time for intimacy, to cuddle, and to talk about your dreams and goals, for you it's only about sex. Do you really think the relationship is going to last long or be healthy? No chance in hell. You may receive the instant gratification of sex now and then, but after awhile it will be as intimate as a monkey humping a football. Does that seem fulfilling to you?

But this is how most of us treat our relationship with money, like a monkey humping a football. We work, work, work, work, to get more money, more money, and more money. Eventually it hurts and your life feels shallow. There isn't any depth to your relationship with money. You're only going through the motions and life lacks its spice.

When your entire focus is on value, the relationship becomes lopsided. Imagine that "value" is a complete being. To represent this "being," let's draw a triangle, as shown below. On the left hand side of the triangle, you have value. On the right hand side of the triangle you have no-value, which is no judgment. Go to the apex of the triangle and there's "value relationship." The apex embraces and includes value and no value so you have a healthy relationship with value. In other words, you give value, but you're not attached to the judgments of value because you embrace no value. The relationship is not lopsided anymore. It's full functioning.

Another way of looking at it is that you need to treat your relationship with money as if you are growing the most succulent tomatoes in the garden. What you need to do is tend to the soil, to the plant, and to the support structures. When you do that the fruit (money) will take care of itself. It's not about the value or the rewards; it's the relationship that counts. Tend to the tomato plant, and its fruit will feed you. Take care of the relationship, and the rewards are plentiful.

CREATING A HEALTHY RELATIONSHIP

Your financial area of life has its own presence. This presence is your Big Mind nature that is undifferentiated, formless, and ready to be molded into form. The current state of your financial situation has come about from the decisions and actions you took, but what determined those decisions and actions were the qualities given to your financial relationship. Your financial area of life has its own presence and is molded into reality by the quality of relationship you give.

What Truth does is unveil those qualities you are resonating with. Love shows you the necessary qualities needed to have a healthy relationship with money. Power is the action that supports and sustains the qualities needed for a healthy relationship.

UNCOVERING YOUR TRUTH

The first step to a healthier relationship with money is to uncover the Truth with your relationship to money. This is equivalent to analyzing and understanding the current environment of your tomato plant. You cannot grow a healthy tomato plant unless you know the truth about its situation—is the soil acidic or balanced, is it the right season, and will the plant receive enough sun?

Here are a few notes about the voice of Truth before you begin. Truth is a quality that is part of our human nature. You never *become* truth, but you can *be* truth. *Becoming* Truth means that you need to get to a future state—that something not in the present needs happen in order for you to become Truth. But it never works, however, because the future isn't real, it's mind made. All you have is the present moment. Even if you want to believe in a past and future that's fine, but when you are thinking about the past and future, which moment are you thinking about them? In the present; therefore, since this moment is the only moment you ever have, you can only *be* Truth, not *become* it.

Why does this matter? When you identify as being Truth, you are the voice of Truth and speaking from its wisdom. You can either speak out loud as the voice of Truth or journal about your current relationship with money as Truth. What's important is that you are Truth, not the Self, which is your name. Therefore, refer to your Self in third person and you're speaking as Truth in first person. For example: *I am Truth. My job is to tell Nick how it is in his life.* Notice how I spoke in first person as Truth and referred to myself, Nick, in third person. If you get confused, the "real life example" in the next section is a guide to help you.

Okay, let's do this. May I please speak to the voice of Truth?

Say "yes," and identify as Truth: *I am Truth.*

Alright, the stage is set. You are Truth. To determine your relationship with money you need to inquire. *What qualities make up my current relationship with money?* Ask to be shown what qualities make up your current relationship with money. What is that relationship like? What is money?

For me, as the voice of Truth, my relationship with money is free and flowing. I feel abundant with money. I can sense appreciation, love, and power with this relationship. I've also noticed times when I slip into wanting it and that I don't have enough.

Pay close attention to the qualities that come out here. Some examples are: intimate, abundant, love, flowing, free, appreciation, patience, or greed, tight, fear, not enough, undeserving, and not worthy. Take note of the qualities that are determining your relationship with money.

96

What is money? Well, money is a medium of exchange. It's a commodity from the free market that makes it easy to exchange goods and services. Another way of viewing money is as service certificates. I render a service, and the individual I'm serving gives me a certificate(s) so that I can extract goods and services from society at my convenience. If I have ten service certificates, I can extract ten service certificates of value from other individuals who offer what I want and need.

What is your ideal situation with money? Where do you want to be with money? Remember to speak as the voice of Truth. Describe the type of person you would be in a healthy relationship with money, and describe how your environment would change.

Now, on a scale of 1-10, 1 being immature and unhealthy, and 10 being completely healthy, mature, and ideal, where do you fall on that scale? This is completely subjective, but it's your life and you are creating it. Realize that if you are anything less than a 10, the relationship is immature and unhealthy. You are actually a 1. Go back to what you have decided as your ideal situation with money. Is the jump from a 1 to a 10, which 10 is your ideal situation, too big of a stretch? If so, how can you bring it down a level or two?

Next step...now that you are uncovering the type of relationship you have with money, let's dig deeper for the Truth. *If your financial area of life represented a relationship with a friend, how would that friend treat you? What type of friendship would the both of you have?* Go ahead and take some time with these two steps and questions. You may not like what you see, or you may be surprised to the type of relationship you have with money, but put all judgments aside. Your goal here is to see the truth and create a healthy relationship with money. Whatever the Truth is to your current relationship, could you accept the situation? If you could, would you allow yourself to be okay with the situation? If not now, when?

The first step for an alcoholic to become sober and healthy is to accept that he is an alcoholic. He must move from denial to acceptance. It does not matter how you got to have your current financial relationship, who wronged you, and how you're going to get out of this mess. What matters is that you are fully okay with your financial situation. Acceptance opens the door for love to heal the relationship. Spend some time the next couple of days or weeks or however long you need reflecting on the Truth with your relationship with money. But as you're reflecting or thinking about it, have the quality of acceptance within your reflection. Ask to receive acceptance—*May I please have acceptance*—and reflect upon the truth to your financial situation.

A REAL LIFE EXAMPLE

Below is a real life facilitation I did with someone based on the two steps to uncovering your Truth above. If you felt stuck in those exercises, I'm sure this facilitation will give you an idea on how to approach the questions to Truth. I recommend reading through the facilitation first, and then go through the guide substituting "Nichole" for your name.

Facilitator: May I please speak to the voice of Truth?

Truth: Yes, I am the voice of Truth.

Facilitator: What is your job as Truth?

Truth: It's to be honest and not judge. I give Nichole the facts and get her to the bare essence of the situation. I let her know 'what is.' No fluff-n-stuff, I am straight to the point so she can get moving towards what she wants.

Facilitator: Since you are Truth, you know the cut and dry version to Nichole's relationship with money. What kind of relationship does she have with money? Describe what the relationship is like?

Truth: The relationship is alright. It could be better because she doesn't make a lot of money. Her reactions vary: neutral, proud, and occasional panic. The panic comes from the belief that she doesn't have enough. Sometimes she lives outside of her financial means. The money seems to run out faster than it comes in.

Facilitator: On a scale of 1-10, where 1 is completely unhealthy and 10 is healthy and mature, where does Nichole fall on that scale? Why?

Truth: I'd say it's a 7. From where Nichole was a few years ago, her finances have improved greatly. She is more responsible. She has money saved. She knows of all her bills and pays them on time. And she has little debt. The reason it's not a 10 is because the money comes in and goes out with little attention on her part. Sometimes she wonders, "Where does the money go?"

Facilitator: If this relationship was like a friend, how healthy is the relationship? What kind of friendship would you expect?

Truth: We're not best friends forever, but the relationship is gradually improving. It's becoming more intimate and present. Nichole is grateful for the money she has and how she is earning it. The relationship is fair and becoming more sovereign. The one thing she would like to change is how the money goes out faster than it comes in. Nichole and her income need to invest more time together.

Facilitator: What is Nichole's ideal financial life? What does financial freedom look like to her?

Truth: The ideal financial life is a place in which she doesn't have to look at her bank account and worry that there's enough. She pays the bills and has a healthy relationship with debt and her focus isn't on debt, but expressing her creativity and providing value. The ideal financial life is one of responsibility and accountability. It's not about having a large bank account, but having safety, sovereignty, and being able to make choices easily to have what Nichole wants.

EXPANDING ABUNDANCE

Once you figure out how to lock into a healthy state in one part of your life, you can use what you've learned to expand it to other parts of your life.

For example, suppose you're already enjoying a great deal of social abundance. Maybe you have a lot of good friends, and you're able to make new friends easily whenever you want. You always have people to hang out with whenever you want. In this part of your life, you've already achieved abundance.

And now suppose you're struggling in the area of finances. Maybe you're in debt, and paying your bills is a burden. Perhaps you have a hard time generating income consistently. Or you feel compelled to take on jobs you dislike to make enough money. In this part of your life, you're still stuck with scarcity.

You can apply what you've learned in the abundant part of your life to rework the scarcity-driven part of your life and gradually raise it up to a level of abundance.

Abundance and scarcity are simply different patterns of relationships. You may have one type of relationship with your social life and another type of relationship with your finances. You may have one relationship with your work and another relationship with your health.

Your relationship lessons can be generalized and transplanted. Just as you can use lessons applied from one human relationship to help you improve another human relationship, you can also apply your internal relationship lessons across different areas of your life.

I recommend that you explore in writing (such as through journaling) how you think and feel about the most abundant part of your life. Answer and journal about these questions:

1. Where are you getting the best results?

2. What's your attitude toward that part of life? How do you feel about it?

3. What kinds of actions do you take in that area?

4. How do you relate to this part of your life? How are you managing this particular relationship, and how is it responding?

5. How do you deal with success in this area?

6. How do you handle setbacks?

7. How do you keep the flow going? Do you have help, or do you manage it alone? Are you active or passive?

8. How did you create these results in this part of your life in the first place?

Then do the same for the part of your life where you're experiencing scarcity. Ask and answer the same types of questions. Aim to get a clearer sense for how you're managing each of these relationships.

Compare and contrast your answers. I'll bet you probably notice some major differences between how you relate to different parts of your life.

Now consider how you can apply what's working from your most positive internal relationships to your most negative ones. What can you do differently? What type of vibe is working best for you? How shall you approach the scarcity-driven parts of your life such that you can bring more abundance to them?

This approach has done wonders for me.

First I worked on financial abundance. Then I used those lessons to achieve time abundance. Next I achieved social abundance. And lately I've been exploring intimacy abundance. The general high-level pattern is essentially the same each time. It starts with creating and holding the right vibe.

Another step involves releasing fear and letting go of attachment to outcomes, putting myself in a place of knowing that I can have whatever I desire. Then I have to work through various blocks and limiting beliefs that are keeping me stuck at the old vibration. And finally, I need to courageously receive the new level of abundance, which invariably requires stepping outside my comfort zone.

For me this process usually plays out over a matter of months, maybe a couple of years max. The main limiting factors are how long it takes me to identify and release limiting beliefs and how long it takes me to summon the courage needed to leave my comfort zone behind and receive something new.

Another tip that can accelerate your progress significantly is to bring people into your social circle that is already enjoying abundance in the area of life in which you'd like to experience abundance, too. So if you want more friends in your life, for example, start hanging out with the most socially abundant people you know. Their vibe will soon rub off on you, and you'll slide into that new reality faster.

Try this for yourself, and be patient. Enjoy the journey of moving from scarcity to abundance, but don't think you have to get there overnight.

10.
Your Heart is Thirsty—Drink!

When you continually practice uncovering Truth in your life, acceptance for the way things are is natural. This Acceptance is not a passive and lazy I-don't-give-a-shit attitude; it's an empowered state of consciousness taking full responsibility for the life you have created, whether it's Self inflicted or out of your control.

Acceptance is a beautiful place to live. You are finally okay with who you are and how life is evolving. The war on life stops; the needing for something different vanishes. There are no uphill battles, wins and losses, or people you need approval from to feel good enough. You are free.

Why not stay in acceptance forever? You can, but acceptance and Truth becomes problematic after awhile. The reason being is because you disown cause and effect; you forget that you are a human being living in a relative world. Sooner or later your Karma is going to catch up. The financial mess you have created isn't going to get better unless you do something about it. Truth transcends the suffering around your relationship with money by turning it into peace and acceptance—a necessary beginning for a healthy relationship with money. But Truth is another mountain peak next to the Self, and you cannot stay on top of the mountain forever or you'll freeze to death. Let me show you what I mean.

Take out a blank piece of paper with no lines. Now draw a big triangle. Rotate the paper until the triangle is inverted—that is, the apex of the triangle is at the bottom. On the left hand side of the triangle you have the Self and all of his characteristics that he identifies with: seeking, control, anger, protecting, greed, victim, love, patience, intimacy, fear, dualism, rationalize, analyze, and on and on. The aspects of the

Self are limitless, and in Zen Buddhism they call the limitless faces of the Self the ten thousand Dharmas. Most of the world is trapped in the left hand side of the triangle, but don't think that the Self is destructive. You need the Self. Without the Self, you could not function in the world; you couldn't use an ATM or brush your teeth in the morning without re-learning the process every time; you also cannot express your Divine infinite wisdom and compassion, and you couldn't ground your creativity.

The right hand side of the triangle is what I've been calling the other shore. This side is Big Mind or nothingness or the formless or Godhead or your Buddha nature. It is seeing things as they are (Truth) without attachment or desire to *be, do, and have.* Looking at the inverted triangle figure, the Self and Big Mind are two mountain peaks. If you have too much Self, the ego dominates your experience. You only know separation and the thinking mind. There are others "out there" and a world you need to conquer and protect yourself from. Unfortunately, too much Self is what most people are stuck in, hence why the world is more problematic than ever.

If you have too much Big Mind, then you ignore the world of cause and effect. You know deep in your bones that everything is one, and you are not a separate Self in the world, but the whole on-going of life. At some point, if you stay stuck in Big Mind long enough, what happens in the world doesn't matter to you. There's no such thing as stealing, so if you steal, regardless of the consequences, it doesn't matter. There's no such thing as lying or cheating or having a body, so the consequences of those actions or how you treat your body do not matter. You are an enlightened human being, but at the same time you're not. You look down upon others as superior because you know the way; a spiritual ego forms. I believe this happens because your human nature catches up and then appropriates Big Mind. In other words, at some point you need to function in the world, so you identify with Big Mind, become "spiritual" and disown the Self; therefore, the Self comes out as disregarding cause and effect and being superior to others.

What you need to do is descend from the mountain into Big Heart. This is your solid ground; the intermediary between the worlds of Big Mind and the Self that embraces and includes both of them, but at the same time transcends Big Mind and the Self. Big Mind is the infinite wisdom of the Universe; the knowing of it all. The Self is the vehicle for the wisdom of Big Mind. Big Heart is the perceiver of Big Mind. It can grasp the qualities and intelligence of Big Mind and then embody those qualities to create your experience of life.

Remember, Big Mind is everywhere and every-when and does not discriminate; therefore, Big Mind is the greed, the suffering, the happiness, the love, the joy, and the fear in the world. When your heart, Big Heart, is left unawake, the grasping, egoic nature of the Self clings to the qualities of fear, control, greed, desire, and suffering. The Self wants the drama and suffering in his life. Why? There are two reasons: 1) the Self believes that through his drama he can get what he desires, and 2), the Self needs separation so he can confirm his existence.

Big Heart is the perceiver of Big Mind. Big Heart reflects and embodies the infinite ocean of Divine qualities into the Self and determines your relationship to a thing, such as your relationship to money. For example, I'm reading a book right now called *The Wild Seed*. I can say that the book has one author, is 265 pages long, and is 6" by 9". I've described the book's characteristics. However, those characteristics don't tell you anything about the book. I've described the book in a cut-and-dry manner. If I say, however, that *The Wild Seed* is fun, inspiring, thrilling, raw, boring, or lame, I'm describing the qualities of the book; I'm creating my experience and relationship with the book. Every quality that the human being recognizes in the world of outer appearances is derived first of all from the inner knowing of his own heart (Big Heart), which contains a complete sampling of the universe of qualities. The Divine (Big Mind) qualities are primary; the heart (Big Heart) is the interior mirror, and the world (the Self) is the outer mirror that embodies the heart's projections of these Divine qualities. [1] Every single relationship you have in life is a pretext for revealing to you the qualities that Big Heart encompasses.

Why then do you have an unhealthy relationship with money? If Big Heart is the perceiver of Divine qualities, and is reflecting those qualities into your life, why is your heart pumping qualities that create an unhealthy relationship with money? Interesting question…the answer is this: because the Self is rubbing soot on the interior mirror of Big Heart. Often times, Big Heart is obscured with conditioned thought, human emotion, and social conditioning. The Self tries to take the job of Big Heart thinking he knows best. But the Self is too small, limited, and needy. Or the Self is too human, as another way of putting it.

To clear the soot from the interior mirror you need consciousness and awareness of where you're coming from in this moment. Are you stuck in desire, fear, anger, and inflating your ego? Or, are you transcending the Self, removing your consuming attention and attraction to the world, and letting a deeper presence guide you?

The individuals that haven't awakened Big Heart and polished off the mirror are the ones consumed by their Self. The heart is cold and sick, numb and asleep, closed and disconnected, and possibly even black. Wake up Big Heart! When you awaken Big Heart, you removed the soot from the mirror and are reflecting wisdom and compassion into your life; thus, creating a healthy relationship with money.

AWAKENING BIG HEART

The cure for an ailing heart is to give it attention and medicine. To awaken and sustain Big Heart, you must give it attention with your presence and the medicine of direct identification as Big Heart.

The body's presence is the doorway to Big Heart. This presence goes beyond the thinking mind and beyond emotion, and directs your attention to the essence of life. Allow me to take you there right now...

Take a few deep breaths. Inhale through the nose, and exhale slowly through the mouth while puckering your lips to a pinhole size. Now, let your body feel the way it feels. Do you feel tightness? Anxiety? Jittery? Relaxed? However you feel in this moment let that be okay. Be with your feelings for a few moments. Locate where those feelings reside in your body. Are they in your chest, stomach, or head? Where's the pain located?

Now, anchor your attention into the aliveness of your hands. Feel the rhythm of the energy pulsating on and off. Be with that for a few moments.

Move your attention from your hands and into the corner of your eyes, right by your temple. Again, feel the energy pulsating around and at the corner of your eyes. Be with that for a few moments.

Next, move your attention to the middle of your chest. Feel the beating of your heart and the energy pulsating within your chest. Stay with that for as long as you can.

Finally, allow yourself to feel the aliveness of your entire body. Feel its energy and how that energy is heavily concentrated in some areas, but not so much in other areas. Observe your body aliveness from head to toe, as if it's one energy field.

Practice this "body aliveness" every day for 15 minutes. Also, take frequent breaks to feel the aliveness of your body as you go about your daily doings. For example, as I sit here and write, I make frequent pauses and anchor my attention into the aliveness of my body, always having an awareness of that presence. If you make this a practice for 30-days, you'll be amazed at how much healthier you'll feel and how your relationship with life begins to work for you, rather than against you.

I AM BIG HEART

My favorite approach to awakening and continually embodying Big Heart and other Divine qualities is what I call *Big Heart Dialogue*. This is a process that incorporates Voice Dialogue techniques, the infinite qualities that encompass the heart, and has Zen Buddhist roots. To go into detail about it here would take too long. This is why books have an appendix; therefore, please visit there.

Here's the essence of the practice in a short metaphor:

Imagine that you, the Self, are like a rough diamond jewel pulled from a river. A diamond in its rough state looks like coal. It is black, uncut and rough, but reveals some of its beauty and potential. The coal appears to not have much value, and at this point it could pass as being dysfunctional. What you need to do is cut the diamond, polish it, and refine its shape into the diamond's fullest potential. The diamond's beauty is revealed when all of its facets are exposed and enlightened.

What we do in *Big Heart Dialogue* is enlighten the many qualities of the heart and the Self by identifying with each quality and speaking as that quality; thus, chiseling the lump of coal into beautiful facets that illuminate and empower the Self.

We are only going to empower Big Heart here, but you can speak to, and empower, many qualities to full functioning: the controller, protector, anger, fear, and the dualistic mind, or Big Mind, Big Heart, No Desire, Patience, and the Full Functioning Human Being. It's a simple process. All you have to do is follow my facilitation. The key is to stay in voice and speak as that voice. Refer to you as either your name or the Self. For example, if I'm speaking to the controller, then I'm speaking from the point of view as the controller, in first person. "I'm the controller. And, my job is to control Nick's life." Notice how I spoke as the controller and referred to me in third person as Nick.

Below is a real facilitation I did with Nichole. I suggest you read through the facilitation to grasp the idea and to learn the technique of being the quality or voice that Nichole is speaking as.

Facilitator: May I please speak to Big Heart?

Nichole: Yes, I am Big Heart.

Facilitator: Okay Big Heart. Who are you again?

Big Heart: I am Big Heart.

Facilitator: Okay, great! I'm just making sure. Now, tell me...how big are you?

Big Heart: I'm as big as Big Mind, but I'm not as sterile. I include the Self—Nichole—and I include Big Mind; therefore, I'm compassion and the heart of the Universe. I'm grounded with one foot in the relative world and one foot in my true essence, Big Mind. People call me "oneness, love, and empathy."

Facilitator: As Big Heart, what type of relationship with money and income do you thirst for? What are those qualities that you want for Nichole?

Big Heart: I desire for a fulfilling relationship that is honest, open, abundant, and flowing. I'm present with money and understand its practicality. I know exactly how much is coming in and I do things that I enjoy to earn money. As Big Heart, my relationship with money is safe and secure, and those are the two qualities Nichole needs to embody the most.

Facilitator: What are the next action steps for Nichole to have a healthy relationship with money and income?

Big Heart: I'd say, first, it's for Nichole to work with the qualities of safety, security, truth, and flowing. All she needs to do is ask to receive those qualities and let them overwhelm her. Next, she needs to open her bank account and sit in presence with it every morning. She needs to acknowledge the money she has and take it in. Next, when she gets paid, take it to the bank. She struggles with receiving, so she needs to acknowledge her income and complete the transaction when she gets paid. This action will help embody power and sovereignty. Finally, as Big Heart, I recommend her to understand how she attracts her income and to be present with her reactions around financial matters.

BIG HEART AND A HEALTHY RELATIONSHIP WITH MONEY

Big Heart is the perceiver of Divine qualities and contains them all. Therefore, you can ask to have a healthy relationship with money and receive the qualities needed to grow and mature the relationship.

At first glance, this looks like a magical process: ask and receive? Then some Deity is going to enlighten you with the wisdom of the ages and your financial situation will be fixed. It's not like that. When you ask to have a healthy relationship with money, you are sitting in presence with your money relationship. You are stripping away thought and the Self from the relationship, and becoming intimate with your money relationship. This will certainly give you an objective view of how you're operating the relationship, but when the Self is relaxed—that is, when the thinking mind has dwindled close to no thought—a relationship filled with quality and love manifest. This isn't any different than having an intimate relationship with your partner. If your relationship is filled with thought, labels, judgments, and criticisms, you are unavailable to truly know that person; it's too clouded with your thoughts about the person. You think you know your partner, but what you know are your thoughts about your partner. When you go beyond your thoughts—that is, allow the thinking mind to think, but you're aware of no-thought—you know your partner's true Self. That's true love because you're tuned into your own presence and your partner's presence. Your heart is open to give your unique qualities and to receive the Divine qualities of your partner.

Here is the outline of the inquiry process you are going to work with for creating a healthy relationship with money:

1. Identify with Big Heart and rest in its presence.

2. Ask to be shown what a healthy relationship with money looks like. Ask to be shown the qualities that would create a healthy relationship with money.

3. Ask to receive and drink the qualities needed for a healthy relationship with money.

4. What next actions would tighten the bond to having a healthy relationship with money (this question is addressed in the next section titled "Big Heart is Power.")

FIRST STEP

The first step is to identify with Big Heart—I am Big Heart (go ahead, say it out loud). Take a few moments and sit as Big Heart. It may be helpful to quietly repeat the name "Big Heart" a few times as if you're speaking the name into the center of your chest. I'll wait…

SECOND STEP

Next step: ask to be shown what a healthy relationship with money would like. You can simply say or think, "As Big Heart, what does a healthy relationship with money look like?" Remember that you are Big Heart, so keep that presence with you by focusing on the aliveness of your body. Allow the healthy relationship to come to you.

As you're sitting in presence with your healthy relationship, what qualities would create a healthy relationship with money? If money were a friend, what type of friendship do you want? Do you sense a presence of patience, intimacy, strength, courage, and sovereignty?

Those could be the qualities needed to have a healthy relationship with money or they may be something totally different. It's also possible to not receive any insight of the qualities needed for a healthy relationship with money. Let that be okay, too. Your mirror may contain a lot of soot from conditioned thought, limiting beliefs, and social upbringings. Have faith that sitting as Big Heart and continually bringing your attention away from thought and into the aliveness of your body, is cleaning the soot off the mirror and creating a healthy relationship with money.

THIRD STEP

Next step: if you know of the qualities needed to have a healthy relationship with money, ask one-at-a-time to have those qualities. For example, if intimacy is a quality needed for a relationship with money, ask, "May I please have intimacy?" and drink that quality; bask as the quality of intimacy. Do this for each quality. Don't think that you have to receive and "drink" each quality during this meditation. You can work with one quality, and the next time work with a different quality.

This practice is working the relationship from the inside-out. What we typically do is go after money in order to be happy, fulfilled, secure, and at peace, so we give our power to money; we think that money is the answer. But our expectations always fail and money never gives us a true sense of safety or fulfillment. When you first ask for a healthy relationship with money, however, you are fulfilling your neediness by taking care of the "why" to why you wanted money in the first place. Imagine relating to the world from a place of fullness rather than from a needy Self. Instead of grasping, clinging, pushing, using people, and getting "what's mine," you bring love into your relationships. Which do you think is healthier: the one who needs and is hungry for money or the one who is already abundant and prosperous? I hope you chose the latter.

BIG HEART IS POWER

Talking about "heart" and "love" can easily lead you to believe that you'll be passive, vulnerable, and a sappy person. Big Heart *does* embody feminine aspects of our human nature, and you'll certainly be more intimate, vulnerable, and open to give and receive, but Big Heart has a masculine side that enforces and empowers. You may know masculine energy as "tough love," as that push to help and get something done. For example, if you know your child is struggling putting together a puzzle, you probably will not console the child, give sympathy, and have good cry on each other's shoulders. What you would do is have empathy and push your child to succeed. You will encourage, praise, and enforce responsibility upon your child. You say that you're giving tough love, but that is the masculine power coming through Big Heart.

Big Heart is the complete Ying and Yang symbol. If Big Heart is pure, it knows at all times when to give feminine energy or when to give masculine energy or the right mix of the two. I remember the time when my fiancé was struggling in her business. She wasn't working with the right clients that pay her well and are fun to work with. What's more, she was overwhelmed and pressured to make her business work. Bills were coming due. She wasn't making enough money to support her needs. And the whirlwind of details was dragging her attention away from what's important for her business to grow.

We were in the bedroom, and she was balling her eyes out. I had two choices: 1) Exercise masculine compassion by encouraging her, showing the path, and helping her to succeed, or 2), to be that shoulder and presence to cry with. I checked in with my heart and chose the latter: feminine compassion. I remained open and vulnerable. I gave her the space and empathy to emotionally go through whatever she had to go through. An hour later, she was done, and thanked me for listening.

A month later, her business shifted. She began connecting with her ideal clients and had plenty of money to cover her expenses. Now, it wasn't me that gave her clarity and power—I'm not a saint, sage, or healer. What I did was get out of the away and let her embrace the qualities that were attempting to be shown. How often do we try to fix someone when they are suffering? When your girlfriend is upset or your child isn't doing something right, we step in and say, "Look, if you do it this way you'll be fine" or "The answer is easy..." Executing the right skills were not the problem, eventually she will learn the skills to succeed. What she needs is to grow her capacity, heart, and strength to be the person who is a healthy match for that relationship. When you successfully align with Big Heart, the healthy relationship you're attempting to create is present. Now it's only a matter of keeping the mirror clean, and polish, polish, polish.

Out of the healthy relationship with money is where your actions and goals come from. What holds many people back is that they do not know what to do. You set an intention to improve your relationship with money and then now what? What actions do you take? This does make logical sense: if you're not a financially responsible person or you're deep in debt, how do you know what actions to do to get out of debt? You are never going to know the complete *how*. And I believe knowing *how* is not that important. There are countless ways to do anything. We would agree that there's one simple way to tie our shoes. But this is not true. Each time you tie your shoes you are doing it differently. You may remember the steps, but how you actually tie your shoes is never 100% the same. If you focus on having a healthy relationship with money, rather than *do, do, do*, you'll be inspired to take the right actions that make the biggest difference given your time, position, and place. And as a side-effect, you will not feel stressful doing the things that need done.

The actions you take are not ineffective unless you are not conscious about them. This means that your actions are ineffective when you're unconsciously acting from fear, overwhelm, and stress. Everything you do infuses the quality of your Being into what you do. For example, a few days ago I had a major headache. Plus, I was running on four hours of sleep. But refinishing the floors at my rental property couldn't wait. I had one day left in Pittsburgh before I flew back home to Maine. Normally I enjoy building and providing beautiful homes to tenants, but that day I was angry, frustrated, and overwhelmed. For about thirty minutes, I was cussing a storm—F this and F that, why don't I have any help, whah, whah, whah...cry more you little baby, right? I finally became aware of what I was doing. I asked, "Why Am I creating this suffering?" It was pointless. Here I am choosing to work and not accepting or enjoying the work. Anything I do from that dysfunctional state of mind will not have a good outcome. I'm poisoning my work and creating suffering for myself. I transcended the overwhelm and anger by accepting the situation and my state of Being. The day wasn't fun, but at least I was at peace with myself and not poisoning the environment with a negative attitude.

A great time to wonder about the actions you need to take is after the *Big Heart Dialogue* practice, or any meditative practice that you partake in. Rather than asking from the small needy Self, "What should I do today," ask "What is it that life wants from me?" The latter approach asks from true need and for guidance from Big Mind and Big Heart. You can also inquire further: "What are the next steps that I need to take to have a healthy relationship with..."

Anytime you look for wisdom from the small needy Self you receive conditioned habits and beliefs. This is not too helpful considering it's your conditioned habits and beliefs that keep you stuck. When you let go of the Self, you allow wisdom and compassion to flow in. A greater intelligence will guide your decisions.

Big Heart is the perceiver of the Divine qualities of Big Mind. Big Heart is the one that creates a healthy relationship with your Self and with the various compartments in your life, such as money. When you ask to receive a healthy relationship with money from the perspective of Big Heart, you'll receive the qualities needed to grow and mature your relationship with money. You're working from the inside-out, and fulfilling your neediness by opening the conduit for wisdom and compassion to flow through. From your healthy relationship with money, goals and actions will be created. A higher intelligence is guiding your decisions. You'll always know what to do when the appropriate moment arrives.

11.
Raise Your Financial Vibration to Embody Power

Over time we tend to fall into financial patterns that generate a fairly narrow range of results. We become comfortable with certain financial experiences; even if we don't like those experiences, they're familiar to us, so we gravitate back to them.

In order to raise your financial vibration (and improve your results), you have to shift your comfort zone. This normally requires pushing yourself through a period of discomfort. You must release the familiar to experience the unfamiliar.

ASSESS YOUR CURRENT FINANCIAL COMFORT ZONE

Answer the following questions as honestly as you can:

1. What level (or range) of income feels comfortable and normal to you, neither being stressfully scarce or excitedly abundant?

2. What's the income level where you'd start to worry if you fell below it?

3. What's the income level where you'd start to get excited if you rose above it?

4. What amount (or range) of cash feels comfortable and normal to you, neither being stressfully scarce or excitedly abundant?

5. What's the cash amount where you'd start to worry if you fell below it?

6. What's the cash amount where you'd start to get excited if you rose above it?

For example, you might define your income comfort zone as $30,000 to $50,000 per year. And perhaps your cash comfort zone is $2,000 to $8,000. Your own figures may vary wildly from these amounts. The only correct answer is whatever feels right to you.

Don't worry about being super-precise here. Obviously there's some guesstimation involved, but try to come up with specific figures to answer these questions. Your goal is simply to get a clearer picture of your current financial equilibrium.

You could have negative numbers here too if being in debt or experiencing a negative cash flow falls within your current comfort zone.

Your answers define your present financial equilibrium. You'll tend to gravitate to this range whenever you step outside it. When you fall below each range, you'll be driven to work harder to get back up again. If you start reaching the high end, you'll be hitting the edge of your comfort zone and will tend to slide back down again (often via self-sabotage or slacking off).

DEFINE YOUR NEW FINANCIAL COMFORT ZONE

Review your answers to the questions in the previous section. Now realize that these figures are totally arbitrary. You probably fell into these patterns based on what you learned from other people. If you had wealthy mentors, your figures are probably higher than most people. If you surround yourself with people who are broke or in debt, your figures are probably on the low side.

Ultimately these amounts are under your control. You can change them if you want. You can choose to stop reinforcing the old comfort zone and push beyond it.

Now define a new equilibrium you'd like to reach. There's no right or wrong answer, but I recommend doubling every number as a good step. When I want to reach a new level, I usually aim for a 3-5x increase because I like to push myself. If it takes me a few years to get there, I'm okay with that. It's a fun challenge to tackle.

CLARIFY AND ACCEPT THE CONSEQUENCES OF YOUR NEW FINANCIAL VIBRATION

Imagine what it would be like to be at your new levels, not in fantasy but in actual reality. How would this affect your lifestyle? What consequences and side effects can you imagine? Can you accept those consequences?

For example, will you need to start making new friends because you can see that some people will hold you back or react negatively if you starting doing better financially?

Erin and I lost a few friends as our finances improved. Some people started acting really weird around us, and it became obvious that they had major limiting beliefs about money, so we let them go. Then we attracted new friends who weren't so blocked in this area. This isn't a bad thing per se; it's just a shift you'll need to deal with.

It's very important to spend some time visualizing what your lifestyle will be like after you shift your financial equilibrium. Imagine going through your daily routine in your new reality. You might be excited at first, but there are always trade-offs. Can you accept all the natural consequences? For example, can you handle paying a lot more taxes? If you double your income, your taxes may more than double. Do you anticipate any problems in your social network? Do you expect that a career change would be necessary, and can you handle that?

If you can't accept the consequences and side effects of your new financial equilibrium, it's extremely likely that you'll make no progress in this area. The gravitational pull of your current comfort zone will be too strong.

For more on this topic, read the article *Fear of Success: What Will Happen if You Succeed?* (http://www.stevepavlina.com/blog/2004/12/fear-of-success-what-will-happen-if-you-succeed/)

BREAK YOUR OLD COMFORT ZONE, AND BUILD SCAFFOLDING TO SUPPORT YOUR NEW EQUILIBRIUM

Now we're getting into the action phase to initiate the shift.

A very effective way to escape your old comfort zone is to change the scaffolding of your life. This requires only a temporary burst of self-discipline instead of having to push yourself every day. If you have to push yourself hard every day, you'll probably fail to complete the shift. A better approach is to make changes to your environment that break your old patterns and begin conditioning new ones.

If you detect that any parts of your reality would conflict with greater financial abundance, you must break them, drop them, or leave them behind. If you want to orbit a new financial planet, you must escape the gravity of your current planet. You can't keep one foot on each planet.

You don't have to get every detail perfect. You just have to achieve a tipping point where you stop resonating with the old levels and start resonating with the new ones.

This is where you start saying, "I quit" to anything that isn't consistent with your new levels. If you're in a dead-end job that can't possibly help you reach your new equilibrium, set a deadline for quitting. If it's clear that your job will only reinforce your old equilibrium, there's no point in pretending you can stay. You don't have to quit right away, but you do need to accept that you'll eventually have to quit.

You don't have to stress yourself over the big changes right away. Start with the easy changes first, especially those that are low-risk. Don't spend money you don't have, but do be creative in altering your environment, especially your home and your social network. Start reinforcing the new equilibrium more than the old one.

This is a good time to clean house. Dump all the old junk that's inconsistent with your new equilibrium.

Review your social network, and start unplugging yourself from relationships that you know will be unsupportive after your shift. Then start building bridges with people you expect will help support you after your shift. This doesn't necessarily mean that you have to make wealthier friends. It just means you need to weaken the bonds with people who would resist your financial growth and strengthen the bonds with people who will support you.

Make a list of other changes you'll implement as more money begins to flow into your life, such as upgrading your computer, overhauling your wardrobe, taking a nice vacation, or buying more organic produce. Imagine that those things are becoming part of your daily routine. Implement those changes when you can afford to.

As you make small shifts one by one, you'll build momentum. The support structure for your old comfort zone will eventually crumble, and you'll gradually create a scaffolding for your new comfort zone.

If you find it too difficult to implement real changes because of too little time or money, then make the changes symbolically. For example, you can draw or cut out pictures that represent your new equilibrium, and then post them on your walls. One time when I wanted to increase my income, I put a small fountain in my office and said to the universe, "This is my wealth fountain. It represents the flow of more money into my life in exchange for the flow of information and ideas I'm giving to others." Then I put other objects around the fountain that represented abundance and growth to me, such as a couple of plants. My income shot up rapidly during that time. I encouraged Erin to try putting a wealth fountain in her office too. She did that and got excellent results as well.

By the time you've completed this step, you should feel that you've burned the ships behind you and that there's no turning back. This doesn't mean burning the food and supplies too! It simply means that you're clearly committed to moving forward. There should definitely be some pain if you try to slink back to your old comfort zone. For example, you may endure some humiliation for begging your old friends to take you back after telling them you have to let them go.

TAKE INSPIRED ACTION

As you continue to scaffold, your old comfort zone will begin to feel less and less comfortable. You'll start feeling more congruent with your new equilibrium, even though you may not see any evidence of it in your reality yet. You might be making $50,000 per year, and even though you've been comfortable near that level for years, now it feels uncomfortably low to you. You start feeling a pressure to make more money. $100,000 per year seems like it would be a lot more comfortable to you.

When I experience this positive pressure, it feels similar to sexual arousal. It's like I have this pent-up energy inside that needs to be released. It's actually a good feeling, more like eustress than stress. The release of this energy is the eventual manifestation of my desires.

When the energy is strong enough, there's a sense of inevitability about it. You can just *feel* you're going to get there. It's as if the manifestation is out of your hands now because the universe is working on it behind the scenes.

For example, I have this sense of inevitability that my book will be released on October 15th. It hasn't happened yet, but I can trust that it can and will happen. I feel the presence of a lot of pressure that needs to be released. When my book finally comes out, I'll probably feel relieved. The pent-up energy will finally flow into physical form.

This is how it feels right before you transition to a new financial equilibrium. There's this build-up of pressure, and you sense it needs to be released. If you aren't at this point, keep working on step 4 until you get there. You simply haven't created enough arousal yet.

At this point you're ready to take some inspired action. Generally the way this happens is that you'll start noticing new opportunities that are consistent with your new equilibrium. Your new energy level will attract them into your life. You'll notice new ways to earn more money.

You don't have to take major risks. Just start acting on the opportunities that present themselves. Your intentions will manifest in the form of opportunities, but you need to actively seize those opportunities.

When it finally comes, your final shift can occur pretty rapidly. One week you're feeling the positive pressure, and the next week the pressure has been released, and your equilibrium has already shifted.

Focus on the opportunities that allow you to create more value for others. Realize that making more money isn't selfish. It's actually incredibly generous, assuming that you earn income by contributing equal or greater value (as opposed to stealing or mooching off others).

If you double your income, it means you're contributing twice as much value to others. The money you earn is an IOU from society. If you have a million dollars in the bank, it means you've given at least a million dollars more value than you received—that's very generous. If you're in debt, it means you're taking more than you're giving. The more value you contribute, the more society owes you in return. If you allow your income to stagnate, it means you're holding back on the contribution side. That's lazy and selfish. Focus on expanding your contribution, and you'll find that society gives you a lot more IOUs.

ENJOY THE RESULTS

When you successfully alter your financial equilibrium, allow yourself to feel grateful for the shift. Embrace the new possibilities and lifestyle changes you can create. Genuine gratitude will help you lock in the changes and prevent you from backsliding.

It may take a while to become comfortable with your new financial position. Don't panic! Just relax and enjoy the ride.

Growth tends to occur in quantum leaps. It's unusual to experience steady linear growth for an extended period of time. What seems like linear growth is often just a form of stagnation. For example, you may get an annual raise that barely compensates for inflation, tax increases, and other expenses, but your lifestyle remains relatively fixed because you didn't increase your contribution. If you want to experience a new level, you must be the one to initiate and sustain the shift.

The point of hitting different financial tiers is to experience them fully and to learn and grow from your experiences. Once you've absorbed the key lessons of a certain level, you're ready to progress to a new level. You're in charge of the pacing.

A PERSONAL EXAMPLE

For me the major growth lessons haven't been on the side of attracting and spending more money—or even embracing more abundance—they've been on the side of finding my true voice and learning to create and share more value. While I agree you can create shifts by focusing on the lifestyle gains, most of my personal breakthroughs have been on the side of creative self-expression. I had to tear down my old comfort zone of being at a certain level of contribution and pass through the uncomfortable zone of stepping up to a new level.

For example, I'm currently going through the shift from blogger to publish author. I can't really say how this will impact my income (it obviously can't hurt), but the biggest part of this shift occurred in my sense of creative self-expression. I had to go through the steps above to create a sense of positive pressure to write a book. I didn't have to do that. I could have stuck to my old comfort zone as a blogger.

For example, my comfort zone of writing was articles in the range of 1,000 to 8,000 words. My book is longer than 10x my longest article.

121

But I also wanted to write a book that was more than a compilation of articles. I wanted to create something unified and coherent. I needed an idea that would fit the long form of a book. This was a big shift that took me well beyond my comfort zone. So that was steps 1 and 2.

For step 3 I had to ask myself, *do I really want to be an author?* It was reasonable to assume that my book would get a lot of attention because of my blog. Did I really want that? How would my friends react if I became a published author? Would that bother anyone (such as people who talk about writing their book *someday* but never follow through on it)? Did I really want more email, more interview requests, and more scrutiny? It took me a while to reach the place where I was willing to accept the natural consequences of this shift.

For step 4 I made a number of small changes to shift my comfort zone. I gave myself permission to blog less often, so I could have more time for my book. I created a chapter outline on my office wall from about 200 colored sticky notes, so whenever I sat at my desk, I couldn't help but notice the rainbow-colored wall in front of me, a constant reminder to work on my book. I told my friends I was writing a book, so they'd always ask me about it; I blogged about it too. That created more accountability and helped burn the bridge behind me. It would have been more uncomfortable not to write the book.

As I created this positive pressure to write my book, opportunities began coming to me. Eventually I got an offer from Hay House and negotiated a publishing deal with them. It all went pretty smoothly because I'd shifted my equilibrium. By the time they approached me, I was ready to become an author. The opportunities came to me, but I still had to act on them. That took a lot of work, but by this point there was no turning back. That was step 5.

Step 6 is still pending. The result that excites me the most is learning how people apply the book's ideas to solve problems and make improvements in their lives. I'm not worried about whether or not everyone likes it; I accept that I can't please everyone. But I can anticipate that these ideas will generate positive results for many people because that's the effect I've experienced. Not a day goes by where I don't consciously and deliberately apply the principles in the book.

So when you seek to raise your financial vibration, realize that it isn't just about attracting more money and experiencing more abundance. Pay special attention to the contribution side as well. If you want to double your income, think about doubling your value output.

How can you increase your contribution? The simple answer is that you either need to serve more people, or you need to deliver more value to each person you serve—or both. Can you go deeper? Can you go broader?

For example, writing a book allows me to go deeper and broader. It goes much deeper than any article or series of articles I've written. There's nothing on this site that compares to what I was able to convey in the book. Secondly, by expanding into an offline medium, I can get these ideas into the hands of a lot more people than I can reach with my blog. People who've never heard of my blog will be able to find the book in their local bookstores, including non-English translations in various countries.

You can create these kinds of shifts even if you work at a regular corporate job. You just have to think about putting yourself in a position where you can contribute more value to the people you serve (deeper), or where you have the leverage to positively impact more people (broader). This may be done by shifting to a more leveraged position within your current company, or it may require switching companies. You might even start your own business. You have many options, but you must be the one to initiate the shift beyond your current comfort zone.

The word comfort might sound...well...comforting. But too much comfort for too long is not a good thing. I encourage you to view comfort not as an accomplishment but rather as a state of decline. If you are too comfortable, you're coasting downhill. You're slowly dying on the inside, while something inside you longs to experience passion and excitement once again.

Instead of long-term comfort, aim for growth. Focus on increasing and expanding your contribution, and your rewards will naturally follow. When considered in isolation, a major financial gain isn't a reward that's worthy of you. It's a hollow victory that can comfort your body, but it cannot stir your soul. The soul-stirring reward is looking back on your life with deep gratitude for all the growth experiences you enjoyed (as well as those you endured) and feeling lovingly connected to all the people whose lives were made a little bit better by your presence.

SHIFTING YOUR VIBRATION TO MANIFEST YOUR DESIRES

Now that you're equipped with *how* to raise your financial vibration and create a new financial reality, I want to focus on the most important step to ensure that your new financial reality *will* happen. For this, let's talk about shifting your vibration.

You are not a physical being in a physical universe. You are an energetic/vibrational being in an energetic/vibrational universe. You are both a transmitter and a receiver of energy.

One of your greatest challenges as a human being is learning how to live as a vibrational being in a vibrational universe.

You don't attract into your life what you want. You don't attract what you think about. You don't attract what you feel. Desires, thoughts, and feelings are all important, but these are more effects than causes.

You attract what you're signaling.

Think of yourself as a vibrational transmitter. You're constantly sending out signals that tell the universe who you are in this moment. Those signals will either attract or repel other vibrational beings, events, and experiences.

You naturally attract that which is in harmony with your state of being, and you'll repel that which is out of sync with your state.

If your energetic self radiates wealth and abundance, your physical reality will reflect wealth and abundance for your physical being.

If your energetic self radiates anger and frustration, your physical reality will reflect that as well.

Since the signals you're sending out at any given moment tend to be fairly complex, your experience of physical reality will be equally complex.

Once you can accept that your vibrational self attracts compatible patterns, it becomes clear that if you want to experience something different in your life, you must somehow change the signals you're putting out.

YOUR VIBRATIONAL HUM

Listen to the vibrational hum of your being. Quiet your mind, tune in to your inner being, and listen to the ever-broadcasting radio station that is you. What types of signals are you broadcasting in this moment?

When I tune in for a moment, I can sense some of the signals that are emanating from me. I can feel that I'm radiating happiness and joy. I can sense that I'm sending out signals to attract positive, loving new relationships into my life. I can sense that I'm radiating financial abundance and increase. I can sense that my energy is very mental at the moment because I'm writing this article.

These are all thoughts, however. The true signal I'm emitting isn't a thought. It's a frequency. I might describe this frequency in words, but I can never get the words quite right because human language is inadequate to the task. If I try to describe my current signal anyway, I might use the following adjectives: flowing, smiling, happy, peaceful, soaring, white, soft, strong, expanding, warm, mindful, smooth, and energized.

I can also tune into signals from my environment. I can sense that my belly is broadcasting satiety since I just had lunch (a mixed green salad and some olives). I can observe that it's 49 degrees F outside. I can hear soft music coming from my computer speakers (sound is yet another vibration). I can subtly perceive Erin's signal transmitting from the next room. I can feel the combined energy of the people reading my articles around the world.

Overall, I can sense that the signals I'm sending out and the signals coming from my environment are in sync. I feel happy, peaceful, and abundant, and my environment reflects that. This is a stable state, one I experience often.

Your energy signature is the summation of all the signals you're sending out. Your thoughts and feelings aren't the cause of these signals though; your thoughts and feelings are actually effects of the signals. If you change the signal you're emitting, your thoughts and feelings will shift as well.

VIBRATIONAL EQUILIBRIUM

Your vibrational being and your environment will tend to move toward equilibrium over time. If your current life situation appears fairly stable, it's safe to say that you're maintaining equilibrium.

For example, if you're financially broke, and if this is a stable situation that has persisted for some time, then it's likely that most of the energetic signals you're exposing yourself to are also vibrating at a similar frequency of broke-ness. This includes the place you live, the people you interact with, your work environment, the events on your calendar, your furniture, and so on. Your being is immersed in a field of these signals, and this encourages you to vibrate at the same level.

If you continue to surround yourself with signals that reinforce your current state, then that state will persist indefinitely. You may be able to get away from it for a while, but you'll keep coming back to it if that's your equilibrium.

SHIFTING YOUR VIBRATION

Creating a temporary shift in your vibration is easy. You can create such a change in seconds. Jump around and move your body. Sing your favorite song. Smile for a minute. Hold a yoga pose. Take a cold shower. All of these will change your state. However, this won't create any sort of lasting change if you return to your old vibration afterwards. If your dominant signal remains unchanged, your equilibrium won't shift.

In order to shift your equilibrium, you need to break the old equilibrium. This means you must create a lasting disconnect between your current vibration and the environmental vibrations that are compatible with it.

There are basically two ways to do this.

First, you can shift your own vibration long enough to create a lasting disconnect with your current environment. If you start transmitting a new signal, you'll soon repel whatever in your environment is incompatible with your new signal. You'll also begin attracting other people, events, and experiences that are compatible with your new signal. Hold the new vibration long enough, and you'll see your whole physical reality change all around you.

You can apply this approach by visualizing your goals very vividly for at least 20 minutes per day. Visualize in such a way that you can feel strong emotions. An emotional shift indicates that you're broadcasting a new signal. The longer you can hold this new vibration, the faster your reality will shift.

The second method is to intentionally replace many of your environmental signals with new ones. Then you must hold yourself in that new environment. This will feel uncomfortable at first because you won't initially be compatible with those new signals. You must allow them to recalibrate your own vibration until you become compatible with them.

You can apply this approach by changing your environmental landscape—physically, socially, and otherwise. For example, stop spending time with your lazy friends, give away your TV, and hang out every day with the most productive people you know. This will feel uncomfortable at first, but eventually you'll start to integrate those new signals, and your own vibrational pattern will soon shift to come into resonance with these new people.

So to sum up, you can either change the signal you're emitting, or you can change the signal soup you're immersed in. Either way can be very effective at creating a lasting change in your vibrational pattern.

CREATING WHAT YOU DESIRE

To create what you want in your life, you must shift your vibrational pattern such that you're emitting a signal that's vibrationally compatible with your goals and desires.

You can identify that new vibration by vividly visualizing your goals until you feel different emotions, and those emotions stabilize at a certain point. Notice how your vibrational inner being feels, not just emotionally but energetically. Then return to your old state, and notice the vibrational difference between the two states. Compare and contrast the old vibration with the new one.

For example, here's how I'd describe the vibration of being broke and deep in debt, a frequency I emitted for many years: tight, knotted, twisted, chaotic, rough, blurry, red, dark, fast, changing, pressed, and squeezed.

Here's how I'd describe the vibration of financial abundance: open, free, clear, bluish-white, flowing, smooth, bright, focused, and intense.

Each vibration has a different energy signature. If I temporarily shift my default vibration to a state of feeling broke (just by imagining it as real), I can feel my vibrational self shifting its frequency too. If I held that vibration long enough, I'd soon find that my physical reality followed suit.

Hopefully it's obvious by now that if you want to shift your vibration, it's a bad idea to consistently expose yourself to incompatible signals. Watch the TV news about the ongoing financial meltdown and the recession/depression, and notice what happens to your vibration. Then notice what happens to your finances in the long run. If you want to experience financial abundance, this is a very bad time to watch or read mainstream news. This is the perfect time to read high-quality books or articles instead.

Learning to sense and control the vibrational frequencies you're emitting is powerful stuff. Once you really get this, you can intentionally shift your frequency at will to experience what you desire.

If you want to experience wealth, you can create that. If you want to experience a new relationship, you can create that too. If you want high energy and good health, you can create that as well.

This isn't to say that it will be easy for you to accomplish all of these things. It takes practice to adjust your vibrational frequency correctly, so be patient with yourself. Rome wasn't manifested in a day.

Part III: Living Your New Relationship with Money

12.
Overcoming Limiting Beliefs

None of us make decisions based on reality itself. We make decisions based on our beliefs about reality. When our beliefs are accurate, our decisions will tend to be effective, producing the results we desire. But when our beliefs are inaccurate, our decisions will often be ineffective, producing undesired results.

We all know how to make decisions *within* the structure of our beliefs. But sometimes we run into dead ends when trying to achieve our goals or manifest our desires. Perhaps we can articulate what we want, but we just can't seem to achieve it, whether it's a particular amount of money, a fulfilling career, a loving relationship, or a certain level of physical fitness. In such frustrating situations, the culprit is often our beliefs. Limiting beliefs hold us back from achieving what we want, turning our technically possible goals into effectively impossible fantasies.

Trying to achieve a goal with a limiting belief is like climbing a mountain while carrying a 100-lb pack. You may begin enthusiastically, but soon each step will be hard and painful, and your progress will slow to a crawl. Instead of pushing yourself to climb harder, a better choice would be to lighten your pack by dumping the limiting belief that's holding you back. Some people, however, become so attached to that 100-lb pack that they won't let it go no matter how restricting it is. Instead they blame the mountain, the rocks, or their shoes for his troubles. But for highly conscious, growth-seeking people, eventually there comes a time to release the old baggage. The lighter pack may feel strange at first, but it will soon enable more rapid progress, and the climb will be more enjoyable as well.

CHANGING YOUR BELIEFS TO ACHIEVE BETTER RESULTS

You already know that you're free to choose your actions (subject to any physical restraints you may be currently experiencing). And of course your actions have consequences. If you take action and observe a negative consequence, the wise advice would be to change your actions. If you take action and achieve a positive result, you'll probably want to repeat that action under similar circumstances. This is just common sense, right?

It's less commonly understood that you're also free to choose your beliefs. In fact, you're even freer to choose your beliefs than your actions because you needn't worry about being physically restrained from believing anything you want. Few people, however, take full advantage of the freedom to change their beliefs. Your beliefs have consequences just as your actions do, and those consequences aren't always positive.

How do you know when your beliefs are producing negative consequences? Look for areas of your life where you haven't been achieving your desired results even after trying many different approaches. You keep trying different actions, systems, or methods, but nothing seems to work. Most likely a limiting belief is preventing you from achieving what you want, so no amount of action will prove effective until and unless that belief is corrected. Many problems which cannot be solved at the level of action can be readily solved at the level of belief. A new belief will enable you to take different actions, thereby producing different results.

Changing your beliefs can be unsettling at first. But like all change, you get used to it. And once you do it enough times, you may even come to enjoy the process.

EXPERIMENTING WITH BELIEFS

For nearly 15 years, I've been experimenting with different beliefs. I basically use a trial and error approach, guided by a balance of intellect, intuition, and input from others. I select a belief that looks interesting, and I install it. After a certain amount of time, I try to discern how this belief is affecting my results. Sometimes this is a challenge, but usually the results are easy enough to detect. A new belief will guide me to think about the world differently, which causes me to look at situations from a new perspective, so I end up taking different actions. Consequently, I produce different results. My income goes up or down. My marriage becomes closer or more distant. I socialize with different people. My eating and exercise habits change. And so on.

If the results of the new belief are positive, I keep it. If the results are negative, I drop the belief. If the results are neutral, which is rare, I usually keep the belief just for the new experience. I enjoy seeing the world from a new perspective.

One of the reasons I opted to start a personal development business is that it would be difficult for me to enjoy long-term success in any other field. At some point I'd alter my beliefs in such a way that I'd shift myself right out of any other career—the old career would cease to interest me, and I'd be attracted to something entirely different. This is why I opt to define my career in terms of its message (the conscious pursuit of personal growth) rather than any particular medium (writer, speaker, blogger, podcaster, etc), as I explained in the article *The Medium vs. The Message* (http://www.stevepavlina.com/articles/the-medium-vs-the-message.htm). This business works well for me because it keeps pace with my own growth. I'm free to change my preferred manner of self-expression as my beliefs evolve. This year my primary outlet is blogging, and I earn most of my income from advertising and donations. Next year I might begin offering workshops and seminars, and after that I might release personal development books, CDs, and DVDs. My original goal was for this business to be an outlet for my own self-expression. It's a business I'm intentionally building to keep rather than to sell.

This is something to carefully consider as you work on your own beliefs. There's always a risk that your new beliefs could make you incompatible with your current job, income, relationship, lifestyle, etc. Personally I feel the risk is worth it. Although my current beliefs are somewhat distant from social norms, they're serving me well.

AN EXAMPLE OF A MEASURABLE RESULT FROM A BELIEF SHIFT

A positive shift in your beliefs can often generate dramatic physical results. For example, by adopting more empowering financial beliefs, my wife and I have greatly improved our financial situation over the past year. Compared to this time last year, both our monthly income and our cash reserves have quadrupled, while our expenses have remained relatively flat. That's a very measurable result.

Several belief shifts contributed to an improvement in my financial situation, but here's a very simple example. Last year I had a belief that said, "Asking for donations would make my web site look amateurish and unprofessional." Naturally I never asked for donations while I had this belief, and of course many other web entrepreneurs share this belief. But I decided to challenge this assumption, so I replaced it with the belief, "Many of my visitors want to help support me financially, and they'd be happy to donate if I gave them the opportunity to do so." This wasn't difficult to do because based on the feedback I was getting, the second belief seemed like it would be more accurate than the first. I knew some people would think asking for donations were downright dorky, but I was OK with that.

So what happened? People started donating. Duhhhhh. Ad revenue was unaffected as far as I could tell. It appears that first-time visitors are more likely to click an ad and leave, while long-term visitors are more likely to donate, especially when they receive significant long-term value from the site. In terms of the monetary amount, total donations have been increasing every month since I added the donations page in December 2005. Currently donations average over $50/day. Although it's not enough for me to live off by itself, it's a nice supplement to ad revenue. I also like that it serves as an additional feedback channel, since people often mention a specific article in their comments when sending a donation.

This is just one example of how a seemingly minor belief shift can unlock new actions and thereby generate new results. Again, the guiding principle is effectiveness. If you desire to improve your financial situation while clinging to beliefs that limit your income-generating opportunities, you'll have a hard time getting the results you want. I happen to think that generating an extra $20K/year passive income stream is a fairly positive result. And it's pretty good compensation for the occasional complaints I receive from fellow bloggers who cling to the belief that requesting donations is lame. I would have agreed with them at one time, but I can think of 20,000 reasons not to.

Let's see if donations buttons start sprouting all over the blogosphere now. Hehehe.

IDENTIFYING CANDIDATE BELIEFS

Where do you find good beliefs to install? I can recommend two good places to look.

First, look within yourself. Write down one of your goals, and then list any beliefs you can think of that might stand in your way. Then go over those limiting beliefs one by one, and create new beliefs to replace them.

For example, suppose you want to adopt a healthier diet. Perhaps you have a limiting belief like, "Healthy foods don't taste good." You might want to replace that with, "Healthy foods are delicious."

Secondly, look outside yourself. Find people who are already getting the results you want, and contrast their beliefs with your own to identify your next shifts. Reading books written by expert authors is a great way to do this, but make sure the author is already getting the results you want or is clearly on their way there. For example, if your goal is to become an accomplished real estate investor, you shouldn't model my entire set of financial beliefs because I'm not a real estate investor. But if you wish to build a high traffic web site and generate multiple streams of income from it, then modeling my beliefs in that area should prove most helpful.

Simply reading the work of other people who are already getting the results you want is helpful, since their beliefs will tend to rub off on you. But there are also some books written specifically about beliefs. For example, T. Harv Eker's *Secrets of the Millionaire Mind* explores 17 beliefs that wealthy people supposedly share, and these beliefs are contrasted with those of the poor and middle class. And of course the all-time classic book on wealth-generating beliefs is Napoleon Hill's *Think and Grow Rich*. I've found such books very helpful in adopting an entrepreneurial mindset. Neither of my parents was entrepreneurial, so I had to unlearn many of the financial beliefs I was taught growing up in order to succeed in business.

INSTALLING NEW BELIEFS

Once you've identified a new belief, you have to install it. I explained the basics of how to do this in Podcast #5: Beliefs (http://www.stevepavlina.com/blog/2005/10/stevepavlinacom-podcast-005-

beliefs/). Essentially you immerse yourself in the new belief until your subconscious accepts it as true and integrates it into your mental operating system. My favorite method is to use visualization, but some people swear by verbal affirmations, especially when combined with strong emotion. The techniques in the article Cultivating Burning Desire (http://www.stevepavlina.com/articles/cultivating-burning-desire.htm) can also be used to recondition your beliefs.

Be patient with yourself because it can take a while for new beliefs to take hold. It usually takes me anywhere from a few weeks to several months before I've successfully integrated a new belief into my subconscious, depending on my internal resistance. If there's no resistance, I can install a new belief in a day, but that's rare for significant changes. It takes time for my mind to accept the new belief as fact instead of merely considering it as a possibility or an interesting idea, and it has to be successfully integrated with all the other thoughts going through my head. Installing a new belief is like getting an organ transplant. It takes a while for your body to accept the new organ, and there's always a risk of rejection.

You'll know when your new belief has taken root because you'll begin to act in accordance with it without even thinking about it consciously. It will feel just like any other belief to you, in principle no different from a belief in gravity.

ENJOYING THE PROCESS

You may find it difficult to shift your beliefs at first, but like any other skill, it takes practice. Don't set yourself up for failure by trying to reprogram your whole life in one day. Start with something small, like getting yourself to enjoy eating a little healthier or conditioning yourself to be less socially phobic. There are no deadlines here. You have your whole life to keep experimenting.

Don't worry too much about straying from social norms. Whenever you want to push beyond average results, you'll find yourself adopting fairly uncommon beliefs. Wealthy people don't hold the same financial beliefs as the poor and middle class. Happy people don't have the same emotional beliefs as depressed people. And healthy people don't have the same diet and exercise beliefs as sickly or overweight people. The more exceptional you want your results to be, the more you have to push beyond the limitations of social conditioning. Exceptional results require exceptional beliefs.

Installing a new belief is like exploring a new dungeon in a role-playing game. What new treasures will be discovered? What monsters will be stirred up? What experience will be gained? Getting that sack of loot and going up a few experience levels is easily worth a few battle scars. And what's the alternative anyway? Spending your whole life as a level 1 human, never knowing the joys of levels 10, 20, and beyond?

If you want to see rapid improvements in changing your beliefs, I recommend Morty Lefkoe's *Recreate Your Life* to tear down your limiting barriers and install empowering beliefs to have the confidence and success you desire.

EIGHT GUIDELINES FOR CHOOSING EFFECTIVE BELIEFS

Effective beliefs are...

1. Accurate. Effective beliefs must be consistent with your observations of reality. Your beliefs cannot contradict any facts you know to be true.

2. All-inclusive. For your beliefs to be effective, they must collectively address your entire field of experience. If you experience things you cannot explain from within your belief system, then your belief system is incomplete. And an incomplete belief system can never be fully trusted.

3. Flexible. Effective beliefs adapt well to new circumstances. They serve you well regardless of your career, income level, relationship situation, lifestyle, etc.

4. Ethical. It is never effective to choose beliefs that lead you to harm yourself or others. Such beliefs are rooted in fear, and fear comes from ignorance. If your beliefs are true, then you can accept reality rather than fear it, which means there is no cause for violence or dishonesty.

5. Congruent. Either your beliefs must be internally consistent with each other, or you must have a higher order meta-belief that tells you how to resolve lower level incongruencies.

6. Consciously chosen. You inherit your initial set of beliefs from your upbringing and societal conditioning. But as a fully awake adult, those beliefs should be identified, examined, and then deliberately altered or integrated. This is an ongoing process that can take years, if not your entire lifetime.

7. Pleasure-increasing and/or pain-reducing. Effective beliefs make you feel good, either by elevating your emotional state directly or as a side-effect of generating results you desire. Effective beliefs also reduce fear; when your beliefs are accurate, certainty replaces fear.

8. Empowering. Your beliefs should allow you to experience whatever is technically possible; they should never mislabel the possible as impossible. Subject of course to ethical/moral considerations, your beliefs should not unduly limit your abilities. If you belief something is impossible for you, then it must truly be impossible regardless of your thinking. If a belief shift would change your abilities (like the placebo effect), then your belief is both disempowering and inaccurate.

Let's consider a couple examples to illustrate these criteria.

BELIEF EXAMPLE 1: MOST PEOPLE JUST WANT TO BE LEFT ALONE

Imagine a young man who believes most people just want to be left alone. Let's call him Paul (not a real person). Paul's belief dictates the terms by which he interacts socially. He has a few friends, and he's fine socializing with people he already knows, but he has a hard time making new friends. He's unlikely to take the initiative because it's too big a risk with a high probability of rejection. Paul doesn't want to annoy people who want to be left alone, so he mostly keeps to himself. His social circle remains small and stagnant, and most of his social connections come from his work. Paul has virtually no relationship prospects because he considers women to be unapproachable except under extremely rare circumstances. If he sees a woman he'd like to date, he remains silent and aloof. Paul feels that to ask her out would be a social *faux pas* because after all, she just wants to be left alone.

How does Paul's belief perform against our criteria? Let's take a look.

1. Is it accurate? I think most people would agree this belief is inaccurate and too pessimistic. The best way for Paul to find out would be to test alternative beliefs and note the results. The problem with this belief is that Paul would rarely ever test it, so he'll gather little or no evidence either way. Perhaps he formed this belief by over generalizing after a bad experience. On those rare occasions when he does push himself socially, his belief will negatively affect his communication style, thus encouraging the rejection he expects.

2. Is it all-inclusive? This criterion doesn't apply because we're taking a single belief out of context here. But this single belief will influence Paul's entire field of social interaction.

3. Is it flexible? No. Paul's belief is unnecessarily rigid. A more accurate belief might be that some people are more friendly and approachable than others. And even the same person will be more or less approachable depending on the exact conditions. Paul's belief is a worst-case scenario, and it will limit him socially even when conditions are excellent. It will also serve him poorly in people-oriented careers, such as sales or communication.

4. Is it ethical? You could make a case that this belief is somewhat immoral. If Paul sees a stranger in need, he'd likely avoid that person instead of offering help. Paul wouldn't become a criminal, but he'd behave apathetically towards others. He might be internally motivated to act, but his belief will cause him to hold back.

5. Is it congruent? That would depend on Paul's other beliefs. There are many popular beliefs that would be incongruent with this one though. For example, if Paul was a practicing Christian who strongly believed in loving service to others, Paul would be internally conflicted. His religion would urge him to help people, but his social resistance would cause him to hold back. At best he might donate money from the sidelines, but he wouldn't feel free to give openly from his heart and express his generosity. If Paul were an atheist, however, there would be no inherent conflict with atheism itself, but there could certainly be conflicts with other parts of Paul's social and moral code of conduct.

6. Is it consciously chosen? Not likely. This was probably a socially conditioned belief or one that developed as an unconscious reaction to social rejection. It's doubtful Paul would have chosen to adopt this belief consciously. If he's consciously aware of this belief at all, he probably wants to replace it, but he may be stuck if he also believes that he can't change his beliefs.

7. Is it pleasure-increasing and/or pain-reducing? On balance, no. This belief may reduce the amount of rejection Paul experiences by causing him to avoiding risky social situations. However, by avoiding a 10-second rejection, Paul kills off the possibility of a long-term relationship as well as abundant new friendships. This belief also keeps Paul focused on his fears, which will likely cause him to experience far more pain in the long run, including the pain of regret. This belief will almost certainly drive Paul's emotional state in a negative direction, possibly for his entire life.

8. Is it empowering? Definitely not. This belief causes Paul to unnecessarily limit himself. Paul will miss opportunity after opportunity. But if he could get himself to take action, some of those opportunities would pay off. He won't ask for the date, for the promotion, for the raise, for help, etc. Technically all of these things lie easily within Paul's power, but this belief will prevent him from tapping that power. Consequently, Paul will lead a far more stagnant life than necessary. His belief effectively makes the possible impossible.

Clearly Paul's belief that most people just want to be left alone doesn't perform too well according to our criteria.

Let's consider a second example.

BELIEF EXAMPLE 2: PEOPLE ARE USUALLY FRIENDLY AND APPROACHABLE

Consider another young man named Chris who believes that people are usually friendly and approachable. Like Paul's belief, Chris' dictates the terms of his social interaction. Whenever and wherever he sees people, Chris is open to interacting with them because he expects they'll be open to it. While standing in line, he'll strike up a conversation with the person behind him. Chris has an abundance of friends and contacts because he's constantly meeting new people. He enjoys a rich social life and goes on dates often because he's always asking. Sure he gets a cold response on occasion, but he knows that everyone has an off day now and then. Because Chris openly interacts with people on friendly terms, people usually respond to him in kind. Consequently, Chris' enjoys an ever-expanding social circle.

How does Chris' belief measure up?

1. Is it accurate? Partially. Like Paul's belief, Chris' is also something of a self-fulfilling prophecy. Even when the people around him are socially neutral, Chris' openness often draws them out. So while Chris' belief may not be totally accurate from a purely objective sense, it is accurate from a subjective one.

2. Is it all-inclusive? This criterion doesn't apply because we're taking a single belief out of context here. But this single belief will influence Chris' entire field of social interaction.

3. Is it flexible? Yes. This belief can adapt well to a variety of social circumstances. The word "usually" gives Chris an out whenever he encounters people who react coldly to him. To him it's just a fluke but not the norm. This belief should serve Chris well across a variety of careers. He could succeed in sales, engineering, or other disciplines. This belief doesn't make Chris an automatic extrovert—it simply opens social doors for him.

4. Is it ethical? Yes. This belief is at least ethically neutral. It enables Chris to freely interact with others in need, but it doesn't compel him to do so, nor does it push him to pester anyone who'd rather be left alone. This belief won't get in the way of Chris' moral code, and it would likely help him wherever service to others is concerned.

5. Is it congruent? That would depend on Chris' other beliefs. But overall it meshes well with popular belief systems. It doesn't create conflicts with Christianity, Buddhism, atheism, or other major philosophies.

6. Is it consciously chosen? Maybe. Typical Western conditioning encourages isolation and social cocooning, but Chris could have been raised within a family and cultural structure that installed this belief. It's also possible that Chris started with a belief like Paul's, realized it was limiting him unnecessarily, and consciously reconditioned himself to adopt this new belief.

7. Is it pleasure-increasing and/or pain-reducing? Yes. While Chris may encounter some rejection as a result of his openness, overall this belief should help him attract abundant positive social interaction. This belief will help steer Chris away from fear and isolation and towards rewarding relationships. It's been said that 80% of our happiness in life comes from our relationships, and Chris will be able to tap into that.

8. Is it empowering? Yes. First, this belief will allow Chris to benefit from open social interaction with others. Secondly, by taking action Chris will gain experience, which will help him make new distinctions and continuously refine his social skills, thus increasing his success rate and reducing the amount of rejection he experiences. For example, if Chris works in sales, he'll become better at pre-screening prospects so that he doesn't waste as much time presenting to people who aren't ready to buy. And in terms of relationships, Chris will become more adept at interpreting subtle signals, allowing him to solve problems before they devolve into resentment.

Overall Chris' belief appears very effective according to our criteria. Such a belief should serve him well for a lifetime.

In reality Paul and Chris would each have their own unique web of thousands of individual beliefs with countless interdependencies. Considering a single belief in isolation has its limitations, but it's a good place to start. Simply becoming conscious of a limiting belief you'd like to change is the first step towards replacing it with a more empowering one.

YOUR HOMEWORK

Take a moment to write down some of the beliefs you have about reality. What do you believe to be true about your health, career, relationships, finances, spirituality, etc? Then go over the eight criteria above to see how they measure up. If you don't like what you see, craft more effective beliefs to replace the old ones. Remember that your beliefs are not mere observations of reality—they shape and create your reality as well. Many of the thoughts you hold most sacred may reveal their hidden falsehoods once you take the opportunity to test one or two alternatives.

13.
Giving Meaning in a Meaningless World

Recognizing your beliefs is probably the most challenging quest you'll have during your conscious growth journey. Questions like, "How do you determine if it is a belief? How do you know which beliefs are contributing to your limited financial situation? How do you effectively and easily eliminate beliefs?" I know I had such questions when I set out to change my relationship with money.

In the last chapter, two methods were given for uncovering your current beliefs: 1) Write down one of your goals, and then list any beliefs you can think of that might stand in your way, and 2), Find people who are already getting the results you want, and contrast their beliefs with your own to identify your next shifts. Both are valuable tools, and will certainly get you on track to uncovering some limiting beliefs about money; however, it's easy to trick yourself into thinking that you don't have a particular belief, when you actually do, and that you have a limiting belief about money, when you actually don't. Let me explain.

I used to write these words on paper, "Money is …" and then write down whatever came to mind: *money is evil, money is a social tool, money is a source of inspiration, money is happiness, there's not enough money in the world, I don't have enough*, and so on. The point of that exercise was to uncover my beliefs about money. The list was long, and every month I invested about thirty minutes doing that exercise. Something always felt "off," however, because I didn't know if they were true. How accurate were they? Was my thinking mind tricking me? Did I really believe two full pages of those beliefs about money, or am I imagining things? Eventually, I ditched that approach because my financial situation wasn't changing.

Fast forward a few days…I was having a conversation with a mortgage broker discussing the opportunity to invest in multi-unit apartment buildings. I asked him what the ball park price range would be for buying, renovating, and then refinancing the buildings. He said the starting price is roughly $500,000 and when I'm done renovating I could refinance close to a million dollars. In that moment I caught myself thinking and feeling, "I'm not good enough to do that" and "I can't afford it." Those were two limiting beliefs I held about money. Is it true that "I'm not good enough"? Of course not. I have plenty of evidence that "I'm good enough" to do anything that I put my mind, time, and energy towards. I also know that there's a price to pay to get good at something, too. The better question to ask is, "Am I willing to pay the price to get x?"

Is it true that "I cannot afford it"? Yes and no. Yes, because I didn't have the cash or credit right now to make the purchase. No, it's not true because I could find money partners or consider creative financing to do that project. Holding those two limiting beliefs were seriously limiting my financial income and available opportunities. And because I was aware of those beliefs in the moment they occurred, I was able to consider other perspectives before making any decisions.

Now here's the point: the best time to discover your beliefs are in the moment they are happening. You deal with them now and they will cease to bother you in the future. Simply recognize what meaning or belief you are giving in this moment, and then separate the meaning or belief from the actual event. This does require awareness on your part. If you ever get the opportunity to have a superhero quality, choose the ability to have profound awareness. You will be a belief eliminating machine. Fortunately, you already know "awareness" from the second section of this book: *Creating a Healthy Relationship with Money*. I believe it's important to see how beliefs occur so you become excellent at realizing the beliefs you have in the moment they happen. This way, you won't have to wait for a superhero moment.

HOW BELIEFS OCCUR

The majority of people believe that the experience of their life happens in this manner: An event occurs > the event determines how they feel > the event and their feelings determine their experience of life. For example, the stock market crashes and you lost 98% of your savings (the event). Since you are broke, you feel worthless and ruined (your feelings, which also magnify your experience of life). You decide to blame the economy and conclude that you are not meant to be rich, therefore, live an unhappy and minimal life (your experience of life).

Here's another example: Your two year relationship suddenly comes to an end. She flat out dumped you. Her dumping you is the event that occurs; therefore, you are angry and feel pathetic, which is how you feel. You decide to never trust women or become intimate with anyone again—that's your experience of life. You believe that all women are evil. What you did here was interpret the event of being dumped as "bad," which lead you to feeling angry and pathetic. To get rid of this "bad" problem, you protect yourself by believing that all women are evil. Since beliefs are self-fulfilling prophecies, you avoid women, intimate situations, and attract more "evil" women. Not good. Let's look at the cure.

Here's the way your life scientifically proven unfolds: An event occurs > the event passes through a series of internal filters, such as beliefs > you distort, delete, and/or make "true" based upon what you believe > you determine meaning(s) for the event > you feel and take actions > you get results in your life. For example, the stock market crashes (the event). You believe that you do not deserve money (that's the internal filter of what you believe). Therefore, you distort the situation and determine the event is bad and a horrible situation (that's the process of distorting and determining the meaning for the event). You feel pathetic and angry and do nothing (that's the feeling and action part). The result you get is depression.

Here's another example: You step on a scale and it reads 110 pounds (that's the event). You believe that you're healthy and fit and health is your natural birth right (that's the internal filter of beliefs). You determine that your weight is a good situation and you feel happy (that's the meaning you're giving to the event). Because of that meaning, you feel happy, fulfilled, and motivated to keep exercising and eating healthy (that's the feeling and action part). As a result, you maintain a healthy weight, look sexy, and feel good about it.

The two things you want to pay attention to are beliefs and meaning. These are the two internal filters that basically create your experience of life. To show you what I mean, let's take the same example above, but change the belief and meaning to see what happens. You step on a scale and it reads 110 pounds (that's the event). You believe that you're fat because every time you look in the mirror your body has love-handles (that's the internal filter of beliefs). You determine that you're weight is bad and you feel fat and depressed and disgusting (that's the meaning you're giving to the event). Because of that meaning you feel depressed and angry. You don't exercise and consistently eat fatty foods (that's the feeling and action part). As a result, you continually prove that you're fat and overweight. You attract the evidence through your body, people confirm that truth by telling you, and you feel disgusting.

I know what you're thinking, "I stepped on the scale and it confirms that I'm overweight." That may appear so, but the reality is that you are comparing a social standard to your situation. Your weight or how your body looks is meaningless; it just is. You can easily change the meaning by appreciating your body, embracing those negative emotions, visualize what you really want to motivate you, and take action that creates a healthy and fit body. By changing the meaning, you invite empowering beliefs to grasp and you change the results of your situation. In order to do this, however, you need to see the meaningless world.

NO MEANING

Every event and situation in life is meaningless. You are the one that determines the meaning to what happens to you in life. You can choose no meaning through the lens of Big Mind, or you can embrace no meaning and meaning through the lens of Big Heart, or you can give absolute meaning, even though it's not true, through the lens of the Self. What you want to do is take control over what you can control. You cannot control the events that happen to you, nor can you control other people. What you can control, however, is how you feel and behave, the meaning you give to events, and what you believe. Ironically, once you shift from trying to control your environment to taking full responsibility of what you believe, the meanings you give, and your feelings and actions, your environmental circumstances change. You are attracted to people and opportunities that are in alignment with your internal processes. Thus, giving you different results and a new experience of life.

The meanings you give to an event and what you believe are two separate things. If you dissolve your meanings with awareness, you are not trapped in conditioned feelings and actions. In other words, you are not fixed with one perspective. You have choice to how you want to feel and how to behave given the current situation. For example, you look at your bank balance and feel awful because it's significantly lower than you thought. In that moment you feel awful, however, you are aware that the meaning you're giving to the situation is "bad." Since you know that you are labeling the situation "bad," the thoughts and feelings of "bad" are gone. You may feel intense, but the labels and judgments are gone, and you're open to consider other perspectives. You decide that it's not a "bad" situation to have low bank balance, but rather, you decide to feel motivated to increase your income. You are now acting resourcefully to get what you want.

You may conclude that awareness over "meaning" lead you to feel different and take different actions—this is true. But this doesn't stop the result from occurring over and over again. Next Wednesday you could check your bank balance and the situation repeats itself: you feel "bad" about a low bank balance. Dissolving meanings when they occur make you free. You are not imprisoned by your emotions or the thinking mind. You are enlightened to be at peace in any situation and to act appropriately given the situation.

CREATING BELIEFS TO EXPERIENCE SOMETHING DIFFERENT

What if you want to experience something different in life? What if you want to change the game to that of a higher income? This is where beliefs come into play. Deciding what to believe will help you notice the opportunities to get what you want and attract the people that resonate with your beliefs. Notice how I didn't say "what you believe will give you what you want." It doesn't work that way. You must do something and pay the price to get what you want. There's nothing magical about creating the life you desire. High income earning people pay a huge price to earn a high income. Some high income earners accept that price and move forward with earning a high income; other high income earners suffer because the price is not worth it to them. I personally do not value accumulating a lot of money. So you won't see me making risky investments, building large companies, managing hundreds of passive income streams, and allocating many hours towards work. Money is important, but I value a different life than being a multi-millionaire or billionaire. Do not become a victim to the magical based thinking of the law of attraction: ask, believe, and receive.

So if you want to change the game you're experiencing, how do you discern between a meaning and a belief in the moment? You figure out, in the moment it is happening, how you are *doing* the meaning you are giving.

Let's say you have checked your bank balance and it is lower than expected. For the past year every time you have checked your balance you feel awful. You know the meaning you are giving in that situation: awful and bad. So it's not really "awful" because that's the meaning you have assigned. You have decided, however, to change your experience of life. Where to start? Consciously identify with beliefs that will give you the best possible opportunities to increase your income. The next time you notice the meaning(s) you give when you view your bank balance, ask, "How am I doing this feeling?" This inquiry helps bring forth the beliefs that are contributing to your current experience with income. You may notice that the way you do the feeling/meaning is that you think "I'm not good enough" and "If I make a mistake or fail, that would be bad. My family will hate me." Those thoughts are your beliefs. Now that you are aware of them, you can apply your favorite belief elimination method, or you can watch the belief with awareness until you no longer believe that you are "not good enough" or that "mistakes and failures are bad."

The question to ask is "How am I doing this feeling?"—substitute "feeling" for "meaning" if you prefer. You are not looking for *why* I feel the way I feel, but rather, *what internal processes are causing me to feel the way I feel*. Behind the meaning or feeling is a belief. And the belief is contributing to your interpretation of that event, to the actions or no-action that you take, to your feelings, to the people you are attracted to, and to your experience of life. Beliefs are that powerful.

Here's the process in review:

1. Notice with awareness a negative meaning or feeling that you're giving when relating with money.

2. Ask, "How am I doing this feeling?"

3. Watch with awareness the thoughts that are zooming by. Normally your beliefs will become known through your thoughts.

4. Take note and apply your favorite belief elimination process.

Does it really take that much work to uncover my limiting beliefs and install empowering ones?

At first it may feel that the situation, your feelings, and thoughts zoomed by so fast that you didn't gather any information. Let that be okay, it's not a race. Noticing that you're thinking and have certain feelings in the moment is a huge win because you are conscious. As your conscious awareness grows, your thoughts and feelings will dramatically slow down. Ninety-eight percent of the time I know exactly how I feel and what I'm thinking. I do not say this to brag, but to give you perspective that a completely conscious life is possible. Yes I admit that I do fall unconscious sometimes. I'll eat too much, get angry without knowing it, make bad decisions, drink too much coffee, etc., but for the most part I'm creating my life the exact way I intend to. This doesn't mean I get everything I want in life, there are outside forces that I cannot control that sometimes block my desires. It also doesn't mean that I do not have blind spots, I have plenty of them. I'm okay with that, and I keep focusing on what I want. If what I want to create is a huge challenge and whole new game level, I usually invest energy into figuring out what I believe and what other people believe who are already enjoying the new game I desire.

Remember, any gain in conscious gives you choice. You cannot do anything dysfunctional to your Self, others, and the world when you're consciously aware of your thoughts and feelings in the moment. Beliefs are a huge part for designing your life, but don't believe that you need to figure out your beliefs to be successful. That's just another trap.

14.
Designing Your Life

HOW TO SET GOALS YOU WILL ACTUALLY ACHIEVE

A major obstacle that prevents people from enjoyably achieving their goals is that they set their goals incorrectly to begin with. This problem occurs because people don't understand the nature of time well enough. When people consider a particular goal, they often worry about the time commitment: If I start my own business now, it could take years to make it profitable. I'm so overweight it could take years for me to get in shape. If I break off this unfulfilling relationship, it could take years to get back on my feet again. Such thoughts are clearly demotivating, but more importantly they reveal a total misunderstanding of the nature of time.

We value our time, so we have a natural tendency to be expedient. And we also want to enjoy the present moment. Consequently, we're disinclined to set goals that will take a very long time to achieve. Who wants to toil for years in order to reach a potentially better someday? Most of us simply don't have the discipline to do that, even if there is a pot of gold at the end of the rainbow. Discipline is not the real issue, however. The issue is a misunderstanding of time.

We tend to think of time as a resource that we spend, just like we spend money. To complete a one-hour task is to *spend* an hour on it. How are you *spending* your day? Where do you want to *spend* your next vacation? How will you *spend* the rest of the year? Time is money, a disposable resource.

This is a silly and inaccurate way to think about time, however. Time is not a resource. You cannot spend time. Time spends itself. You have no choice in the matter. No matter what you do, the time is going to pass anyway. It doesn't matter if you do one thing or another for the next five years. Those five years will pass no matter what you do.

In reality you are never in the past or future. You exist only in the present moment. Even when you remember the past or envision the future, you're still thinking those thoughts in the present. All you really have is right now. And that's all you ever will have. You can't control the passage of time, but you can control your present moment focus. That's all. No past. No future. Just right now.

So if the only thing that exists is the present moment, then what sense does it make to talk about long-term goals? How do you actually achieve anything?

First, understand that you can only achieve anything in the present moment, and you can only enjoy those achievements in the present moment. You can't achieve anything or enjoy anything in the past or future because you're never there. That's obvious, isn't it? But too often people act incongruently with this fact. It's very difficult to achieve a goal that's based on an inaccurate model of reality—such a goal will surely be an uphill struggle.

The purpose of goal-setting isn't to control the future. That would be senseless because the future only exists in your imagination. The only value in goal-setting is that it improves the quality of your present moment reality. Setting goals can give you greater clarity and focus right now. Whenever you set a goal, always ask yourself, "How does setting this goal improve my present reality?" If a goal does not improve your present reality, then the goal is pointless, and you may as well dump it. But if the goal brings greater clarity, focus, and motivation to your life whenever you think about it, it's a keeper.

Many people set goals and then assume the path to reach the goal will require suffering and sacrifice—a recipe for failure. A better idea is to set a goal and pay attention to the effect it has on your present reality. Set goals that yield a positive effect on your life whenever you think about them, long before the final outcome is actually achieved. Treat goal-setting as a way to enhance your present reality, not as a way to control the future.

Suppose you set a goal to start your own business. You imagine some future point where you're enjoying being your own boss, doing what you love, and making a great income—nothing wrong with that. Then you think about how much work it will be, the risks you'll face, and other discouraging thoughts. You've left the present and are dwelling in the future, which is only an illusion. Bring yourself back to the present and realize that none of those things have happened. You're just making them up. How silly it is to make up things you don't even want! And your imagination isn't accurate anyway.

Now try this: Think about starting your own business and imagine how great it will be when everything is running smoothly. Now stay in the present and consider how this goal can improve the quality of your life right now. Not a year from now. Not five years from now. Not even tomorrow. Right now this very minute. What does the goal of starting your own business do for you here and now? Does it give you hope? Does it inspire you? Does it promise solutions to some current problems? Allow those thoughts to churn through your consciousness for a while. Consider how the goal of starting your own business improves your life right now. And of course if you can see no improvement, then drop the goal and consider a different one.

Think about some goals you might have set if not for the imaginary obstacles you focused on. Do you want to lose a certain amount of weight? To enjoy a new relationship? To enjoy a more fulfilling career? Stop imagining doom and gloom on the path to get there, and simply focus on how each goal can improve your present reality. What does the thought of physical fitness do for you right now? What does the thought of finding your soul mate do for you? What does the thought of a fulfilling career do for you?

As you think about how your goals improve your present reality, eventually you'll feel motivated to take action. At the same time, you'll begin attracting resources into your life that will help you achieve your goals. There's no need to force yourself—you'll find yourself naturally drawn to take action as you keep bringing your focus back to the present. When you think about a goal in a way that motivates you right now, it's only natural that you'll begin taking action congruent with the goal.

When you set goals that increase the quality of your present reality, then what does it matter how long it takes to achieve the final outcome? Whether it takes one week or five years is irrelevant. The whole path is fun and enjoyable. More importantly, you feel happy and fulfilled this very moment. This drives you to take enjoyable action, so you're productive too.

Whatever goal you set, you have the option of envisioning a path of sacrifice and suffering by focusing on the illusion of the future, or you can allow the goal to inject your present reality with new hope, enthusiasm, and motivation. Even though it seems like you're setting goals for the future, you're really setting goals for the present. The better you understand this, the more easily and enjoyably you'll achieve your goals.

If you adopt this goal-setting mindset, you'll find yourself setting different kinds of goals. The size and scope of the goal will cease to matter. The most important factor will be what effect the goal has on your present moment when you think about it. When you really grasp this concept, you'll begin to adopt a lifelong mission instead of just a collection of disjointed goals and preferences. It doesn't even matter if your mission can be achieved in your lifetime. What matters is the effect it has on your present reality. So you can feel free to adopt a really enormous mission, even one which may be unachievable in your lifetime, as long as that mission inspires and motivates you. If the mission is so big that it disempowers you, dump it. But if it really inspires you, go for it.

I recommend you abandon the concept of SMART goals. SMART = specific, measurable, action-oriented, realistic, time-bound (there are many variations on this too). This model sounds intelligent, but it's based on an inaccurate understanding of time. Instead of thinking of your goals as time-bound projects, consider each goal in light of its effect on your present reality.

I know this is a very different way of thinking about goals, so it's only natural that you may have some resistance to it if you're deeply ingrained in a time-bound model of goal-setting. So ask yourself this: How well is your current goal-setting model working for you? On a scale of 1-10, how would you rate your performance at setting and achieving meaningful goals? I'd be surprised if you're higher than a 5. Pushing yourself to get better isn't the solution. The whole paradigm is broken to begin with. It's like trying to push a cart with square wheels. You don't need to push harder—you need a cart with round wheels. The square-wheeled cart looks really slick, and from a certain perspective, it seems like it should work OK. But reality itself is the ultimate judge.

CREATING YOUR VISION

When you write down your goals, your primary aim is to create a new vision for what you desire to experience next in life, while improving your present reality, so that you can begin to make that vision a reality.

So what do you do when you sit down to write a vision for your life, and you're coming up with a lot of blanks that you just aren't sure about?

Guess.

It really is that simple. Just take a stab at it. Don't even worry about making your *best* guess. Just make any guess that seems remotely reasonable.

Now take that guess and run with it. Write 1-2 paragraphs to describe the vision that pops into your mind when you think about that possible direction.

Make sure your vision is written with positive, present tense statements. Add some emotion to your vision. Include how you expect to feel ("I'm thrilled to be…", "I'm feeling deeply grateful as I…").

Don't worry about whether your guess is right or wrong at this point. Truthfully this isn't a matter of right or wrong. It's a matter of suitability for you. You're free to make whatever choices you desire. You just want to identify choices that make sense for you. You want to make choices where you can expect a very positive outcome.

Now re-read that vision statement once or twice per day, and as you read it, imagine it as already real. See yourself there. This should only take a minute or two to do the visualization part for a single goal… maybe 30 seconds once you're accustomed to it.

As you imagine your vision as real, notice how you feel about it. Do you feel really, really good about it? Does it appeal to you on an emotional level? Or do you feel neutral or negative about it? Do you feel some hesitation or resistance?

Quite often, something will feel a little bit off when you visualize your vision. That's perfectly fine. If it's a vague feeling of unease, just keep renewing this same vision on a daily basis for several more days. Allow your mind to expand and play with the vision a little more each time.

Eventually you'll get a sense of whether the vision is a keeper or if it needs some tweaking.

Your vision may be just right to begin with. Maybe it feels great every time you imagine it. You know you want it. You're practically lusting after it. That's great. You've found a keeper. Hold on to that vision, and keep renewing it each day. This will help to imprint the vision onto your subconscious. Usually within a month or less (sometimes much less), you'll see evidence that this vision is already becoming real for you.

Another possibility is that as you imagine your vision, your mind will begin to tweak it in different ways. It will twist it in a slightly different direction or add more details to improve it. Keep renewing that vision until it becomes a keeper, or it becomes clear that the vision just isn't working.

And finally, you may encounter a situation where your vision just doesn't quite come together in a way that feels good to you. Maybe it's internally incongruent. Maybe it doesn't mesh well with some other part of your life. In that case, ask yourself, *What is it about this vision that fails to delight me?*

Take note of the details of the vision that aren't working for you. It can be helpful to write them down. This is a time where it's okay to be negative. Identify the parts of the vision that don't feel right.

Now ask yourself how you can re-engineer those broken parts of the vision to create something better. Maybe the problems are minor and you can swap in different details to improve the vision. Or maybe the problems are so deep that you feel it's best to throw out the whole vision and start over from scratch with a totally different direction. Or maybe you're somewhere in the middle.

However it turns out, that's perfectly okay. You're using your imagination to beta-test your vision, running the vision through your feelings as a filter. If it doesn't feel right to you, you know that something is off and needs tweaking.

If you continue to hold a vision that feels off, your negative feelings will block you from allowing it to become real. So it's important to get your feelings on board. Holding a vision that doesn't feel right is a waste of time. Holding a vision that makes you feel nothing special is also a waste of time.

Once you update your vision to correct the problems, repeat the process. Write out your new vision. Then visualize it as real on a daily basis for several more days. Notice how you feel about it. Use your feelings to identify problems. Then revise the vision to take a stab at correcting the problems.

This is an iterative process. You probably won't get your vision just right on the first attempt. You probably won't get it right on the second or third attempts either. But with each pass, you'll get closer to your true desires.

When you eventually have a vision that passes your emotional filters, it tends to manifest very quickly. I've seen some amazingly fast transformations occur in my life when I reached that point. Sometimes a new vision shows up the very next day, like it was just waiting for me to become a match for it. Other times I'll see breadcrumbs leading me right to it.

I review my written visions each morning. I have a few paragraphs of vision statements for each area of my life: career; finances; health; relationships, family, social life and family; workflow and order; personal and spiritual; and lifestyle, travel, and adventure. You don't have to use the same categories. I just find it helpful to make sure I'm creating a vision for each important part of my life.

If you don't create a vision for each part of your life, someone else will do it for you. The intentions of others will fill in the blanks. You're always working to fulfill some vision. Either you're creating and fulfilling your own vision, or you're working on someone else's vision for you. There is no neutral. If you aren't creating your own vision, then you're obediently fulfilling a blended vision created by others, such as the vision that you should be a good citizen and taxpayer, that you should relate to people a certain way and live a certain kind of lifestyle, and that you should manage your affairs a certain way until you die. If you're in love with the vision that society is expecting you to live out, then there's no point in creating your own vision. But if you'd like to hold the reins of your own destiny and direct your life path more consciously, then you must absolutely create a vision for yourself.

By default, you are visualizing the status quo. Without a grander vision to occupy your thoughts, you will naturally succumb to the habit of thinking about what you're already getting, and you'll often feel some emotions when you do so. This is exactly how you hold the intention to manifest more of the same. So by default, you are automatically holding intentions to keep getting what you're getting.

This is why it's rather silly to complain about your problems. Sometimes people come to our discussion forums and write really long posts to explain what they're experiencing in life and why they don't like it. What they don't realize is that what they're doing is the exact process necessary to ensure that they'll experience more of the same. They're imagining their past and present as they write about it, and they're feeling strong feelings as they do so. They are using the power of vision to create a future that resembles their past and present.

If you want to create something different than what you're already getting, do NOT do what I described in the previous paragraph. It's stupid. This is the exact opposite of an intelligent solution. Only do this if you want to be stupid. And if you catch someone doing this, please refer them to this chapter, so they can hopefully understand why it cannot possibly work, and so that they'll get some motivation to start creating a new vision—even if they have to guess at first.

Instead of reviewing and rehashing what you don't want, create the vision of what you do want. If you feel a need to post something online, post about your dreams and desires. Write a really long, emotional post about what you most want to experience next in life. This way you won't make the terrible mistake of reinforcing what you're already getting. I like to do this publicly at least once a year by writing about my primary focus for the upcoming year in advance. What's really cool about that is that when I share my vision in public, some people will find that my vision appeals to them too, and they offer to help me make it a reality. That help wouldn't come to me if I didn't feel so good about what I wanted to create that I was willing to share it publicly. Your willingness to share your desires publicly is a good test of how ready you are to experience them in reality.

If you don't like what you're already getting, the best thing you can do is to ignore it. Turn your back on it. Stop dwelling on it. Only pay the minimal amount of attention to it that is truly essential. Turn the bulk of your attention (and emotion) to the new vision you've created. Spend more time living in the new reality you're creating as opposed to the old one you wish to leave behind. This will quickly draw that new reality into your life in physical form. Don't worry about trying to be perfect at this. Just do the best you can. The more you can turn your attention away from the past and towards your new vision, the better. The more you practice this, the easier it gets.

"Going with the flow" only makes sense if you're going with the flow of your own vision. If you don't have a clear vision and try to live in such a way that you go with the flow, all you're doing is going with the flow of social conditioning. It just means you're going with the flow of the default social vision for you. There will be a flow that you'll experience in that case, but it can be chaotic at times, and it's generally very slow moving. But if you love what you're experiencing and you love the current pacing of your life, then technically there's nothing wrong with going with the social flow. It's an option that's available to you.

Personally I'm not a big fan of going with the social flow. I find it tediously slow. With my own clear vision, I can create something in less than a month that would otherwise take years to create if I went at the pacing of the social flow. An individual can greatly outpace a pack that moves at the speed of its slowest member.

Keep tweaking your vision as you feel the need to do so. Keep renewing it once or twice per day. Feel the feelings of being there. Eventually you'll create a vision that feels so good that you'll find it immensely pleasurable to just sit back and imagine it as real. You may reach the point where you'd rather live in your new imagined reality than in your current physical reality. That's what creates the shifts that make your vision a reality.

15.
Visualize Your New Reality

Did you ever see the TV show *Sliders*?

In that show a group of four people would "slide" through a portal between dimensions, spending each episode in an alternate version of earth. For example, they might enter a reality where the Nazis won WWII. Or in another reality one of them might be a famous performer.

Another TV show that can give you the right idea is *Quantum Leap*. In that show a man spent each episode in someone else's body in an alternative time and place.

Imagine you're a Slider or a Quantum Leaper, and you just slid through a portal into your new desired reality—into that new YOU as well. You're already there living it. The whole reality already exists in some alternate dimension, and you're now experiencing it as real.

Put yourself in the shoes of that new person. Witness through his/her eyes how s/he goes through a typical day. Imagine that you're in an episode of *Sliders* or *Quantum Leap*.

What time do you get up in the morning? Who's sleeping next to you? Where are you? How do you feel? What do you eat for breakfast? What do you do in the morning, afternoon, and evening?

You must imagine yourself as already being there. You want to reach the point where it feels natural and normal to be there. After all, this is your reality, isn't it? So of course it will feel normal in a way. You're already used to it.

Initially the Sliders/Leapers were freaked out when they entered the new reality. It took them a while to figure it out and understand it. Eventually they got used to it and were able to get things done within that reality.

This is what will happen when you visualize a new reality for yourself. At first it may seem like an alien environment. You'll have to play around with it for a while before you get used to it and it starts to seem normal to you. It's very important that you push beyond that freak-out phase. You must shift from thinking about your visions as FANTASY to seeing them as REAL.

A good movie to watch is *Being John Malkovich*. That will give you more insight into how to slip into an alternate reality and imagine life through the lens of your new character.

Ideally, visualizing your future should be very much the same as remembering your past. Just as you would recall and mentally review what you did yesterday, that's how you want to imagine your new reality. What are the highlights of your typical day, and how do you feel about them?

Notice that emotional memories are much stronger than routine events. Such memories can draw the past back into your present, but they can also draw a powerful future into your present if you create powerful new memories of the future.

PARTIAL VISUALIZATION

One of the most common mistakes people make is that they fall into the trap of doing partial visualizations. They only imagine one or two aspects of their new reality but not the entire big picture. Or they'll imagine something that makes them feel a certain way, but it wouldn't actually be a part of their desired reality.

For example, you may imagine seeing a pile of cash on your table and counting the bills. A lot of people suggest this exercise as a way of manifesting more money. I think it's a lame idea though.

If you really had financial abundance, would you actually have a pile of cash currency in your home? That seems unlikely. If you were already living it, playing with your money or obsessing over it would be silly and immature. That's the sort of thing someone would do only if they weren't already living it.

Partial visualizations manifest partial results. You may attract part of what you want, but it will be unstable because you've only locked on to some and not all of the necessary frequencies required shifting into that new reality. You may be able to visit it briefly, but you won't be able to stay long.

When I was around 24-25 years old, I read the book *Think and Grow Rich*, and I started doing partial visualization exercises to attract more money into my life. I imagined having about half a million dollars as a pile of cash on my bed. I felt the texture of the bills with my fingers. I saw it as very real and imagined what it would feel like to have that much cash all at once.

Sometime after that (I don't recall how long—a few months maybe), I entered into a new game publishing deal with a total advance of $675,000. I soon received the first installment in the form of a check for $50,000, which was the biggest check I'd ever received at that point in my life. It appeared that my intention had manifested.

However, this situation was incredibly unstable. The publisher turned out to be extremely corrupt. First, they screwed up the deal with seemingly insane delays and nonsensical decisions. Then they unilaterally breached our contract. And finally they tried to sue me (unsuccessfully) to recoup the $50K advance. Looking back, it appears that their goal was to tie up my team's project so that it wouldn't hit the market, while they had another team developing a potentially competing game. The initial $50K I received was spent on early development for a game that was never released. In the end I was left with a busted project and more debt than when I started. If I could have afforded the legal fees (which I couldn't at the time), I may have been able to successfully sue them for breach of contract, but that simply wasn't how I wanted to do business. I wanted to spend my time making games, not giving depositions.

Years later this same publisher was publicly exposed for a massive accounting scandal, and the company and several officers were sued by the SEC. If I recall correctly, their CEO was fined $10 million and had to step down. That came as no surprise to me and many other developers who worked with them.

Not a good manifestation!

Although it seemed promising in the beginning, this attempt to manifest money completely imploded and left me worse off than when I started—aside from learning some very tough lessons, which in retrospect turned out to be quite valuable.

I hope you can learn from my mistakes here and not succumb to the trap of partial visualization. In order to manifest your desires, you need to lock on to the total package of frequencies and the full range of emotions that you'll experience in your new reality. And one of the best ways to do that is to get really, really clear about what you want.

COMPLETE VISUALIZATION

Don't just visualize one small part of your new reality, such as having more money come to you. Visualize the entire alternate reality you wish to enter, in as much detail as possible.

It's okay to focus on one area of your life at a time. I personally find it rather difficult to visualize a whole new life for myself that covers career, finances, health, relationships, my daily habits, spiritual development, personal development, etc. So I generally focus on one area at a time, but I do my best to make sure it's congruent with my desires in other areas too.

A few years ago I focused on creating financial abundance. Then I worked on social abundance (having lots of friends). Now I'm working on intimacy abundance (creating deeper relationships). All of these parts of my life are working beautifully right now. This process definitely works. Sometimes it works so well it scares me a bit.

Career and finances are good areas to visualize together since most people generate income via their careers. Don't just imagine yourself having more money. Put in some detail about what is sustaining that flow of money. How is it being maintained?

My initial attempts to manifest money flopped (or made things worse) because the big picture was incongruent. I was trying to pull money out of thin air, figuring it would come to me like magic. Well, this isn't magic—not really.

Similarly, in the area of social abundance, I didn't just manifest friends with magic. I had to see the big picture. This required thinking about what kind of friend I'd be. I thought about the friends I wanted to attract, and then I imagined what kind of friend I'd have to be in order to attract them to me—and to maintain good relationships with them. This made it clear that I had to work on myself too in order to step into that new reality. I had to become a better friend to others so I'd be worthy of those new relationships.

I know some people who are working really hard at manifesting new relationships. But all they do is imagine the other person coming to them and loving them. That's a partial visualization, and it fails consistently. Honestly I don't think I've seen this approach ever work out. People do attract new partners this way, but the matches aren't compatible.

Suppose you're trying to attract a new woman by visualizing her in your life. She's everything you desire. She's a perfect match for you and absolutely amazing as a human being. You can't help but fall in love with that new reality.

But will she fall in love with you—realistically? A new reality is something you're going to make REAL—it's not a fantasy!

If you think your new reality is too good to be true, then it is too good to be true.

What do you have to offer this woman? She may be *your* best possible match, but are you *her* best match as well, or will she have better options than you? Will she have to compromise her values and settle for less than she's worth to be with you? Will you be able to maintain a relationship with someone like that? Are you worthy of her?

These questions can hit people like a ton of bricks because they reveal our inadequacies. But we still need to address them.

When you visualize your new reality, you must imagine yourself *being* the kind of person who can attract and hold on to all the good stuff you wish to manifest. That means you're going to have to work on yourself and grow into that kind of person.

I know one woman who's been trying to manifest the perfect relationship for years. She goes on a lot of dates, yet she remains perpetually alone. It's obvious to me—and to many who know her—why that's so. The simple reason is that the man she desires wouldn't find her attractive at all. I can't even see that being a remote possibility. She's a kind-hearted person with a successful career, and she doesn't have a problem getting dates, but her personality is a total mismatch for the kind of man she wants. She doesn't fathom what such a man would find attractive in a relationship partner, so she lives in denial of the fact that he wouldn't be attracted to her. So she's always dating people where there's no two-way chemistry. If she keeps doing what she's been doing, she'll either remain alone indefinitely, or she'll eventually settle for an unstable connection with someone she doesn't find attractive or who doesn't find her attractive.

In the area of career and finances, what kind of person will you have to become in order to attract and hold on to the abundance you desire? What will it take to be worthy of that kind of flow?

When I was in my 20s, a $50K sum was too much for me to hold on to. I could attract such a sum on rare occasions, but I couldn't retain it. It would slip through my fingers like water.

Eventually I stopped doing partial visualizations and began seeing the big picture. I realized I'd have to become a man who was worthy of abundance. This may mean something different to you, but to me it meant that I would need to be a kind and generous person who created a lot of value for others. That felt congruent to me. If I were a greedy bastard who was all about me-me-me, I'd feel I didn't deserve that kind of flow. In my visualizations I felt *really* good about centering my career around service to others, and I could see that this would be consistent with attracting and perpetuating a constant flow of good stuff through my life—money, good health, low stress, loving relationships, fresh opportunities, etc. The total package just made sense to me.

I had to work a lot on myself to step into that new vision of me, but it definitely worked. In the past five years, I've put out enough free content to fill a couple dozen books. That feels really good to me. And resources flow to me so easily that I simply take it for granted that I can relax and enjoy whatever I want to experience in life. This works because it's a congruent and stable situation. I use my creativity to put out a lot of value for others, so naturally I receive a lot of value in return. But in order to reach this place, I had to go through many internal shifts to step into this new reality.

In the area of social abundance, I do my best to be the kind of friend that's worthy of having amazing friendships. I support and encourage my friends to pursue their dreams, but I also love to joke around and have fun. Consequently, I attract and maintain relationships with like-minded people. I'm really good at attracting people who are loving life, who enjoy helping people, and who are very encouraging and supportive of me too. And I naturally repel people who wouldn't make good friends for me.

In order to manifest what you desire, the total package must be congruent. There must be harmony between what you're attracting and what's attracting you. Too often people fall into the trap of trying to attract something that would naturally repel them, such as trying to manifest a flow of money without creating any value, or trying to attract a loving relationship without becoming a loving and attractive person.

This is largely common sense, which many people seem to lose sight of when trying to apply the Law of Attraction.

Will a health nut be attracted to a lazy couch potato? Will honest, conscious business people want to do business with someone who creates little value and is in only in it for the money? Will an adventurous growth-seeker be attracted to someone who's timid and security-minded? Even if these situations were to manifest, they're unstable and usually won't work out well unless there's a strong attraction in some other area to compensate.

Manifestations can occur rapidly and powerfully once this harmony is achieved. But until that happens, results tend to be minimal or negative.

WRITE IT DOWN

Imagining your new reality can be tricky if you try to do it all in your mind.

You may find it helpful to sit down and write out what it will be like to experience your new reality, in as much detail as possible.

For example, if you want to attract a certain type of person into your life, write out a detailed description of that person. Then you can use that as a guide when visualizing. Another option is to create a vision board by assembling a collection of photos or images (physical or digital) that help you imagine the big picture.

I recently stumbled upon an old journal entry where I wrote out several pages describing in detail what I wanted to experience in life. My life at the time was nowhere close to that reality. I put an incredible amount of detail into it, even including personality descriptions and physical attributes of imagined people, such as how tall they were or that they wore contact lenses or were left- or right-handed.

What really freaked me out is that there is now a person in my reality who matches someone I described about 95% accurately. This person was not on my radar at all when I wrote this journal entry. I wrote it in February 2001. My life was in a completely different place back then.

Most of what I wrote about back then has already manifested. I'm now living it. Other parts of my reality have shifted so much that parts of my vision that seemed so far away are not nearly so distant now. I can actually see steps that would make more of them possible and realistic. The big picture is sliding towards me.

I was talking with Erin about this last week, and she asked me, "Why did you put that kind of detail into it? Why did it matter to you that an imaginary person was near-sighted?"

My best answer is that I found that a copious level of detail made it easier to see it as real. The vision became more believable. If the new reality is to become real, the people within it must be real too, not imaginary archetypes. Real people have height and weight. They may be near-sighted or left-handed. They may have pimples or unshaven faces. They wear certain types of clothes. They have unique personalities.

If you suddenly slid into your new reality, you would instantly observe all of that detail. It would be right in front of you. So put it in front of you now. Create it in your imagination. Clarity creates believability, which gives rise to stronger, crisper vibrations than fogginess.

It takes practice to get good at this, but the more you practice, the richer and more vivid your visualizations will become. That richness makes it easier to lock on to the new emotional states you're aiming to create.

16.
Don't Act As If

Why is it that sometimes you can be really clear about a goal, make a plan to get there, and take action on it, but even after years of pushing yourself, you still have little to show for your efforts?

Maybe you made some progress, but perhaps it wasn't enough to justify the effort. Meanwhile it seems like so many other people are able to achieve similar goals much more quickly. This can be frustrating.

What is it that causes you to run in circles?

A common goal achievement strategy looks something like this:

1. Define your outcome.

2. Make a plan to get there.

3. Take lots of action.

4. Refine your approach as needed.

5. Persist until you succeed.

This method will indeed work for certain types of goals. But for other goals, it will actually cause you to run in circles. You'll burn a lot of time and energy, but you won't reach your goal in a reasonable period of time.

The method above tends to work okay for goals that don't require much inner change. Your current thoughts, beliefs, feelings, and behaviors are well aligned with your outcomes. You don't have to change on the inside. You just have to take certain basic actions that you're already comfortable with, and you'll get there.

For example, if you set a goal to organize your home office, and you're already a fairly neat person, and you know how to organize, and you like the feeling of having everything in its proper place, then you can use this process to achieve that goal. You can imagine your home office the way you'd like it to be. Then make a to-do list of the action steps to get there. Then set aside a weekend to make it so, and go through the steps one by one until you're done. If something unexpected happens, you can adjust your plan on the fly. This is an achievable goal for you, and if you feel motivated to make it happen, it's clearly within your power to get it done in a reasonable period of time.

On the other hand, suppose you set that same goal to organize your home office, but your thoughts, beliefs, and feelings aren't aligned very well. Maybe you're not particularly happy with the work you do, and having a cluttered office makes it easier to distract yourself from depressing thoughts and feelings. Maybe you worry about having more responsibility. Maybe you fear that your life lacks variety. Maybe you've been eating a crappy diet, and it's bringing down your energy levels, making it hard to feel motivated to de-clutter your office. Maybe you've piled up so much clutter that you now view it as a monumental task. Maybe you're a habitual pack rat and have a hard time throwing things away, even if you haven't used them in years.

For this second person, the goal achievement process previously described usually won't work. It may look good on paper, but it can actually have an adverse effect, causing you to run in circles. You may set a goal to have a neat office and make a to-do list just as the first person did, but it won't yield the same result for you. Even if you make a dent in the clutter, you'll re-clutter it within a few weeks. Then you'll beat yourself up, resolve to "stop procrastinating" and "finally get organized," and try again. Fast forward five years, and your cluttered office still looks pretty much the same, despite investing a lot of mental and emotional energy in trying to improve.

This doesn't mean you're broken, lazy, or impotent. It means you're using the wrong process for your particular goal. If this process isn't working for you, stop using it. A good process produces good results.

A TALE OF TWO VIBRATIONS

Albert Einstein is famously quoted as saying that we cannot solve problems at the same level of thinking we were at when we created them.

In the case of our first person organizing her home office, she already thinks of herself as a neat and organized person. She likes being organized and feels good about it on the inside. When she sees clutter in her environment, she immediately recognizes it: "This isn't me." It feels wrong to her. It's below her standards to tolerate it for long. Perhaps she just got busy, and things piled up temporarily, but she knows that being neat is congruent with who she is. She may have been at a lower level of thinking when she created the clutter problem (stressed, overworked, tired, etc.), but that isn't her normal state of being. Once her life is "back to normal," she feels a strong desire to fix the clutter problem. Clutter isn't congruent with who she is.

We can say that it's part of her *vibe*—her collection of thoughts, feelings, and beliefs—to be neat and organized. While clutter may arise from time to time, it's in her nature to return to a state of order again and again. Something must knock her down to a lower level of thinking, such as stress or illness, in order for her to take actions that create clutter. And even then, she knows she'll eventually clean it up when she's back to her normal self.

With our second person, however, being neat and organized isn't part of his vibe. His normal, default experience is to create and tolerate clutter, even if he doesn't like it. He's a match for clutter. His thoughts, feelings, and beliefs all support the creation and maintenance of a cluttered environment. When he does feel like getting organized and he's able to get himself to take action, it's a peak state, and it usually doesn't last for more than a few days. Even if he can get himself to hold that state long enough to organize his office, he'll simply re-clutter it in the following weeks when he's back to his normal level of being.

Can you think of goals in your own life where your experience was like that of the first person? And other experiences that were more like the second person?

ARE YOUR GOALS CONGRUENT WITH YOUR VIBE?

You can use the previously mentioned goal achievement process (or something similar) when your situation is like that of the first person. But it doesn't work well in the second situation.

Think about some of the goals and projects you'd like to accomplish. Which ones are already a good match for your current level of being? Which ones are not a match for your current vibe?

For example, if you set a goal to earn $1 million this year, but you've never earned more than $50K in a year before, it's safe to say that the first goal achievement process will cause you to run in circles. That's because your vibe is incongruent with that goal.

However, if you've earned $400K, $600K, and $800K in each of the last 3 years, and it feels normal to see your income increase significantly each year, then the first goal achievement process can work just fine. Your current vibe is already a good match for this goal.

FOOLISH PLANS

When your default level of thinking and feeling (i.e. your current vibe) is not a good match for one or more of your goals, don't try to use the first goal achievement process. It will almost certainly run you in circles. The reason that happens is that you're trying to achieve a goal at a level of thinking at which it cannot be achieved. You may come up with a nice-looking list of action steps, but they'll be the wrong actions. When you try to work on that list, something will feel off. You'll find yourself procrastinating massively, for instance. This doesn't mean you don't want the goal. It means you're trying to use the wrong process to get there. You'll probably experience lots of clunky starts and re-starts to try to get yourself moving, but you won't move much.

For example, if you've never earned more than $50K in a year, and you decide to earn $1 million this year, but your vibe is stuck below the $50K level, then when you make a to-do list for how to achieve your million-dollar goal, it won't be a realistic plan. It will be a fantasy. Your plan will be like a child's plan to build a space ship. It won't be something you can realistically implement, and it won't look much like the plan that a true soon-to-be millionaire would use.

Your plan will probably be cluttered with actions that don't even need to be done, at least not by you personally. It will include a lot of unnecessary busywork. It will focus on actions that won't produce strong results under real-world conditions.

If someone who was already earning $1 million per year looked at your plan, they'd likely see it as unbalanced and off-base. Even if they were starting from scratch, their plan to earn that first million wouldn't look very much like yours.

Don't bother to create plans for goals that you aren't already a good match for. Such plans won't work in the real world. First you have to get yourself to the level of thinking at which your goal can be achieved. After you get to that level of thinking, then you can start identifying action steps, and those actions will make sense.

So what do you do if you have a goal that doesn't mesh well with your current level of thinking and feeling? How do you bridge the vibrational gap between where you are and where you'd like to be? You need to use a different goal achievement process for that.

17.
How to Achieve Your Stretch Goals

For the sake of convenience, let's use the term "stretch goals" to refer to the types of goals for which you aren't already a good match.

Such goals are of course relative to the person setting them. Buying a new car wouldn't be a stretch goal for someone who can easily afford it, but it could be a stretch goal for someone who's broke and struggling with unemployment. The first person can simply walk into a dealership, pick a car, pay cash for it, and drive away with it. The second person may be looking at tougher challenges to overcome.

Jack Canfield likes to refer to these as *breakthrough goals*, perhaps because when you achieve such a goal, you're breaking through to a whole new level of being.

VIBRATIONAL ALIGNMENT

People don't experience the same level of difficulty in achieving similar goals because each person has a different degree of vibrational alignment (or lack of alignment) relative to the goal. A goal is only *easy* or *hard* relative to your vibe. Some vibes are weak matches for certain goals. Other vibes are strong matches. The more strongly your vibe matches a goal, the more easily and effortlessly you can achieve that goal.

For example, if I wanted to earn an extra $10K this month, that would be a fairly easy goal for me to achieve. I could probably do something this weekend that would generate an extra $10K by the end of the month. My vibe is already a good match for receiving such sums. It feels normal to me. But since the goal wouldn't cause me to stretch, it isn't very inspiring either. As far as goals go, it's a bit dull.

For someone else, earning an extra $10K this month might be a seemingly impossible fantasy. Their thoughts, feelings, and behaviors create a different vibe. Whereas I see ease and simplicity, they might see struggle, obstacles, or lack of opportunity. They might also become overly excited about the idea of earning an extra $10K (which suggests it isn't normal for them), thereby positioning the goal in the realm of fantasy instead of possible reality.

To yet another person, the goal of earning an extra $10K this month might be right in the middle—enough of a challenge to be interesting and motivating, but not so challenging as to appear impossible. For this person it's a stretch goal. They see it's possible, but they aren't sure how to make it a reality yet.

Your vibe largely determines which goals you're even willing to set. If your vibe is too far out of alignment with a particular goal, you'll never bring yourself to set such a goal. That would be self-delusion at best, like a scarcity-minded person setting the goal to become a billionaire. The mind won't believe the goal, so the person won't take the actions needed to get there.

When your vibe is a very close match for a goal, you probably won't even think of it as a goal. It will simply be a task to do, like making dinner or taking your dog for a walk. For me, writing a new article is a basic task which I often do for the sheer enjoyment of writing. So we could say that my personal vibe is a very close match for the goal of writing an article.

When your vibe is somewhere in the middle, you have a stretch goal. Your vibe is enough of a match for the goal to enable you to set the goal and take it seriously, but not yet enough of a match to experience the achievement of the goal.

One of the best reasons to set goals and work to achieve them is the vibrational shift you must undergo in order to achieve new goals, especially stretch goals.

MATCHING VS. MISMATCHING VIBES

There are two types of vibes to think about with respect to any goal:

1. Vibes that match the goal

2. Vibes that don't match the goal

When your vibe is in the first category, then achieving your goal is relatively easy. You will still take action, but your actions will flow easily, and they won't feel terribly effortful. Taking action will often feel like play. The actions you choose will be the right actions that will move you closer to your goal. You'll probably experience many synchronicities too. Great opportunities will come to you. You'll see good evidence that real progress is happening. Other people will notice that you've shifted.

When your vibe is in the second category, the path to your goal will seem difficult and littered with obstacles. You'll notice the obstacles and will probably feel a strong desire to procrastinate, and you'll often indulge in distractions. You will identify actions to take, but they won't be the right actions. When you take action, you'll often feel resistance, either from inside yourself or from the external world. Getting to your goal will feel like work more than play. You may invest a lot of time and effort into your goal, but you probably won't get there. Months or years may pass, and you'll have little to show for it.

These are the extremes. Depending on the degree of alignment between your vibe and your goal, you'll probably fall somewhere in the middle. Some aspects will look like the first example, while other aspects will resemble the second situation. This means that your vibe is a partial match for your goal. Some parts of your vibe are very well aligned with your goal, while other parts are opposing your goal.

STOP USING FORCE

Now here's the tricky part to understand, so please read this next bit carefully.

When your vibe is a good match for your goal, you'll naturally have a sense of the right actions to take and synchronicities will show up to guide you as needed. You won't have to struggle to figure out what to do next. Most of the time, the next action to take will be fairly obvious, and it will feel good to you. It will be an action you want to take. You won't have to force it.

However, when your vibe is a poor match for your goal, you'll come up with some actions to take, but they'll be the wrong actions. You won't have a strong inner feeling of clarity about them. You'll have a lot of doubts. It will be hard to choose a path, and even when you do choose, you won't feel certain that it's the right path for you. When you do take action, you'll be acting under a cloud of doubt and uncertainty. You'll also have a strong tendency to procrastinate and delay.

A common prescription for people in the second situation is to use *force*. Take more action. Fight procrastination. Push yourself harder. Eliminate distractions. Focus! Do it now! Get to work!

This doesn't work well. It's like trying to push two opposing magnets together. Even if you do achieve a goal this way, it will be difficult to sustain it, and a fall is inevitable. Your vibe and the goal are constantly resisting each other. As soon as you let down your guard, they repel each other.

Imagine trying to get up at 5am when your vibe isn't a match for being an early riser. Instead of popping out of bed feeling alert and refreshed, you feel tired and sleepy and hit the snooze button. When you are a match for such a goal, however, you can arise early with ease. The goal requires no struggle at all. It's just your normal wake-up time. No big deal.

It's safe to say that if a goal seems like a big deal to you, this indicates that your vibe isn't yet a match for that goal.

When you notice that you're trying to force a goal, stop for a moment and think about it. Why is this such a struggle for you? Why are you fighting what you claim to desire? Why are you sabotaging yourself? Why do you keep procrastinating?

Ask yourself, *Do I really want this goal? Is this a good goal for me at this time?* It's okay if it's a stretch goal. Just be sure it's something you really want. It's perfectly okay to desire a goal that may seem like it's beyond you right now.

If you realize that you don't really care enough about this goal to take it seriously, then let it go. If you don't desire to do what it takes to become a match for the goal, there's no point in fussing over it. Drop it, and accept the consequences of that decision.

I often see this pattern with people who go to college because their parents expect them to. They pick a major that others will approve of. But they don't enjoy the coursework, and they don't even want to work in that field. That's a no-brainer recipe for vibrational resistance. Then these students wonder why they procrastinate on their studies and don't feel motivated. Sure it takes courage to choose your own path, but you aren't here to live up to other people's expectations.

Now if you still feel good about the goal and you still want the out-come, that's perfectly fine too. Just because you aren't a match for the goal doesn't mean you should drop it. Some of the best goals will re-quire you to shift your vibe in order to achieve them. It could be said that the vibrational shift is an even greater accomplishment than the external goal. For example, aligning your vibe with abundance can be a greater accomplishment than earning some specific sum of money. Once you've integrated the vibe of abundance, your whole life is trans-formed, not just your finances.

ORBITING VS. ACHIEVING YOUR GOAL

Let's assume for now that you have a goal that you like, but you aren't yet a vibrational match for it. What's the next step?

Well, many people would say that the next steps are to make plans and start taking action, but for a goal of this nature, that approach doesn't work well. It will usually cause you to run in circles.

It's like trying to push two opposing magnets together. You can push with great force, but that isn't a wise idea. If you want the magnets to stick, then it's easier if you flip one of the magnets around. If you do that first, then you can pretty much let go, and the magnets will attract each other. You may give them a nudge, but forcing them together isn't necessary.

Now this is a very simple analogy, so let's expand it a bit. Your vibe is much more complex than a single magnet. Your vibe with respect to any single goal is like 100 pairs of magnets. Some magnets have their poles aligned to attract each other, but some are repelling each other. When you try to achieve your goal by taking direct action, sometimes you're in the flow, and sometimes you're out of flow. Some parts of your vibe are pulling the goal towards you. Other parts of your vibe are pushing the goal away.

You don't have to be in perfect 100% alignment to achieve your goal. You just have to make enough shifts such that the overwhelming force is attractive rather than repulsive. But it has to be strong enough to overcome inertia and any repelling forces.

If there's too much repelling force or inertia and not enough at-tracting force, then you'll fall into the trap of running in circles when you try to take action.

The Earth and the Moon attract each other gravitationally. But they don't crash into each other. The Moon just runs in circles around the Earth. But what if we could somehow slow down or stop the Moon's motion relative to the Earth? Then the Earth and the Moon would attract each other till they collided. This would be bad for people on Earth, but the Earth and Moon would become one. Similarly, if you wish to become one with your goals, you'll need to work with the various forces and motions that are present until a collision course with your goals becomes inevitable. This is essentially what it means to become a vibrational match for your goal. If you're not a match, you'll end up orbiting your goal instead of reaching it, despite having a lot of gravity on your side.

UNDERSTANDING THE NEW VIBE

Now here's another tricky part, so read this carefully and ponder it a bit.

The #1 reason people struggle to achieve their stretch goals is that they don't have a solid understanding of the matching vibe.

Because they don't understand what the new vibe looks like and feels like, they don't understand the right actions to take. So they take the wrong actions, they struggle, and they get results they don't want.

The most important thing you can do to achieve a stretch goal is to deepen and clarify your understanding of the matching vibe. What will your thoughts, feelings, and behaviors be like when you've already achieved the goal? What kind of person will you be when you're already there?

Someone who earns $1 million per year doesn't have the same vibe as someone who earns $50K per year. The thoughts, feelings, and behaviors of each person are very different. If you're earning $50K per year, and you set a stretch goal to earn $1 million per year, the first thing you must do is study and understand the vibe you'd be emitting if you were already at the $1 million per year level. It will be very different than your current $50K vibe. Energetically speaking, you won't be the same person.

Your greatest risk of failure stems from the problem of projecting your $50K vibe onto the $1 million goal. You can't use a $50K vibe to create the action list to achieve this goal. You have to use the $1M vibe to create the action list, and you can't do that until and unless you understand the $1M vibe well enough.

Most people don't do what it takes to understand the new vibe. They project their old vibes forward in time, but that doesn't work. It only keeps them orbiting the same goal, running in circles for years.

You must figure out which of your 100 internal magnets are aligned with the new goal's magnets, and which aren't aligned. When you dive into action without this understanding, the odds of success are very low. The opposing magnets will simply repel each other, and you'll be kept in orbit indefinitely. The closer you get to your goal, the stronger the opposing force will be. This may look like you're sabotaging yourself each time you get close to your goal. Forcing it won't work, it will only frustrate you. Then you'll say to yourself things like, "Why is this taking so long? I should be much further along by now." or "Why do I keep procrastinating?"

HOW TO LEARN THE NEW VIBE

There are many ways to deepen your understanding of the new vibe that pairs with your goal. Here are some suggestions.

First, be humble as you enter this process. Admit that you don't yet understand the new vibe. If you did understand it, you'd already be coasting effortlessly to your goal. Accept that if you're struggling, it's because you don't understand the new vibe well enough. You might also be clinging to some false assumptions about it.

Try to set aside any preconceived notions about the new vibe. Start with a blank slate. Open your mind to new possibilities. Don't pretend to know something you haven't yet experienced. If you aren't already living it, it's safe to say that you don't know it yet.

It may help to think about a goal you've already achieved. Remember your vibe before and after the goal was achieved. Think about the goal of learning to drive a car. Notice how different your vibe was before you learned. It probably seemed like a big deal. You may have put the goal on a pedestal. You may have felt a bit stressed about it. But as you got closer to achieving this goal, your vibe shifted to the point where driving seemed like no big deal. If your vibe didn't shift, you still wouldn't be able to drive yet. We could say that practice is what helped to shift your vibe, but we could also say that you shifted your vibe by spending time with people who already had the right vibe (i.e. experienced drivers), and you picked up the right vibe (not just the know-how) from them. Once you matched the vibe of a confident driver, you could drive confidently too.

This leads us into the next step. If possible, identify people who've already achieved the goal you want to achieve (or something similar). Buy their books, and read them for starters. Join clubs where these people are members. Do whatever it takes to get face time with such people. Don't admire such people from a distance. You need to connect with them in person, and preferably one on one. This means not over the phone and not over the Internet. In person means in person. This is easier than it sounds if you make it a priority. When you hang out with such people in person, you'll learn so much about the new vibe you wish to create. Some inner shifts will happen automatically. This is very important. Don't blow it off unless you prefer to orbit your goals instead of experience them.

So if you want to be a millionaire, go to places where millionaires hang out, and spend time getting to know them. Talk to them about money. Don't worry about getting how-to tips. You won't be able to apply them yet anyway. Instead, get a sense of the other person's thoughts, feelings, and beliefs about money. Contrast their vibe with yours. What's different about their vibe? Why is it that they're a match for having lots of money, and you aren't? The vibrational differences tell the story.

If you're shy or socially dorky, go to a park or coffee shop in a wealthy neighborhood. Sit down, shut up, and observe. Listen to people's conversations. Do this again and again until you start getting a clear sense of the vibe of such people. Contrast their vibe with yours. What's different about them? Are you willing to embrace this vibe?

Notice that such people don't usually say, "Holy frak! I can't believe I have all this money! It's so unreal!" Having lots of money is just normal and routine for them. It's no big deal. That's the vibe you want to understand. If you think having a lot of money is a big deal, that's why you don't have it. That's the vibe of wanting money and not having it. The vibe of having money is totally different.

Next, spend time visualizing yourself as already having the vibe needed to achieve your goal. You'll learn about this vibe partly from being around people who've already achieved your goal. Visualization can help you personalize the vibe. Other people will give you clues with respect to where you need to make shifts, but your vibe is uniquely your own. Your wealth vibe, for instance, won't be quite the same as someone else's. However, you'll still have a lot in common with other wealthy people when you make the shifts that work for you.

I recommend spending about 10 minutes per day visualizing how your life will be different once you've achieved your goal. How will you really think, feel, and behave on the other side of that goal? Try to make as few adjustments as possible to your current vibe, just enough to realistically see yourself in that situation and having it feel normal to you. This is important. Realize that if you're going to achieve this goal in reality, then it's still *you* on the other side, with all your dorkiness coming along for the ride. It's not your higher self or your ideal self. It's just a slightly adjusted version of your normal, everyday self.

Try doing it like this. Imagine a scene that represents your goal. Now put your current self into that scene. This is the person you are right now, your normal self. Imagine yourself going through that scene as if it were completely real and happening right now. You just quantum leaped right into it. Do your best to imagine this not as a dream or fantasy, but as solid reality, like a real event that's happening today, perhaps a few hours from now.

Now let your character interact with the scene. How would you realistically react to what's happening? What you want to understand is your character's vibrational interaction with the vibe of the scene. This will tell you where some of your magnets are pointing in the wrong directions. The more realistic you can make this scene, the more you'll learn from it.

Daydreaming isn't the same thing as visualizing. You can visualize yourself being in a sex scene for the purpose of taking care of yourself, but that isn't the same thing as visualizing a sex scene that you actually want to experience in reality. Your mind can tell the difference between fantasy visualization and a serious goal. Otherwise you'd manifest lots of sex just by imagining it. You can imagine anything you want, but it won't become real until you match the vibe of that experience too, and that part takes a bit more work.

For example, suppose one of your goals is to live in a mansion and have a staff of servants. In most of your visualizations, you imagine how great it will be, but that doesn't get you any closer to your goal.

However, when you take the time to imagine it as 100% real, and you plop your current self into that new reality, you notice some issues coming up.

Maybe you feel nervous and anxious living in such a big place. Perhaps you feel uncomfortable telling your servants what to do—maybe you feel bad about the idea of other people cleaning your toilets and making your meals. Maybe you also feel some excitement about having such a cool place to live, but that also suggests a mismatch because if you actually lived there, it would probably feel normal to you. You might appreciate your home, but you probably wouldn't feel excited about living there every day.

Take notes about these experiences. Write down things like: I don't feel good about paying 20x bigger tax bills. I don't like telling other people what to do. I'd feel stressed if I had to earn hundreds of thousands of dollars per year minimum just to cover my expenses. What are the thoughts, beliefs, and feelings you have that indicate you're still a mismatch for your goal?

Sometimes it's the extended consequences of the goal, rather than the goal itself, that reveal a lack of alignment. For example, if you want to be a famous actor, what do you think about being in the public eye? Can you handle public criticism from people who don't know you? Can you accept that as being a normal part of your life, or does that seem like something you'd want to avoid? If you want to achieve a goal, you must accept the logical consequences of that goal. If you resist the consequences, you resist the goal.

Now ask your mind to show you what vibrational adjustments you need to make to be congruent with your goal. Imagine that your character is downloading a new personality subroutine. Let your adjusted self interact with the scene anew. Allow your mind to keep making tweaks until your character seems to be a comfortable, natural fit for the scene. Get a sense of your character's new vibe. What's different about it? What had to be changed?

Again, take some notes that you can refer to later. You may notice things like: My new character is more confident. My new character jokes with the staff; he appreciates them but also retains an air of authority. My new character feels that it's easy to earn enough to cover all the expenses; this isn't a big deal.

A very helpful final step is to broadcast your desires (http://www.stevepavlina.com/blog/2010/02/broadcast-your-desires/). Share your goal openly with the people in your life, and talk about it seriously as if you intend to make it real ASAP. Notice how the people in your life react to your announcement. This will quickly reveal which relationships in your life are helping you become a match for your goal and which are holding you back. You'll need to drop or transform the relationships that will otherwise hold you back. Don't get clingy since that just holds everyone back and builds resentment. Accept that you're here to grow. You'll have the opportunity to connect with much more compatible partners anyway, so no worries about being alone.

TURNING REPULSION INTO ATTRACTION

This process will help you create a vibrational to-do list. This is even more important than your action list. Once you take steps to adjust your vibe to be in harmony with your goal, the action steps will begin to flow rather easily.

What's a vibrational to-do list? It's a list of the personal development work you need to do in order to become a match for your goal.

Ultimately it will include three types of growth experiences:

1. You'll shed limiting beliefs and perspectives that align with the old vibe, replacing them with new truths that align with the new vibe.

2. You'll shed negative relationships that are bad match for your new vibe, and you'll add positive new relationships that are well aligned with it.

3. You'll stop feeding your power to excuses and obstacles, and you'll begin emitting a more powerful vibe that draws your goal increasingly near.

These personal growth experiences are the inner magnets that you must re-align. Let's consider each category in turn.

NEW TRUTHS

Suppose your goal is to earn $1M per year. That's about $80K per month. If you currently earn $50K per year, then this may seem like a very large sum. But if you were a match for this goal, then $80K per month must look and feel like a normal sum to you. It's just your regular paycheck. There's nothing special about it. If you're going to turn it into a big deal, then you're pushing this goal away.

So your new truth might be, "Earning $80K per month is normal. It's easy and natural for me."

To help you align with this goal, you might go to your bank, withdraw $1000 cash, and carry it around in your wallet every day. That may feel uncomfortable at first, but keep doing it till it feels normal and natural to you. How does it feel to carry two hours' worth of pay in your wallet? It's no big deal. Embrace your new truth, and it will help you create a more abundant vibe. If you want to earn 20x more money, then you need to change your relationships to money by a factor of 20. A $1000 sum in your new vibe is equivalent to a $50 bill in your old vibe.

If you can't make little adjustments like this to get started, then you aren't yet serious about your goal, are you? Are you going to make it real or not? If you're going to make it real, then you'd better get used to dealing with larger sums of money as if it's a totally normal experience for you. So start building that comfort now. Otherwise you'll repel those larger sums because you'll freak yourself out when they start to show up.

NEW CONNECTIONS

Suppose your goal (once again) is to go from earning $50K to $1M per year. When you imagine yourself as already there, it becomes clear that some of your current friends won't be able to handle it. So part of your inner work will be to either (1) drop these people from your life, so they stop blocking you, or (2) have some deep conversations to transform these relationships, so these people can get behind your goal.

Build new relationships, too. What kinds of people would you have in your life if you already achieved your goal? Start building those relationships now. They'll actually help you get there. Don't do the "I'm not worthy" thing. If you're going to make this goal a reality, then you're going to have to overcome those feelings of unworthiness. You might as well start now.

The same goes for family members. In my early 20s when I decided to start my own business, I distanced myself from my parents and siblings because they were so immersed in the employee mindset. I had to be around other entrepreneurs to understand the vibe of success on this path.

Don't cling to relationships that aren't a good match for your goal. This is an area where you may really have to do some house-cleaning. Yes, you'll see a lot of relationships come and go. That's part of life. You'll get used to it. If you want to be a match for having lots of growth experiences, then you'd better embrace the idea of seeing your personal relationships shift around a lot. Otherwise, you'll be a match for stagnation and foot-dragging. This sort of shifting is nothing to fear. It can be quite exhilarating to connect with a variety of cool people in your lifetime. Clinginess isn't a vibrational match for growth.

EMBRACING YOUR POWER

The third area for personal development work is to notice where you're giving your power away, and begin to reclaim your power. It's time to stop making excuses, stop blaming others, and accept the full consequences of what it will take to achieve your goal.

Suppose you want to have a threesome (sexually). Obviously there are plenty of people on the planet who are willing to engage in this, so it's certainly possible for you to have such an experience if you're willing to do what it takes to make it a reality. It's certainly not that difficult action-wise. Ask enough people, and you'll get some yeses. Arrange a time to get together, and have fun.

And yet despite the simplicity of this goal, you can massively overcomplicate it if you give your power away.

Suppose you ask your current partner, and she says no. You can blame her for being a stick in the mud, or you can try to convince her (a form of force), but you'll probably end up with a bad experience if you go that route.

You can also accept your partner's no and learn to live without the threesome. But if this is a strong desire for you, then this will only build resentment. Settling for less than you desire certainly won't lead to greater happiness and fulfillment. It may appear a more socially acceptable choice in some circumstances, but that's just another instance of your feeding your power to something that blocks you (the delusion of being socially accepted by others in this case).

The deeper inner work is to ask, *Why am I with a partner who doesn't naturally want the same things I do? Why am I settling for less than I desire? Why am I being so clingy with someone who wants different experiences than I do?*

To make the threesome real (not merely a fantasy), this inner work has to be done. These apparent conflicts need to be resolved. You have to learn to use your power to feed your desires, not obstacles.

If you were already a strong match for having threesomes, you could make one happen this week, perhaps even today. I know someone who claims to have had 500+ threesomes. For him it's a fun but also an easy thing to experience. He can go out and make it happen with two women he just met, and he certainly doesn't look like a swimsuit model. While most people block such an experience from happening, he directs his power to creating the experiences he wants to have.

I hope you can see that logistically, this really isn't that difficult of a goal. The action steps are pretty basic, mostly involving some communication. But if your vibe isn't a good match for such an experience, then it may appear to be virtually impossible for you. It will seem like the external world is opposing you, but that isn't the case at all. Your own vibe is what's creating the mismatch. If you adjust your vibe enough, the goal becomes easy and straightforward. It may even happen on its own without your having to ask.

Achieving stretch goals requires fixing the magnets that aren't turned the right way. This includes dropping limiting beliefs and false assumptions, dumping disempowering relationships, and letting go of excuses and blame. If you avoid this inner growth work and try to jump ahead to cause-and-effect action steps, you'll simply orbit your goal.

DO THE PERSONAL GROWTH WORK

Once you've identified the personal growth work you must go through in order to become a match for your goal, then get busy working on it. If you're conscious about it, you can compress lessons that would otherwise take years into a few months or weeks, creating big shifts in a short period of time.

There are tons of methods you can use to do this personal growth work. This website is filled with them. Here are some examples:

1. Journal to gain new insights (contrast the old vibe with the new one).

2. Have deep conversations with people who are intelligent and aware.

3. Meditate on feelings of gratitude and appreciation.

4. Keep visualizing yourself as already there; feel it as real.

5. Disconnect from people who aren't a match for your goal.

6. Join a club that will help you align your vibe with your goal.

7. Move to a new city that's a better match for your goal.

8. Replace the books on your bookshelf with books that match the new vibe.

9. Donate possessions that aren't a good match for the new vibe.

10. Catch yourself giving your power away, and reclaim it by directing it back towards your desires.

11. When someone says no to your desires, say no to that aspect of your relationship with them (or to the whole relationship, if necessary).

12. Create new empowering belief statements to replace old limiting beliefs.

13. Hang out regularly with people who can naturally help you align with your goal (i.e. people who inspire you in that direction).

14. Intend and expect to reach your goal.

15. Use the word "when" instead of "if" when talking about your goal.

16. Blog about your goal or talk about it publicly (this will reveal mismatching relationships and help attract compatible connections too).

17. Conduct experiments like 30-day trials to immerse yourself in the experience of a new vibe.

18. Change your diet, clothes, etc. to eat, dress, and live as if you're already there.

19. Put up pictures or other inspirational messages that represent the new vibe.

20. Read books written by others who emit a vibe that's compatible with your goal.

21. Go to lectures, workshops, seminars, and retreats that will help immerse you in the new vibe.

22. Forgive people who've wronged you, and release the hurt and resentment.

I think you get the idea. The exact processes you use here aren't that important. Last year, I went to a talk where Joe Vitale asked everyone in the room (a room full of professional speakers and authors) to shout out their favorite personal growth processes. He had two people writing them down on a large white board. Within 10 minutes the board was completely filled, and they still kept going by writing over the previous items. This drove home the point that there are countless ways to do inner work.

Use your favorite three-letter acronym process. Get therapy. Poke yourself with your finger a few times. Go to Sedona and consult with the vortex aliens. Whatever. The specific process doesn't matter. What works best for me may not work at all for you, and vice versa. The important thing is that the processes you use are helping you become a match for your goal. Don't stick with a process that isn't giving you results.

Results in this area may involve a lot of inner processing, but they should still create tangible effects. For many years I've wanted to travel a lot more. But I didn't have the right vibe for a travel-rich lifestyle. I had limiting beliefs about how difficult it would be to make travel a regular part of my life. I had home-centric relationships that didn't support a travel-rich lifestyle. I gave my power away to reasons (i.e. excuses) for why I couldn't travel as much as I wanted to. I did some serious inner work to resolve those blocks, and as I did this, travel began showing up in my life very easily. Now it seems normal and natural to travel often. Two weeks ago I was in Canada. This week I spent a couple days in Sedona (consulting with the vortex aliens, no less). And next week I'll be in New Orleans. Travel has become an easy and natural part of my life. It took some inner work to integrate the frequent traveler vibe, but I'd say it's pretty well integrated now. I like being a travel slut.

When you've integrated the new vibe well enough (perfection isn't necessary), you'll find that the right actions begin to flow with ease. It feels natural and casual. There's little or no resistance. When you want to experience something that's aligned with your vibe, you just create it. It's no more difficult than making a meal.

Now here's the rub. The personal growth work will not be easy. It may be very challenging. But this is the area where you'll make the fastest progress when working towards goals that you aren't already a good match for experiencing. Once you resolve the alignment issues, the goal almost takes care of itself. You won't have to worry so much about problems like procrastination and self-sabotage.

If you want to get through this part faster, read my book *Personal Development for Smart People*. It covers the 7 fundamentals of personal growth and how to speed up the process, regardless of what type of goal you're trying to achieve. I've alluded to 3 of those 7 principles in this article. For the others I have to refer you to the book because it would take way too long to explain them properly in a chapter (and this one is already pushing 8000 words). A full book was necessary to do this topic justice.

AVOID DELUSIONAL ROLE MODELS

I feel very fortunate because I have a privileged perspective that isn't available to most people. I get to observe lots of people going after different goals, and I get to see who succeeds and who flounders. And because I'm exposed to all this raw data, I'm able to learn patterns that most people don't have the opportunity to learn within their lifetimes.

One thing that's become very clear is that when people succeed, they tend to get there by taking actions that are easy and natural for them. Force doesn't work well. Force can sometimes get you to a goal, but the form of the goal will be a bit off from what you wanted, and it will be hard to hold onto it. When you achieve a stretch goal using this vibrational alignment process, however, it's easier to hang onto it afterwards—and to further build upon it. And you'll enjoy the process of getting there so much more.

This is a personal process, however. You have to keep coming back to what works for you. You have to stop projecting false imaginings onto other people, especially people you've never met. That's delusional thinking that will only push your goal further away.

For example, if you set a goal to become a millionaire, search your thoughts for the kinds of images that come up. What associations do you already have in your memory? Where did you learn them? Are they accurate? Do they apply to you? Did you pick up fictional characters from TV or film for your role models in this area? When you think of millionaires, do you imagine Ebeneezer Scrooge or Gordon Gecko? Do you imagine millionaires that you've only seen on TV but which you've never met face to face? Such mental clutter will screw up your vibe in this area.

Go back to basics and re-learn the right vibe from scratch. Admit that you don't really understand the true vibe of what it's like to *be* an actual millionaire in the real world. I have many millionaire friends, and none are anything like the way I've seen wealthy people portrayed in fictional books, TV shows, or movies. Their real vibes are totally different than the fictional versions. Their vibes are also quite different than what I'd have expected based on interviews I've seen with other millionaires, or from what I've read in books written by millionaires.

When you only experience certain people through indirect media, don't pretend that you know the person being represented. It's too easy to project false assumptions and beliefs onto someone else when you only connect from a distance. If you later interact with such people one-on-one and face-to-face, those interactions will often throw you for a loop. The other person's vibe won't be what you expected.

Obviously I've shared many details about my life via my blog, but it's safe to say that someone who spends 30 minutes chatting with me one-on-one in person will *know* me significantly better than someone who's read all of my articles but has never met me in person. The second person will have a lot more information about me, but the first person will have a much better understanding of my actual vibe. I feel the same about others. If I haven't met you in person, then I don't claim to know you at all.

I can't tell you how many times I've met someone in person who's clearly shy and introverted, but from their blog postings, you'd think they were a social butterfly. In most cases, they didn't intentionally create a false image to deceive people. It's just that their real vibe doesn't get transmitted over the Internet. This leads people to project all sorts of false assumptions onto them, making it hard to use such people as good role models.

One of the reasons it's so important to favor in-person communication (especially when you want to understand a new vibe) is that your skin cells are covered with tiny antennae that pick up electro-magnetic fields emitted by other people (such as their heart waves and brain waves). Every human being is like a walking transmitter and receiver. This aspect of our biology, however, is essentially a local phenomenon. It drops off massively if you're more than a meter or two away from someone. Even watching someone from a stage is too far. You really want to be no farther than the distance of sharing a meal together. That's when you'll learn the most about someone else's vibe. Of course you'll learn even more about someone's vibe if you sleep with them, but you don't have to take things that far.

Consequently, if you've never spent any real time with me in person, then it's not such a good idea to use me as a role model for any goals I might have achieved that you also want to achieve. If you only know me from my blog posts or podcasts or from watching me give a speech, you don't really know what my normal daily vibe is like. You're better off finding someone local who can serve as a role model, someone you can hang out with in person, if only for a short time. If you use primarily Internet-based role models, you're probably going to spend a lot of time running in circles instead of achieving your goals because it will be very hard for you to lock onto the right vibe. You'll merely be creating a false projection that doesn't much resemble the real vibe that matches the goal.

THE PROCESS IN REVIEW

Here's what our overall process looks like step by step:

1. Define your outcome.

2. Develop a deeper understanding of the new vibe that matches the goal (get face time with people who've achieved it, visualize yourself as already there).

3. Contrast your current vibe with the new vibe to see where you're out of alignment (use contrasting visualizations, broadcast your desires).

4. Identify the personal growth work necessary to adjust your vibe (new truths, new connections, smarter application of your power).

5. Use your favorite processes to do the personal growth work until you achieve enough alignment to experience the flow of inspired action.

6. Allow the flow of inspired action (not force) to guide you to your goal.

7. Enjoy the harmonious manifestation of your goal.

It's a simple process in essence, and it works amazingly well.

No goal is out of reach with this process. But what if you can't find any role models for a particular goal?

Then you'll have to rely more heavily on visualization. This may require more experimentation to find the right vibe. It's one reason that new goals that have never been accomplished before by anyone usually take longer to achieve. It takes a while to figure out the right vibe that aligns with the goal. For example, human beings are always building faster computers than the ones that exist today because the vibe of "building a slightly faster computer" is already known and understood by enough people to make that possible. However, the vibe of "building a sentient android" is not yet understood and integrated, so we don't have a Mr. Data yet.

Some fun areas for vibrational "play" involve exploring spaces with stretch goals that no one has ever achieved before. Can you figure out the vibe that aligns with the goal? Can you do the personal growth work to become a match for that vibe? Or will you stick to the vibes that represent a "been there, done that" experience for someone else?

What about the action steps? When your vibe becomes a strong match for your goal, you don't even have to think about the action steps. That would be like telling you how to make dinner. There are countless resources to inform you about the action steps to take. When your vibe is a match for your goal, those action-step resources will tend to effortlessly flow to you. If it seems like the action steps are unknown or a struggle, then you need to do more work on aligning your vibe with your goal.

18.
Quality and Contribution

I remember reading in one of Donald Trump's books that he'd buy cheap clothes and shoes because he didn't think the more expensive ones were worth the money, even though the cost difference was negligible relative to his income. Then he finally splurged (I think it was on a $2000 pair of shoes), and he was impressed by the difference in quality relative to a much cheaper pair of shoes. The construction was much better, the shoes were significantly more durable, and he ultimately saved time and money by not having to replace them as often. At his income level, saving that extra time is more important than saving $2000.

Now you may think a $2000 pair of shoes would never be a wise purchase, but recognize that as the dollar-value of your time increases, the quality of your purchases becomes more and more significant. Think of it like this. If it takes you 100 hours to earn $2000, then buying a $2000 pair of shoes would likely be a poor trade. But if it takes you 10 minutes to earn $2000, then maybe it's not a bad trade at all, and it would be worthwhile for you to trade those 10 minutes for the best shoes you can get, especially if they may last you for a decade. Two thousand dollars may seem like a lot of money, but if it's only 10 minutes of your time, it's not too significant.

Even if you consider what you could do for others by giving away that $2000 and foregoing the shoes, if you're capable of generating that much value in 10 minutes, you could obviously do a lot more for others by contributing through your work vs. fussing over such a small amount (small relative to your total value-generation potential). Who cares what shoes you wear if they help you provide millions—or even billions—of dollars of value through the course of your lifetime? If you're capable of doing such a thing, by all means enjoy the best shoes money can buy, and just keep doing what you're doing.

QUALITY AND INCOME

The importance of quality is relative to the value of your time. The quality-cost tradeoff doesn't scale linearly, so when you want something of better than average quality, you usually must pay a premium for it. To get something twice as good as the average, you may have to pay five times as much. For most people that isn't a reasonable trade, but as your time becomes more and more valuable, it may be wise to pay 80% more in order to get that last 20% gain in quality. The time and headaches you'll save will more than make up for it, as will the potential enjoyment from the increased quality.

When Erin and I were fresh out of college, we'd often buy the cheapest stuff we could get—cheap furniture, cheap clothing, cheap used cars. That just seemed intelligent to us. Why spend more when you can get by with something almost as good for a lot less money?

Eventually we went from being cheap to being value-focused, so we looked for the best quality-cost tradeoff. In the long run, cheap often ends up costing more, not just in money to replace or repair items that wear out quickly but also in lost time dealing with the shortcomings of those excessively frugal purchases. We started buying well-made items that would last instead of the cheapest we could find, even if we had to pay more for them. And this actually saved us money in the long run.

When our income was close to the average, consumer products of average quality seemed just right for us. But as our income shot above average, it made sense to pay those premium prices for a modest boost in quality, at least in certain situations. The time-quality tradeoff became more significant than the cost-quality tradeoff.

For example, when Erin and I bought our new house last month, we went for a significant upgrade. The new house has more than twice the square footage of the old house, it's in one of the best neighborhoods in Las Vegas, and it cost more than three times as much as our old house. But the payments (mortgage, insurance, utilities) are only around 20% of our income, so it's hardly a financial burden. Erin now has her own office instead of having to share it with our bedroom, so she's a lot happier and more productive. Plus we both really enjoy living

198

in this new house, which puts us in consistently more positive states while we're living and working here.

As another example, I recently bought a new laptop PC. In fact, this is the first article I'm writing with it. I spent about $1700 on it (purchased online with free shipping). I probably could have gotten something 80% as good for about half that price, but since the price difference is less than a day's income, that marginal quality improvement is a worthwhile tradeoff for me, especially since it's a tax-deductible business purchase and something I'll be using frequently. If I could have found a better model with the specs I wanted, I'd have gladly paid even more for it.

THE OUTRAGE SCRIPT

Several years ago, I'd have viewed such purchases as extravagant, wasteful, or imprudent. But I started asking questions that led me to some new insights. How could anyone possibly justify spending $10,000 a night for a hotel room? What kind of person would pay $100,000 for a car? Who'd be crazy enough to spend $200 on a dinner? Are such people completely nuts, throwing away good money just to show off? Don't they realize that if they bought a cheaper but still adequate car they could use the rest to put a few kids through college? And what kind of person eats $200 in a single meal?

I eventually saw that these questions were a function of scarcity thinking. I call it the "outrage script." Have you ever run the outrage script?

Personally I found it difficult to dump the outrage script. It was ingrained in me from a young age. I partially learned it from my grandparents. They were delightful people, very loving and generous with their grandchildren, but having lived through the Great Depression, they had a lifetime subscription to the outrage script. I eventually dropped this script when I saw that the more outrage we feel towards abundance-minded people who experience no lack whatsoever, the tighter we are with our own money, and the less we ultimately contribute. I don't know if you'll agree with that, but I think you can at least agree that running the outrage script surely does no good for anyone.

You won't often see abundance-minded people running the outrage script. Instead you're more likely to see them running the gratitude script. That script looks something like this: Isn't it wonderful that certain people are generating so much value—and so efficiently—that they can easily afford to pay $10,000 for a hotel room, thereby helping to create new jobs and keep money flowing through the hard-working service industry? Isn't it great that people can afford a $100,000 car in order to fund new innovations that could benefit us all? Isn't it outstanding that people can buy a $200 dinner, encouraging the best chefs to create new culinary delights and to help the wait staff support their families? While it would be unusual for someone to phrase their questions like this, the common element is that they recognize that spending money is itself an act of contribution because spending is giving.

THE CONTRIBUTION SCRIPT

Even better than the gratitude script is the contribution script. Here's how this script sounds: What could I do to create so much value for others that spending $10,000 for a hotel room would be easily affordable and a great way to reward myself and my friends for a job well done? I could adapt the other two examples as well, but I think you get the idea. Money isn't a scarce resource unless you make it one. Money becomes abundant when social contribution is abundant.

How does the concept of quality relate to the contribution script? First, as you contribute more and more value to others, the ability to enjoy better quality is your natural reward. Secondly, upgrading the quality of your surroundings can in turn increase your ability to contribute. These two aspects serve to create an upward spiral. The more you contribute, the more you can contribute. It's all good.

Unfortunately it's easy to fall victim to mental blocks that keep you out of this positive spiral. Running the outrage script is one example. Another example is feeling that your best contributions won't make much of a difference, so why bother? Try to see these blocks for what they are. Think about them consciously, and ask yourself if they're really true. Whatever bothers you most about people who are contributing (and being handsomely rewarded for it) is a pointer to something you must work on within yourself.

THE QUALITY-CONTRIBUTION BALANCE

Ultimately the physical stuff in your life is a reflection of your life's inner quality, not the cause of it. When you've found and accepted an inspiring purpose and are feeling totally fulfilled by it, that inner fulfillment works like a magnet, drawing unto you the physical surroundings that are congruent with it. You could refer to this as "fake it till you make it," but I think it's more accurate to say, "As within, so without." You don't need to fake anything. You just need to recognize that your inner world and your outer world are constantly influencing each other, and a glaring deficiency in one will induce a similar deficiency in the other.

Over the past year, I've had the opportunity to speak to some very financially successful people, and I keep noticing this quality-contribution connection. One friend I spoke to last week runs a business that earns $15 million a year and has dozens of employees, and it's growing like gangbusters. When I asked him how he manages his life without being overwhelmed by stress, he said he just absolutely loves his work. He also mentioned he takes week-long vacations every six weeks, gets massages, enjoys relaxing spa days, and spends plenty of time with his family. On the one hand, you could consider these the rewards of success. On the other hand, you could make a case that they're contributing to his success. I think they are two sides of the same coin. The more you contribute, the more you'll enjoy your life, and the more you enjoy your life, the more motivation, energy, and willingness you'll have to contribute.

Your quality of life and your social contribution will tend to remain congruent, so if you want to see improvement in either area, you must create a temporary positive imbalance. Raise one side, then the other, and create a new equilibrium. An even better approach is to commit to seeing both sides grow together, so the whole system has a positive momentum without becoming seriously unbalanced. This kind of change takes time, so don't pray for an overnight miracle. Be patient with yourself.

If you want to increase the quality of your life, focus on increasing your contribution. And if you want to improve your contribution, take steps to upgrade the quality of your surroundings. Ultimately the two are inseparable, but you'll often find that one side or the other is lagging behind, thereby dragging down the whole system. Is your contribution suffering because you aren't being adequately supported with a positive environment, good friends, and reliable tools? Or is the quality of your life suffering because you're wearing yourself out from over- or under-contributing, while blocking the abundant flow of rewards into your life? What can you do to restore balance and re-align yourself with that upward spiral?

THE ABUNDANCE MINDSET

If the $10K hotel room seems like an extravagant expense, it means you're out of alignment with the mindset that's capable of producing $10K of value very quickly. It's not the expensive room itself that helps you contribute. What helps you contribute is thinking about what it would take to become the kind of person who could afford to stay in a $10K hotel room without thinking twice about it—because that's a person who's capable of generating massive value very efficiently.

At an average level of income in the USA, there's not much difference between a dime and a penny, right? It's a small amount either way or not particularly significant. Would you fret over a price difference of 9 cents? Hopefully not. But for some people on this planet, 9 cents is a fair amount, and to pay a dime instead of a penny for something would be regarded as extravagant and wasteful.

Similarly, at higher levels of income (and value creation), $10K is nothing. It's just a penny. It's insignificant. It's pocket change. There's virtually no difference between a $10K hotel room and a $100 hotel room—the price difference is meaningless, so why not pay that extra "9 cents" for a nicer setup?

The point is that if you harbor the outrage mindset towards "extravagant" purchases, you're keeping yourself out of alignment with becoming the kind of person who could generate that much value easily. Hence, you're severely limiting yourself.

If you want to look at it from the opposite angle, start applying the outrage script whenever you see people overpaying a few pennies for a purchase: "Are you insane? You could have bought that apple for 5 cents less at the store down the street! You must have money to burn!" They'll think you've lost your mind. Similarly, this is how very wealthy people think about the price difference between a $10,000 vs. a $100 hotel room. If you were to complain that they should stay in a cheaper room to save $9,900, they might look at you like you're nuts.

Fretting over pennies probably seems foolish to you. Similarly, to those who are capable of generating massive value (and being paid accordingly), fretting over $10K is equally foolish. People who can spend $10K on a hotel room know that $10K is not a lot of money.

I believe the outrage script is a big mistake. It holds people back more than they know, and my intention was to try to shed some light on that. If you think any amount of money is "a lot" or "too much" or "extravagant," you're resonating with scarcity, not abundance, and you're preventing yourself from becoming the kind of person who can generate that level of value. Why do this to yourself? Why hold back if you're capable of contributing so much more?

It was this realization that helped me increase my own income several times over during the past year alone, and I didn't have to work harder or longer to do it. I realized that if I think of some arbitrary amount of money as huge or extravagant, whether it's $10K or $10 million, then I'm out of alignment with being able to earn that much money, which means I'm out of alignment with being able to generate that much value for others.

Remember that money is social debt. The size of your bank account is a measure of how much society owes you for the value you've already contributed. If you think $10K is a large sum, it means you probably aren't in a position to generate $10K of value for others very easily. If you can dump that unhealthy mindset, you can open yourself to generating far more value in much less time. When I started thinking of $10K as a small sum, I soon found it very easy to earn $10K. Earning $10K is about as difficult as making a sandwich.

Start where you are, and stretch yourself to let go of those limiting beliefs that hold you back. If you think it's fairly easy to earn $10 or $100, try to open your mind to the possibility that maybe, just maybe, it could be equally easy (maybe even easier) to earn $500 in the same amount of time or less. One you've reached that point, push on to $1,000, and keep going from there. When you think that a certain amount of money is "no big whoop," you'll find a way to earn that much, and that means you'll be contributing more value to others. The money you receive as compensation is your receipt.

19.
The Foundation for Abundance

How we can talk about creating abundance when it seems we live in a world of scarce resources? Aren't these in conflict? Isn't an abundance mindset just an exercise in self-delusion?

SCARCE RESOURCES

Certain resources on earth are in limited supply and are being depleted quickly. Perhaps the #1 example of this is oil. Oil is being pumped out of the ground faster than it can be replenished by the earth.

It takes energy to pump the oil out of the ground, and not all of the oil can be retrieved in an energy efficient manner. It doesn't make sense to spend 100 units of energy in order to extract only 90 units.

The easy-to-get oil is already scarce, and companies are going after the harder-to-get oil at much greater risk and expense. It's easier to pump oil out of the ground than it is to build offshore oil rigs and pump it up through the ocean floor. There would be no rational justification for engaging in costly offshore oil drilling if land-based oil supplies were abundant. The very existence of offshore oil drilling is a clear signal that oil is becoming scarcer. Even oil rich nations like Saudi Arabia are engaged in offshore drilling, which is a tacit acknowledgement that they're running out of oil.

It's only a matter of time before this resource runs out. As it becomes increasingly scarce, shortages will occur, and oil prices will surge. Industries that depend heavily on oil will have to cut back. Aren't we already seeing this happen?

At present there's no resource that can substitute for oil's versatility nor its integration into modern society. Oil is used to run farming equipment and transport food. It's used in plastics—your home is probably filled with petroleum-based products. Even the tires on your car are made with oil, about 7 gallons per tire. It's not a resource that can be easily replaced. As oil runs out, some lifestyle changes are inevitable.

STORY

There's no need to deny that certain resources are scarce. Scarce resources are part of the story of earth.

If life is a dream, then what sense does it make for there to be scarce resources? Can't you just think your way into limitless abundance?

Limits and constraints make for interesting story. If there are no constraints, there's no story. Life in a constraint-free world would be incredibly boring.

Abundance isn't the same thing as limitlessness. If you lived in a truly limitless world, would you feel a sense of abundance? More likely you'd suffer from gluttony, boredom, and laziness. It would be a disappointing and uninspiring dream to endure.

This may appear unintuitive at first glance, but abundance requires scarcity.

GRATITUDE

Abundance and scarcity are equally valuable teachers. They both teach us gratitude, but in different ways.

When there's a constant presence in your life, you'll tend to take it for granted. You'll come to expect that it will always be there. But when you have to do without for a while, it gives you the opportunity to appreciate what you have even more.

It's the shifting between phases of abundance and scarcity that teaches us what we value most.

I take time every day to appreciate the good things in my life, partly because I've had the experience of not having them. I know these experiences are temporary.

I'm grateful for the freedom I enjoy because at one point I was in an 8′x10′ jail cell, feeling what it felt like not to have that freedom.

I'm grateful for the money that flows through my life because I was broke for many years, went bankrupt, and got kicked out of my apartment because I couldn't pay the rent.

I'm grateful for the friends I have because I know what it's like to feel alone and friendless.

I'm grateful for the health I enjoy because I know what it's like to be sick.

When I use the Internet, I feel grateful for how amazing it is and how it lets me connect with people all over the world. I remember what it was like when I didn't have access to this amazing wonder.

In two days I'm traveling to Canada to visit my Rachelle. We haven't seen each other in a month and a half. Being apart for so long makes it hard to take each other for granted. It helps us appreciate each other much more. I'm very grateful that she's in my life.

However, when there's a glut of abundance, I'm more likely to take things for granted. That's when scarcity may become the more valuable teacher.

When I've spent a few weeks with Rachelle, for instance, I may not feel as appreciative of her on Day 20 as I did on Day 1. But after saying goodbye to her at the airport and then experiencing a few days alone, I become more acutely aware of just how much I appreciate her, and I look forward to seeing her again.

It's the contrast between abundance and scarcity that helps raise our awareness of what we value most.

The abundance mindset isn't about acquiring and securing more stuff. It's about appreciating life fully and feeling grateful for what life is teaching you.

GRATITUDE FOR THE STORY

Can you actually feel grateful for the scarcity you experience because it's teaching you new truths about yourself?

When I was deep in debt, knowing I was going to have to declare bankruptcy, I felt I had nothing more to lose financially, so I decided to stop feeding so much of my power to that part of my life. I'd been telling myself I couldn't have a good life if my financial life was broken. So I gave myself permission to feel good about the other parts of my life and not let the lack of money drag me down so much. After all, it was just a number. Why was I giving it so much power over me?

I started paying attention to what I did have, and I learned to appreciate it more deeply. I appreciated the food I was able to eat. I appreciated that I somehow still had a roof over my head. I appreciated the weather. I appreciated the ocean, the beach, and the sunrise.

I appreciate that I could breathe. I appreciated running and meditation. I appreciated my relationships. I appreciated my health.

It was in late 1998 and early 1999 that I began to do that. And 1998 was the last year I felt to be a scarce one (and perhaps the first half of 1999). After that I always seemed to have plenty. Even the money situation turned around within a year. That was my first financially positive year after 6 years as an entrepreneur. I experienced 12 more good years in a row after that.

I'm glad these events were part of my story. If I had achieved lots of good things earlier in life, I don't think I'd appreciate them as much as I do now. Despite having a lot of good stuff in my life these days, I don't take it for granted. The sweet stuff is sweeter because I know what bitter tastes like.

THE STORY OF LOSS

Everything you have in this world is temporary. One way or another, it will vanish from your life. If it's physical in nature, it's impermanent.

Earth's resources will eventually be used up. Your human body will be used up as well. Even the Sun will eventually burn out. And it's expected that the known universe itself will eventually end.

Loss is part of the story of life. When we lose something precious to us, we deepen our understanding of its value.

Humanity is burning through some of the earth's scarce resources. That, by itself, is not a problem. The real problem is that we don't properly appreciate those resources. It's okay to pump oil out of the ground and use it. The earth doesn't mind. But are we truly appreciating what the earth is giving to us?

Do you realize that all of the "stuff" in your life is a gift of the earth? If it's physical in nature, it was probably made from something that was pulled out of the ground. Human creativity played its part of course, but do you realize that the raw materials of the items in your home came from the earth? You're literally wearing pieces of the earth on your body.

Now realize that all of this is temporary. You'll either lose it before you die or when you die.

The great story of loss is that everything in this physical reality will eventually be taken from you. Do you accept this, or do you resist it?

APPRECIATING SCARCITY

According to Elisabeth KÃbler-Ross, the five stages of grief are denial, anger, bargaining, depression, and acceptance.

Clinginess shows up in the first 4 stages, but when we get to acceptance, we finally let go and make peace with reality.

I think there are stages beyond acceptance, however, and gratitude is certainly one of them. When we can see the important role that loss plays in life, we can learn to appreciate loss itself. It's an important part of our story. Loss helps us grow.

Without loss we'd be too likely to take the good parts of our lives for granted. They'd eventually become hollow and meaningless to us. When we lose them, however, we become intensely aware of the value we once experienced.

As we move into an abundance mindset, we recognize that the true value we experience can always be recreated. Real value isn't scarce. We may lose a loved one, but we can experience love again.

Scarcity teaches us what true abundance means. Scarcity helps us understand what we value and what we don't.

You may not value oil specifically, but by appreciating what oil has done, you may come to appreciate technology, and by appreciating technology, you may come to appreciate human empowerment, sharing knowledge, making new discoveries, and connecting with people.

TRUE ABUNDANCE

Abundance doesn't require unlimited physical resources. Having limitless oil or some suitable replacement won't help us feel more abundant. It will simply lead us to take more things for granted, and we'll underappreciate what we have.

Abundance isn't about having more, more, more. It's about learning what we truly value and realizing that we can in fact create that value if we so desire.

In some ways this dream world is much smarter than our limited individual personalities. It brings us what we truly desire, even if that conflicts with what we explicitly ask for. The universe is completely and 100% on your side. You can try to make an enemy of it, but it never abandons you. It simply outsmarts you by doing an end run around your stubbornness.

To create an abundance mindset, you may need to shed a lot of false desires. You may need to stop feeding your power to what you don't want. And you may need to start appreciating all the goodness that's right in front of you, but you've been too blind to pause and appreciate it.

If you think that scarcity in the world is a bad thing, take another look. You're seeing scarcity because you need to see it in order to grow. You need to see war in order to appreciate peace. You need to see unfairness to appreciate fairness. You need to see disease to appreciate health. If you didn't need to learn these lessons, you wouldn't keep summoning scarcity as your teacher.

Don't close your eyes to the scarcity you perceive. Let it sink in fully. Feel the sense of lack. And when you've learned the lesson you need to learn from it, withdraw your power from it, and use it to create the abundance you desire.

HAPPINESS

Aligning yourself with abundance is the same thing as aligning yourself with happiness.

There are many false road signs to happiness in this world. Most of them lead to dead ends.

Material wealth is one example. If you think that having "more" will lead to happiness, go ahead and try it. You may learn this lesson by gaining *more* and still feeling unhappy, or you may learn it by failing to reach the level of *more* that you desire. Eventually you'll become so frustrated that you decide to explore a different path.

I put some energy into improving my finances, but I didn't feel happier or more abundant when I achieved those goals. What gave me the greatest feeling of happiness was taking time to appreciate the good things in my life. The interesting part is that this had nothing to do with the things. It had everything to do with how I was using my power.

I learned that it makes no difference what my finances are doing. They can go up or down, and it doesn't affect my happiness. I always have the ability to feel grateful. Sometimes I feel more grateful when I have less vs. when I have more.

One of the reasons I placed my work into the public domain and no longer copyright it is that I realized that owning a lot of intellectual property doesn't make me any happier than when I owned none. When I tried feeling grateful for it, I realized it wasn't the ownership that mattered to me. Nor was it the body of work that I created in the past. I discovered the deeper truth that I'm grateful for the opportunity to express myself creatively. I'm grateful for the ability to connect with people around the world. I'm grateful for the chance to learn and grow.

I don't need to make more money or acquire more prestige or gain more web traffic in order to be happier. I can be happy simply expressing my creativity. Certain tools like a computer and the Internet help me do that, and I'm grateful for them as well, but if they were all stripped from me, I could still express my creativity with sticks and stones. Even if I ended up paralyzed, I could build new creations within my mind, and I could still feel grateful for the ability to do that.

However, I've noticed that the more I remember these lessons, the less often scarcity shows up in my life as a personal teacher. I'm getting better at making choices with respect to happiness as opposed to making choice on the basis of *more*. I pass up obvious avenues for advancement in my business if I don't think they'll increase my happiness, even if they might increase my income. From an entrepreneurial perspective, it may appear that I run my business strangely, but I run it happily.

DISCARDING FALSE PATHS

The existence of scarcity in the world helps us identify and discard the false paths that won't give us a true sense of abundance.

I believe that a true abundance mindset isn't about how much stuff you can acquire. I think it's about realizing how little you need to create happiness. Could you lose all your stuff and still feel grateful? Can you still use your power to create the experience of caring, generosity, and happiness even in the presence of lack?

I also think that life stops hammering us with certain lessons once we learn them. My money problems didn't go away because I became aggressive about making more money. They stopped arising when I let go of my fear of not having money and when I stopped empowering the belief that I couldn't have a good life without money.

What helped me most was thinking about what my life would be like if I actually became homeless. I could live on the beach and sleep under the stars each night. I could work on my social skills. I could learn to get better at drawing. I'd have lots of freedom. I could learn new languages from bilingual homeless people. I could go to libraries and read. I could meditate and go running each day. I could write a book about the experience. I could even do volunteer work to help people. I soon realized that even if I had no money at all, I could still live a pretty cool life. It was within my power to do so.

Once I realized that my money situation absolutely did not have the power to sentence me to a miserable life and that in fact, I could still lead an interesting and fulfilling life no matter what, my whole being lightened up. It seemed as if reality said to me, "Ok, great…it took years, but you finally got that lesson. Now let's move on to these other lessons over here." There was no more need for major scarcity to keep arising for me in this particular area since I learned what I needed to learn.

An expanded version of this lesson that I've been learning recently is that I don't need non-physical property either. I don't need to own anything at all to be happy. I think I'm going to enjoy writing without the burden of ownership. The creative part is what I enjoy most. I don't need to own what I create.

SUSTAINABILITY

Some people desire to create more sustainability in the world, which is partly about shifting away from non-renewable resources and towards renewable resources.

I don't presently consider myself a proponent of the sustainability movement though. I think there are more beneficial growth lessons to be learned from cycles of excess and scarcity than there are from long-term sustainability.

If my own life had been more balanced, I doubt I'd have learned as much as I did. I think it would be boring and depressing to live as many animals in nature do, so I wouldn't use that as my model of environmental harmony. I think there are good reasons humans create such huge imbalances—and why we have the capacity to continue doing so. These imbalances provide us with amazing growth lessons, teaching how to expand our power and our wisdom simultaneously.

Some would say that today our power has gotten ahead of our wisdom. I tend to agree. This, however, motivates us to increase our wisdom. When our wisdom pulls ahead, there will be a stronger drive to increase our power.

On a deeper level, I see this as the balance between Truth, Love, and Power. These are the primary ways in which we experience growth, and all three have the capacity to expand.

When Truth gets too far ahead, then we have theories we cannot test and grand ideas we cannot implement. This motivates us to come together and collaborate (Love) in order to achieve new breakthroughs (Power).

When Love gets too far ahead, we connect to such a degree that we begin to lose our individual will and drive. We stagnate and do the same things day after day. You may see this kind of imbalance arising in your life if you spend tons of time socializing online. Eventually you begin to feel empty inside, like you're just spinning your wheels. This negative feeling can't be resolved by throwing more socialization at it. To correct this imbalance, you need to incorporate more learning (Truth) and creative projects (Power) into your life.

When Power gets too far ahead, we abuse ourselves. We get good at creating what we don't want, so we create a lot of it. This motivates us to pay more attention to our relationships (Love) and to listen to our true desires (Truth).

If we truly appreciate a natural resource, we'll be motivated to find ways to use it efficiently to create good value for ourselves. If we don't appreciate a certain resource, we may push it to the point of extinction and then deal with its absence afterwards.

How many of the now extinct species did we appreciate? Do you miss them, or are you okay living without them?

Is oil a resource that you truly appreciate, or is it one you'd be okay living without? Do you feel grateful for all that oil has added to your life? Do you hate it and want to see it go away? How does the unfolding story of earth reflect your feelings in this area? How does it give you new insights into what you value most?

For me the lesson of oil has to do with prioritizing my values. Using oil has consequences, some of which I perceive as negative and some as positive. Which of those consequences am I willing to accept? Which am I not willing to accept? And what does this tell me about my values? I learn a lot about myself by witnessing the story of oil unfolding in my reality. It's a wonderful teacher.

LESSONS FROM YOUR STORY

The story of earth is taking us through some interesting lessons these days. When faced with these lessons, we have a choice. We can choose to resist them, in which case we'll feed more power to them and see them expand. Or we can choose to learn these lessons now, which give us a chance to move on to new lessons.

If you don't appreciate something in your life, then why is it there? It's there because you keep feeding your power to it. You keep noticing it and paying attention to it. If you didn't do that, then for all practical purposes, it would be invisible to you.

The reason you're creating this drama is so that you can have a growth experience. It is there to teach you something important, such as what you truly value. You'll keep creating this drama in different forms until you're able to learn the lesson behind the drama. That lesson will ultimately take you to a deeper level of Truth.

If you try to shortcut these lessons, your solutions will never last. The deeper part of your being—the part that wants to grow—will simply keep manifesting the lessons as new dramas in your reality. You create with your whole being, not just with your thoughts or feelings.

Some people are currently experiencing interesting and dramatic lessons with respect to unemployment. Many didn't appreciate the jobs they once had and which are now gone. Now they are job-free, and some don't appreciate that either. They may finally get a new job, and they may dislike that too. They'll continue to live out such cycles until they realize that the common element in all this scarcity isn't the presence or lack of a job. It's their ongoing lack of appreciation.

If you were looking to employ people, and someone came to you for an interview, and you sensed they didn't appreciate their previous employer, and they didn't appreciate what they learned from unemployment, and they probably weren't going to appreciate the job you could give them, would you hire them? If you were going to hire someone, wouldn't you choose someone that would truly appreciate what you can offer? Wouldn't you favor someone with a record of appreciating their previous work history as well? Would you rather work with an appreciative person or with an unappreciative one? What would you want if you were the employer?

What kind of employer would hire an unappreciative employee? Perhaps an employer who's desperate, ignorant, or self-punishing would do so. Is that the kind of person you'd want as your boss? Are you likely to enjoy that job?

My career life turned around when I learned to appreciate the value of work itself. I realized that the value I get from work isn't about how much I get paid or who hires me. It's about the opportunity to express myself creatively. Once I realized that, I always enjoyed my work. I feel grateful that I get to create something that didn't exist before. I also realized that being creative is more important to me than a steady paycheck. I'm glad that life brought me experiences to teach me this lesson, even though they were difficult to learn.

Can we enjoy abundance in a world of scarce resources? Of course we can. Scarcity is one of our best teachers. It steers us away from false paths and teaches us what real abundance means to us. We don't need more money or success or "iStuff" to be happy. We can choose to feel grateful for what we value most, and through that feeling of gratitude, we can empower its expansion.

APPRECIATING ABUNDANCE

When you observe financial well-being in others, especially very lavish well-being, do you sometimes condemn it? If you do so, you're simultaneously condemning your own well-being.

This doesn't mean you need to praise those aspects that don't resonate with you, but don't waste your energy on condemning them. Instead, turn your attention to the aspects you can appreciate, and this will soon attract more well-being into your life.

Notice that if you desire greater abundance while thinking negatively towards those who already have it, you're putting out conflicting intentions—I want more abundance; I hate excessive abundance—which means you cannot and will not progress. You'll merely continue to manifest lack.

Think of someone who enjoys a degree of abundance that bothers you on some level. Perhaps imagine a wealthy corporate CEO that got paid what you feel is excessive compensation, even as their company lost money. Imagine this CEO spending that money lavishly—fancy cars, expensive vacations, a huge mansion, a staff of servants. Now look for a seed of appreciation within that imagery, and expand it.

Do you find it difficult to appreciate someone in this situation? If so, then approach it from a different perspective. Imagine that someone who lives on less than $1 per day and who doesn't have access to clean water and reliable meals is doing this same exercise, and she has selected you as her example of lavish living. Your lifestyle seems incredibly abundant to her, far beyond anything she's known during her life and seemingly unattainable for her. Would you expect her to judge you harshly for having what she does not? Would you have her condemn you as a heartless and greedy bastard? How would you like her to feel about you?

Now return to the original exercise. Put yourself in the place of that CEO. To you this lifestyle feels normal, not lavish or excessive. As you see it, so many others are living in lack and scarcity. You know you can't help them by joining them in lack. You can be generous with them of course, and you do so to the degree it feels good, but you don't want to give so much that it disempowers them, do you? Instead you would rather inspire others to create their own happiness, assisting them where you can but being careful not to rob them of their own creative power.

People do not want to see you in lack, but they cannot rob you of your power either—that is something you must learn to develop. Do not fight against the abundance you desire, especially when you see it in someone else. Instead, think of relating to this more abundant person as you would want someone in greater scarcity to relate to you—as

216

an example of hope and potential, not a perfect or flawless example, but an example nonetheless.

Part IV: Letting It Flow

20.
A Fixed Income Is a Sucker's Bet

Do you live on a fixed income, earning the same amount of money paycheck after paycheck? Maybe you pick up a cost of living adjustment or a raise now and then (or suffer a pay cut or reduction in hours), but barring any major changes like getting promoted, fired, or laid off, is your income fairly stable and predictable? Do you have a good sense of what you're going to earn during the next 3 months? Would it be exceedingly unlikely for you to earn double or triple—or half—of that anticipated amount?

If this describes you, then who decided to fixify your income? Who made that decision?

You made that decision, didn't you? You decided to earn a fixed amount of money per month. You can trace your decisions back to some moment where you said yes to a fixed income.

Are you aware that saying yes was entirely optional? In fact, if you give it some thought (which I'll encourage you to do), you should be able to see that accepting a fixed income is a rather stupid choice, all things considered. A fixed income is a sucker bet.

How is that choice working out for you so far? Are you blissfully delighted with it? Do you like knowing that you'll earn the same amount of money month after month? Does it feel comforting to know how much you're going to make? Or is there some part of you that's bored and frustrated beyond recognition?

Do you like the stability of it? Is it truly stable, or is your feeling of security rooted in a hopeful illusion? If some individual can decide to turn off your income with the words "You're fired," it's hardly stable. If that's your situation, it's safe to say your income is unstable and conditional rather than stable and secure. We can say that all income is conditional, but how stable are those conditions? Does someone else wield the power to turn off your income?

For the sake of argument, let's assume that your income seems reasonably stable, secure, and predictable. Perhaps you work in a high-demand field, and you're really good at what you do, so even if you lost your current job, you could quickly find a new one doing similar work for similar pay. That may be a stretch for some, but for the sake of this article, we don't even need to pluck that low-hanging fruit. There are plenty of other cuts awaiting a splash of lemon juice.

DOWNSIDES OF A FIXED INCOME

Aside from its predictability and possible stability, virtually everything else about a fixed income is negative.

First off, a fixed income lacks flexibility. It cannot adapt well to changing circumstances. This means that fixed incomes can get pummeled in a variety of ways.

If expenses rise unexpectedly and surpass your monthly income, then you have no choice but to draw money from cash reserves or investments or go into debt. If your expenses later return to normal, this debt may be temporary, but you'll still end up paying extra interest or losing interest on your depleted savings/investments, which takes money out of your pocket.

If you spend more, you can't simply earn more to compensate. This turns unexpected expenses into threats. They become something you relate to with fear or worry about. What if the car breaks down? What if someone gets sick? What if prices go up? Such events are part of life. It makes no sense to fear the inevitable. Stuff is going to break, including expensive stuff that costs a lot to repair or replace. If getting an unexpected bill stresses you out, your mindset is a mismatch for reality.

If expenses rise above net income for too long, you can sink into debt for a long time and waste a great deal of money paying interest to someone else. Many people remain stuck there till they die. If their fixed incomes are too close to their expenses, taxes, and debt payments, then getting out of debt becomes hopeless. Hope can only be restored by focusing on the income side.

For this reason, people on fixed incomes often spend an inordinate amount of time fussing over their expenses. Otherwise they may risk depleting their savings or going into debt. They want to fulfill their desires, but their income limits their ability to do that.

"I can't afford it" is practically a mantra for fixed income people. They sacrifice their true desires in order to stick to their budgets, totally oblivious to the fact that no one is forcing them to waste their lives on expense-tracking tedium. If they desire something with a price tag, but they can't afford it, they rule it out as impossible for them—as if their fixed income is the final arbiter of their desires. Eventually resentment builds. They start resenting the unfairness of the economy, of people who set the prices, of business in general, of money, and so on. The bad guy is somewhere out there. Nope...the bad guy is the stupid choice you made to fixify your income. Wise up and stop doing that to yourself.

People look really pathetic when they act financially helpless. This isn't how human beings should relate to themselves.

"Hi, there's something I really want. Actually, it feels like the perfect match for me, but I just can't afford it because I'm on a fixed income. Help me! Can you give me a price break or something? I really, really want it!"

"How about if you give me a break and stop pretending to be helpless?"

"No, you don't understand. I'm on a tight budget. I really can't afford to pay full price."

"Now you're just making yourself look foolish. Who fixified your income in the first place? You did! Why are you putting it on me to work within the limits you created for yourself? You're asking me to fit an elephant inside a breadbox. Why don't you raise your limits? Raise them high enough to be well beyond your desires, so you can easily afford whatever you want."

"I can do that?"

"Yes, you've always been free to do that."

"Well, I dunno about that. I don't think my boss will give me more money."

"Screw your boss then. Why do you want a boss anyway?"

"But that would mean making major changes in my life."

"Yes, it would."

"I don't think I'm ready for that. It's too risky."

"There's no additional risk because you've already lost the connection to your desires. You're already stuck in a situation where you aren't experiencing what you truly want. Life doesn't get any worse than that. To do nothing ensures a continuation of the worst possible outcome—being perpetually unfulfilled."

"But it could get worse. I could be even more unhappy."

"If you do nothing, it will indeed get worse. That's a given. Your desires will slip further and further away as you disconnect from your heart even more. Life doesn't get any worse than that. The only hope lies on the path of change."

"So it's to be torture then?"

"Yes, until it kills you."

"I can cope with torture."

"Suit yourself."

"So how about that price break?"

"Fezzik, tear his arms off."

FOOLISHLY GUARDING FOOL'S GOLD

It's funny how people strive to protect that which is worthless. The state of being unhappy and unfulfilled is worth absolutely nothing. If that's where you find yourself, you're already at rock bottom.

You may think that you'll have to risk some of your stuff (possessions, money, etc) to make big changes in your life. That may be true, but if you aren't happy right now, then all of that stuff is of zero value to you anyway. If you try to maintain your stuff at the expense of your happiness and fulfillment, then you are indeed a complete idiot. You're trying to sell your very soul, aren't you? You're entering into an agreement that says, "I agree to be perpetually unhappy and unfulfilled in exchange for cash and goods worth $X." Add up the value of all the stuff you believe you'd have to risk to make big changes. Does that value of X make this agreement a wise choice?

Risk the stuff. It's worthless anyway. But don't make the insane choice of sacrificing your happiness for stuff.

SWITCHING TO A VARIABLE INCOME

Earning a variable income, where you have the flexibility to earn a different sum of money each month, has a lot more to do with mindset than anything else. It doesn't matter if you have a job, run your own business, or enjoy multiple streams of income. Those are just different vehicles.

The key is to recognize who determines your income. You do. You may have financial and economic realities to deal with, but ultimately you set the prices for what your time and efforts are worth financially, you decide what skills to develop and what kind of training to undertake, and you determine what kind of value to create and deliver to people. The most powerful choices are under your control.

If you deliver pizza for a living, you can expect to be paid for that particular skill based on its market value. Pizza delivery guys are easily trained and replaced, so you can expect to earn very little from such a job. Don't blame the job for what it pays. No one is forcing you to choose a low-paying, unskilled job. If you try to squeeze more money from a job than the job is worth in the larger marketplace, eventually your boss or customers will figure out that you're being overpaid, and you'll be replaced by someone cheaper.

On the other hand, maybe you want to inspire and motivate people for a living. This takes a lot more skill than delivering pizzas, but it's in much higher demand relative to the supply. In general, people are willing to pay a lot more to be inspired and motivated than they're willing to pay for a hot pizza (unless you live in Naples). If you develop a high ability to inspire and motivate people, and you build the means to deliver your value to a sizeable number of people, you can eventually earn more in an hour than the pizza guy earns in month.

You not only have the ability to develop your skills within a particular field, but you can also switch fields repeatedly. If you want to earn more, then keep building skills and changing up how you combine and express those skills to maximize the value you're able to create and deliver, thereby maximizing the income you're able to generate. The opportunities to do this are endless as long as you remain flexible and alert.

Your income is not fixed unless you decide to fixify it. It doesn't matter if you're getting checks from the government as your only income source. Those checks may not increase in size, but they aren't the only checks you're capable of earning. If you don't like the size of those checks, go out and earn different checks.

A FIXED INCOME IS A SUCKER BET

Take note that while you're receiving a fixed income, someone higher up the chain of command is enjoying a variable income at your expense. When you receive a fixed income, you're actually creating a variable amount of value, but the income generated by your excess value is being siphoned off to line someone else's pockets. They're profiting from your ignorance. How generous of you! It may seem like they're taking on more risk, but keep in mind that if they go down, you go down too. You share in the risk, but you don't share in the upside. You do realize you're giving away the farm here, don't you?

If you're going to work, then why not receive and enjoy the fruits of your labor instead of giving most of your earnings away before you even see them? You're already creating value, aren't you? If you want to be generous, consider giving some of your excess value away to charity. I donate some money each month because it feels good to do so. But I donate to non-profits and charities that spend their money on things I want to support, not to stock-holding officers or investors who are already making millions a year.

Stop pretending to be helpless when it comes to how much money you make. Your paycheck has no power over you—except to the degree you give your power away. You may be working in a system where the higher ups have every financial incentive to keep you powerless so they can keep siphoning the value you're creating, but ultimately you're the one who chooses to walk through that door each day. You don't have to keep doing that. You can get up and leave right this minute if you want. Many people are much happier for having done that.

You are the final arbiter of your desires. If you want something with a price tag, you have the power to earn the money to pay for it. You decide how much you earn. You decide how much you spend.

When you realize that you choose your income, you can focus your energies on creating and delivering as much value as it takes to earn whatever you want. Be intelligent and deliberate about it. Make abundance a priority in your life. This is a lot more fun than fussing over expenses and nitpicking your taxes. Once you develop a modicum of skill, you'll find that it's a lot more fun to earn an extra $10K than to save $10K. You can earn $10K in an hour if you develop the mindset and skills to do so. No one is stopping you from doing that.

EARN $10,000 IN ONE HOUR?

Many books on time management recommend the practice of thinking of each hour of your time as being worth a specific quantity of money. It's an extension of the "time is money" concept. First you figure out what your hourly rate is, and then you use that as a guide to determine where you should spend your time. If you want to earn more money, then you must first mentally raise your hourly rate, so you can start doing activities that are worth more. For example, if you currently earn $50/hour and want to earn $75/hour, then you have to do less and less $50/hour work as you shift to doing $75/hour work. Brian Tracy advocates this type of thinking in his time management programs, as do many other time management experts. I've used this model myself in the past.

I've spent a lot of time considering this paradigm, and at present I have only one problem with it.

It's stupid!

It's possibly the stupidest paradigm you can use for income generation.

While it seems enticing on the surface, in the long run it will hurt you more than help you. Let's take a look under the hood.

THE GOOD

On the positive side, if you tell yourself that your time is worth $50/hour, then that can help you focus. It can make you aware of those activities that clearly aren't worth $50/hour that you might still be doing, especially if you track your time usage with a time log. Once you become aware that you're wasting time on low payoff activities, then you can begin reducing, eliminating, or outsourcing those low payoff tasks. For example, you could recruit a part-time personal assistant to offload much of the $10/hour and $20/hour work. My wife runs an online vegetarian magazine, and she has a staff of people working for her including an assistant, editors, and writers to offload much of the work that can be done at a lower hourly rate than her own. It works great.

This seems like good common sense if you want to improve your productivity. If you can earn $50/hour, then you should spend as much as your work time as possible doing $50+/hour work, shouldn't you? Recruit others to do any work that pays less. The benefits of this particular optimization may be hidden in a large corporate environment where personal productivity isn't strongly linked to pay, but it's very noticeable if you're self-employed.

THE BAD

The big problem is that when you tell yourself your time is worth $50/hour, you're simultaneously telling yourself that it isn't worth $75/hour or $200/hour or $10,000/hour. You're programming your subconscious mind to limit the range of opportunities you will notice. Because you won't be on the lookout for $10,000/hour ideas, you'll overlook them completely. If you tell yourself you earn $50/hour, you'll think in terms of $50/hour opportunities.

Thinking in terms of an hourly rate may help limit your downside, but it also severely limits your upside. And that's a really bad trade-off, bad enough that it requires me to dismiss this whole paradigm as utterly stupid. There's no way the upside of turning some $20 hours into $50 hours can compensate for missing those $10,000 hours. That's penny-wise, pound-foolish.

One $10,000 hour is worth 200 $50 hours. That's more than a month of full-time work! You don't need too many of those huge payoff hours to pick up the slack of some of those less productive $0-20 hours, but if you miss out on even one of those $10,000 hours, it's a crippling blow that overwhelms all other thoughts about financial productivity.

In the long run, your greatest financial risk isn't whether you made the mistake of succumbing to doing $20/hour work when you could have done $50/hour work. Your greatest risk is missing those $10,000 hours. And most people miss out on them completely. It's ironic that people think of being a salaried employee as being low-risk and being an entrepreneur as high-risk. The reality is just the opposite. One of the reasons I chose the entrepreneurial path is that it's just way too damned risky to be an employee. I'm not kidding. It's easy to hit a good number of those $10,000 hours as an entrepreneur, but it's a lot harder to do so as an employee.

How many $10,000 hours did you enjoy this year?

How rare is it for a $50/hour salaried employee to experience even one of those $10,000 hours in the entire course of their career? Pretty rare I would say. Certainly not a normal, expected occurrence. But this isn't because such opportunities don't exist—it's because your limiting beliefs about how much your time is worth prevent you from noticing them. Simply choosing to believe that it is possible will open the door to allowing it to manifest. You don't need anyone's permission to believe you can come up with an idea that you can implement in less than an hour that will earn you an extra $10,000. Such ideas are naturally plentiful, but you won't notice them until you adopt the right mindset. Right now as you're reading this, such an opportunity is practically staring you in the face, and you're completely oblivious to it. It's just like how my colorblindness prevents me from ever seeing the color red as other people can; it's beyond my ability to perceive.

Once you release the brakes and embrace the idea that a single hour of your time could be worth $10,000 or more, you'll almost immediately begin to notice such opportunities. I suspect you'll uncover the first one in less than 48 hours.

THE UGLY

What the heck is $50/hour work anyway? Who determines what an hour of your time is worth?

If you're self-employed, then you set your own hourly rate. And that's fine if your work requires hourly billing. But don't fall into the trap of thinking that all of your working time is worth that same hourly rate. If you do that, you'll begin to tune out much more lucrative opportunities.

If you're an employee in a corporate environment, then your salary sets your hourly rate, depending on how many hours you typically work each week. And in this high-risk situation you have a double problem. First, you have the previously mentioned challenge of getting yourself to think outside the hourly rate box. But secondly, in corporate environments it's rare to find fair incentives for employees to have such breakthroughs. If you have one of those $10,000 hours on the job, you probably won't share in the rewards. You'll just enjoy your usual $50 pay for that hour, while the company keeps the other $9950 you've created. At least entrepreneurs and self-employed people get to keep the whole $10,000.

Whom does the hourly rate mindset benefit? It benefits those who get to keep the extra value above and beyond that rate. But because this paradigm suffers an imbalance between value creation and reward, I think it also cripples the will to generate those $10,000 ideas. If you aren't going to benefit from the extra value you create, then why bother to create it?

The solution is to think like an entrepreneur, even if you're an employee. If you can devise and implement an idea in one hour that ends up saving your company $25,000 a year, I'd say you damn well deserve to be paid $10,000 for that hour of your time.

But too often employees don't bother to negotiate such terms with their employers. They willingly submit themselves to the tyranny of the hourly rate. Having been an employer myself though, I'll tell you that if an employee came to me and said she had a low-risk idea that would put $25,000 in my pocket and which could be implemented independently by her in an hour, and she asked to be paid $10,000 only if and when the idea proved itself, I'd be pulling out my checkbook. In fact, I'd ask her if she had a twin I could hire too. But if you don't negotiate such deals in advance, then by default the employer receives all the value above and beyond your normal hourly rate.

If I ever found myself an employee (which I can't imagine happening), I'd be on the constant lookout for those $10,000 ideas. I'd befriend someone who had the authority to pay bonuses in the manner described above, even if I had to work my way up the chain of command a bit. Then I'd look for simple ways to increase the company's revenue or cut its costs that would produce tangible, measurable results. And I'd negotiate the ability to either be paid a fixed sum if the value can be determined in advance or to share in a certain percentage of whatever value was created.

If I found that my boss didn't have the necessary authority or the will to authorize this sort of thing, then I'd keep going up the chain of command until I found someone who did. It's simply a matter of finding someone who will directly benefit from my extra value creation. It could be a stock-owning VP, the CEO, or even an investor. People who have a direct financial stake in the enterprise will not want to see profit-creating or cost-cutting ideas being squashed unreasonably, but beneath this level, you might run into a lot more closed-mindedness. But fortunately those who share in the profits of your ideas will normally have the authority to overrule those who don't. So don't let your boss get in your way. If you develop the habit of implementing $10,000 ideas, you'll soon be the boss anyway.

If I found myself working for a company or organization where this level of flexibility was impossible, I'd quit and go work in a less draconian environment. There are enough progressive companies around now that it isn't necessary to work for one of the unenlightened ones.

ALL HOURS ARE NOT CREATED EQUAL

My income isn't based on how much time I spend working. It's a function of the value I create. I can work a whole month and produce less monetary value than I do in one breakthrough hour. Every hour is unique.

I stopped thinking in terms of a fixed hourly rate many years ago. In practical terms an hour of my time could be worth $0, or it could be worth $10,000 or more, depending on what I do with that particular hour. Much of the time I pursue activities that don't generate any income at all, even though I still consider it to be productive work. Answering email doesn't seem to pay too well, and I don't get paid an hourly rate for writing blog entries and articles. But sometimes I'll get an idea which I can implement in just 30-60 minutes that will earn me an extra $10,000 over the course of a year, often continuing for many years thereafter. So the concept of an hourly rate, even an average hourly rate, is meaningless to me.

In the normal course of my work, those $10,000 hours are becoming more common. I normally have several a year, along with some $1000 hours, $5000 hours, and so on. Usually the money doesn't come right away, but it still blows away the concept of an hourly rate. It wouldn't even be accurate to say that it's those other hours that make the $10,000 hour possible. Sometimes the $10,000 is just a random idea from out of the blue, or maybe it's something that comes to me from a book or another person.

Almost always the $10,000 hour is the result of a great idea. And great ideas can strike at any time. When I get one of those $10,000 candidate ideas, I'll normally drop everything and implement it right away. If it flops (and usually it does), I've lost an hour, but I still learned something. Most of the time it isn't a total loss. I end up with a lot of $10, $50, and $250 ideas too. But I can afford to endure dozens of those relative flops for the chance to hit just one more $10,000 idea. And when it works, I must say it's pretty darn nice.

It's not that $10,000 is a lot of money per se. The idea isn't to make just $10,000 here and there. It's to make $10,000 for only one hour's worth of work. That's what makes the entrepreneurial game so much fun. You never know when one of those $10,000 ideas will strike. Imagine working each day with the real possibility that you could earn an extra $10,000 that day, completely out of the blue. If your normal hourly rate for a full-time job was $10,000, you'd be earning $20 million per year, and in that case $10,000/hour would be no big deal. But if you earn something closer to $50/hour, then one of those $10,000 hours is a major breakthrough. And the truth is that those $10,000 hours are a lot more accessible than you might think.

Regardless of whether you're an employee, self-employed, or otherwise entrepreneurial, don't cap your income by thinking in terms of an hourly rate. Once you free yourself from this punishing paradigm, you'll invite the opportunity to enjoy some of those $10,000 hours. It's really just a matter of giving yourself permission to experience them.

STOP FUSSING OVER EXPENSES AND TAXES

When it comes to reducing your expenses and taxes, you have to do a lot of tedious work. It's not fun, at least not for any sane person I've met. Yet people with a scarcity mindset spend a lot more time nitpicking their expenses and taxes than they invest in boosting their income. Not a good trade off—not by a long shot.

When you try to minimize your expenses and taxes, you'll eventually reach the point of having to make tough calls that could reduce your quality of life. On the expenses side, you may have to do extra expense tracking and budgeting, which takes time. Or you may begin to sacrifice quality to save a few bucks on your purchases.

On the tax side, you'll have to fill out more paperwork and do more accounting to take advantage of more deductions and save more money. Is that really what you want to spend your precious life doing?

Consider that when it comes to expenses and taxes, you have a hard limit of $0 and can go no lower. Once you're spending the bare minimum, that's it—you're done. So your maximum ideal gain is to spend nothing at all. And even if you could take things that far, your quality of life will surely suffer. You'll be wasting so much time going out of your way just to save a few extra dollars here and there. Sacrifice and scarcity will be your constant companions. That's no way to live.

In the long run, it's much more productive to focus your time and energy—not to mention your precious life—on the side of generating more income. You have no hard limit on that side. For all practical purposes, the sky is the limit. With commitment and persistence, you can boost your income by many multiples of what you might save on the expense and tax side.

Working on the income side is a lot more fun to boot. You get to spend your time creating value and receiving money with gratitude instead of worrying about whether or not you can afford to splurge on organic produce.

For my taxes, I pay an accountant to do all the paperwork for me. That costs extra money, but I don't worry about it. I also procrastinate endlessly when it comes to doing any sort of accounting work. I do the bare minimum I can. I keep everything in good order, but I don't balance the accounts very often. At tax time I let my accountant work his magic to figure out the best deductions for me, but if I have to do extra work that I don't want to do just to save a little more money, I simply decline. That way I get to spend more time on the value creation and delivery side, not to mention the enjoyment of life side. The pay is much better on that side, both financially and emotionally.

Last year my accountant told me I could save more money by deducting the business use of my car. All I'd have to do would be to keep track of mileage when I drive my car for business reasons. There may have been some other ways to claim this deduction, but they still required me to do more tracking, analysis, and/or paperwork. That seemed like a stupid waste of life, so I told my accountant to skip that deduction—not worth it to me. I'm not going to waste more time on stuff I don't enjoy just so I can save an extra thousand dollars on my taxes. The IRS will surely have no trouble taking the extra money, and I'm happy to spend my time doing more of what I enjoy, which will easily enable me to earn enough money to cover that missed deduction many times over. I'd actually lose money if I tried to take that deduction. It's yet another sucker bet for those who choose to live in scarcity.

When it comes to my expenses, I don't maintain any sort of budget, either on the business side or personal side. Budgeting is boring to me, so I don't do it. I simply spend whatever I feel like spending. When my expenses rise, expectedly or unexpectedly, I don't worry about it. I don't have to worry. I know that if I begin to overspend, I can always restore balance by over-earning just as easily.

Earning money is fun. Spending money is fun. Both activities are interchangeable. Fussing over expenses and taxes isn't remotely fun, so that isn't part of the equation—that kind of stuff gets triaged.

My latest credit card bill for my business is $1010, which is on the low side. Most of it is stuff that gets auto-billed each month. I was too busy earning money that month and didn't have as much time to spend money. The bill before that was $6900. Ah yes, the Bermuda conference. I had a lot of fun spending money that month. The bill before that was somewhere in between. My personal credit card bills fluctuate similarly. Every month I pay off every balance completely, so there's no revolving balance and no interest charges.

I "waste" money on unnecessary expenses all the time. I overspend on little things. I don't fuss over trying to save money. I assume that whatever I can spend, I can earn. That wasn't always the case though— it took years to train up to the level where I could earn enough to cover my desires.

Years ago I had a friend who absolutely hated waiting in line. He saw it as a personal insult. He used to say that all stores and restaurants should have a separate cashier for people who are willing to pay 50% more, just so they'll never have to wait in line. I thought he was nuts at the time, but he was simply trying to maximize the value he got from life. Waiting in life sucked too much value away.

I really don't know how much money I earn each month because I only look into it a couple times a year. It's just video game gold anyway—doesn't really matter what the exact figures are. I have a general feel/vibe for how the cash is flowing week by week, and in terms of spending I do my best to go with the flow. Is my bank account growing or shrinking? I like to see the numbers keep growing. I check my account balances a couple times a week to take their pulse. I earn money from multiple sources pretty much every day, so my checking account is perpetually refilling itself, but I want to make sure there are no big surprises like fraudulent charges. Some months it's hard for me to guess what I actually earned within +/- $5K. I simply don't care to keep track. It's somewhere in the tens of thousands each month, more than enough to live off.

I do the same with my book. I have no idea how many copies it's sold. Can't even fathom a guess within +/- 5K copies. I haven't asked my publisher for a sales update this whole year. It's great that we're up to a dozen languages for translated versions, but as for the money and sales, I don't really care. I'll sort it out when the royalty statements start coming. It will be more fun to be surprised.

Even though this may sound financially irresponsible, I think it's just the opposite. My bills always get paid. I'm paying down my mortgage much faster than necessary. My car is 100% paid for. I'm sharing this with you because it actually works, even though it may sound counter-intuitive.

Managing your finances in real life—the fun way—is very much like earning gold in a computer role-playing game. Earning money is play. Spending money is also play. If you aren't having fun, you're missing the whole point.

I think it's truly irresponsible to waste your precious life on things you don't enjoy, like fussing over your expenses or taxes. Does it feel good to you to sacrifice quality of life to keep a tight grip on your finances, when you could be making plenty of money if you simply spent more time doing what you love and providing value for others? Would you rather do something creative and have plenty of money to splash around, or spend your time dealing with cheap items that keep breaking down? I think you deserve the best that life has to offer you, but you have to step up and claim it. No one is stopping you from doing that.

CASH RESERVES

Suze Orman recommends maintaining a short-term cash reserve (not counting long-term investments) equivalent to about 6 months of expenses. I think that's a wise idea. A decent cash reserve gives you a lot more flexibility, whether your income is fixed or variable.

I maintain a liquid cash reserve at all times to have a cushion for any unforeseen expenses. I like to see that reserve be at least $50K, preferably closer to $100K. That way if something unexpected happens like a wacko filing a frivolous lawsuit because he spilled boiling water on himself while attempting my brown rice recipe, or crashed his car while attempting to drive after a week on polyphasic sleep, I can easily afford a decent hitman—just kidding.

When your income source is fairly vulnerable, like if you could get laid off or fired and spend a lot of time out of work, you may want to maintain a bigger cash reserve. But when you assert more control over your income and maintain more options for responding to financial setbacks, you don't need as big a reserve.

If you have multiple streams of mostly passive income, and if it would take a major upheaval to threaten those sources even if you stopped working for a while, you may be fine with a 2-month cash reserve or less. If I suddenly need more cash, I have lots of options that could easily be implemented in less than 60 days. I could do another joint-venture promotion. I could create and sell an info product. I could do another book deal and get an advance. Even so, when I focus on feeling abundant, I naturally attract a bigger reserve than I need.

Cash reserves are useful because there's a lag between creating and delivering value and receiving income from it. Some income sources have low lag time. For example, when someone registers for my workshop and pays by credit card or PayPal, the money is in my bank account within a few days. Some sources pay monthly, such as affiliate deals. Others pay quarterly, semi-annually, or less frequently, like book royalties. Some pay "whenever." A cash reserve helps to smooth out fluctuations. It also keeps you from incurring stupid bank fees from bouncing checks. Having a bank balance that's too low can lead to a lot of time wasted as well as unnecessary stress.

How do you build a cash reserve? You can get there by skimping on expenses, but that gets really tedious and boring after a while, so I don't recommend it. Focus on creating more value, training up your value-creating skills, and building a bigger client base for whatever service you provide. It all comes down to getting better at creating and delivering value.

I certainly didn't make sacrifices to build a cash reserve. I just kept doing what I enjoyed. I stayed alert for new ways to express and deliver value to people. Sometimes it was as simple as asking, "What else can I write about that could help people in some way?" I didn't have to focus on earning money. When you get good at creating and delivering value, money finds its way to you.

LUCK OR CHOICE?

Why do I find myself in this "lucky" situation where I get to do what I want, earn what I want, and spend what I want? If you think luck had anything to do with this, you're crazy, deluded, and otherwise insane. This happened by choice. I created this career and financial situation deliberately. It wasn't easy to figure out how all the pieces would fit together—it took years—but it was definitely worth it.

How long it takes you to hit your desired financial stride is irrelevant since the time is going to pass anyway. You can spend that time creating the life you desire, or you can stay stuck with something you don't want. You might as well work toward what you desire, unless you want sacrifice and scarcity to accompany you all the way to the grave.

Recognize that a fixed income is a sucker bet. It's like drinking soda. It doesn't matter that lots of people do it—that doesn't make it any less dumb. There's no good reason to sacrifice yourself to line someone else's pockets. Don't be a sucker.

You're free to opt out of the fixed income sucker bet whenever you want. When you do this, rest assured that the other suckers in your life will bark at you for pouring lemon juice on their cuts, and the higher ups won't appreciate that you saw through their scheme. But you'll be free to decide how much you earn. You'll be able to write your own paycheck, not with airy-fairy wishful thinking but with a commitment to creating and delivering the best value you can, regardless of how you choose to express yourself.

Of course having a variable income isn't all fun and roses. It takes time to get the hang of it and to get a good feel for how to balance the flow of earning and spending. It took me about 5 years before I achieved basic competence with it. I made tons of mistakes during that time, but I learned from them. After that it was pretty easy to maintain stability.

If you pursue this path, maybe you can figure it out in 2 years. Maybe it will take 10. Again, the time is going to pass anyway. If you drop the fixed income mindset, you'll end up in a pretty sweet place once you eventually figure it out.

As you probably noticed, I made up some words in this chapter. You're free to coinify your own words too. This is your reality after all. You make the rules. Just as you can subscribe to other people's verbal patterns, you can also subscribe to other people's income patterns. But you don't have to. You never did have to. Just because a pattern is popular doesn't mean it's the best pattern for you. Give that some thoughtification.

21.

Getting Money to Flow Your Way

It's amazing how much time and energy people waste stressing over money, reacting to financial setbacks as if money is life itself.

For my son Kyle's 5th birthday earlier this month, he received the board game *Trouble* as one of his gifts. The game involves mostly luck plus a small amount of skill (easy enough for a child to grasp).

Our family has played this game together several times so far—we often play games together after dinner. Erin plays the game fairly calmly, but my eight-year old daughter Emily and I totally ham it up when we play—screaming for certain die rolls to come up, giving each other high fives after dealing the leader a setback, verbally strategizing as if we can control the odds, and laughing uproariously.

Kyle, however, takes the game far more seriously. When he's in the lead and one of his pieces gets knocked back to the starting position (a common setback in the game), he may get so upset he can barely continue playing. Even when he wins a game, he's reticent to play again. We try to explain to him that it's just a game (and mostly blind luck at that), but he hasn't yet reached the level of maturity where he can grasp that kind of abstraction. He gets so attached to his pieces that any kind of setback is seen as a personal blow.

Interestingly, Kyle has actually won more games than Emily and I have. But he doesn't enjoy his victories as much as Emily and I enjoy our defeats. The game seems to be a fairly stressful experience for him. When he wins, his happiness is brief, and he seems to dread it when we say, "Let's play again." Now he still seems to enjoy playing the game— we certainly don't force him to play—but his attachment makes it more stressful than fun for him.

On the other hand, Emily and I have so much fun when we play that you'd never know if one of us was winning or losing. Every minor gain leads to outlandish celebration. You'd think we just won the lottery each time we captured a piece. Because we don't take the game personally, we enjoy it a lot more.

Of course this is a metaphor for how people relate to their finances. Many people play the game like Kyle plays *Trouble*: feeling stressed and worried because there's this underlying fear of loss. A significant financial setback is seen as a serious personal blow. Even financial victories can't be enjoyed much because the next setback could come at any time. Any uncertainties serve to increase the stress and worry, which leads to the desire to clench down really hard and try to control every known factor, to avoid any potential risk. Another possible reaction is to check out from the game entirely and refuse to play (except as absolutely necessary), lamenting the great unfairness of it all.

How would you react to a player who played *Trouble* like this? If it's a young child, no big deal, right? He'll outgrow that phase soon enough. But what about a grown adult who plays this way? What advice would you give such a person? How about, "Chill out, dude…it's just a game. Don't take it so seriously."

What's the point of playing the game *Trouble*? Is it to win? No. The point is to enjoy the experience and have fun. What's the point of playing the money game? Is it to amass a fortune? Of course not. You're going to lose it all when you die anyway. The point is to enjoy the experience, have fun, and grow from it. The money game isn't your enemy. It's your teacher.

Just as Kyle needs to learn not to take the game *Trouble* so seriously, many people need to learn not to stress out over the money game. If you lose all your money, sure it stings a little, but it really isn't the end of the world. There's always another opportunity to get back in the game. Going broke or bankrupt isn't a death sentence.

Nine years ago Erin and I lost a round of the money game. We got kicked out of our apartment, went bankrupt, and had to start over from scratch with almost zero cash and minimal income. But guess what, we're still playing the game, having fun, and learning from it. Those early losses simply helped us become better players. Isn't this a better approach than whining about the loss and saying, "That's not fair! I'm never playing this stupid game again!"

Don't blame the money game if you're a bad player. It's not the game's fault if you suck at playing. Don't blame the other players either, especially the ones you perceive as more skillful or more lucky than you.

In terms of being able to win equally, the money game may not seem particularly fair. That's irrelevant though because winning isn't the point. This isn't a game that can be won with any sense of finality anyway. However, in terms of the opportunity for growth, the money game is very fair. If you play full out, you will undoubtedly grow from it.

It's much more fun to play the money game like Emily and I play *Trouble*. We keep ourselves in a fun, light-hearted state, so no matter what happens, we enjoy it. Even though the game is supposed to be competitive, we celebrate each other's victories. We'll even celebrate Kyle's victories to help encourage him.

Although *Trouble* is mostly luck, skill plays a much bigger factor in the real life money game. If you play the money game scared, you'll tend to do very poorly. If you're worried about losing your pieces (i.e. your money), you'll play the game way too tight. But if you see it as a fun game, you'll loosen up, and you'll feel more comfortable playing in a larger field.

Money needn't be a stressful or worrisome part of your life if you treat the money game as a fun growth experience. If you don't take your financial life so seriously, you can learn to enjoy the process of shifting from a scarcity mindset to an abundance mindset. There's no mandate that says you must stress yourself out about money, regardless of your current financial situation.

Even though real life may seem more serious than a game of *Trouble*, you can still laugh in the face of defeat and enjoy the game regardless of circumstances.

Play the money game for fun and growth, including the fun and growth of the other players. Don't stress over whether you think you're winning or losing. The more important question is: Are you growing?

HOW TO MANIFEST MONEY

The most important aspect of manifesting money is to approach it from the right heartset. Think of your heartset as the overall vibe of your relationship to the activity of attracting money. How would you describe that relationship? Is it greedy, needy, excited, hopeful, etc?

If you approach this process from a place of neediness, clinginess, scarcity, or too much seriousness, you'll most likely fail. That's the right vibe for attracting nothing—or for making things worse by attracting unwanted expenses—but it's not the right vibe for attracting money.

So if you come at this from a place of saying, "I really need $1000 to pay my rent next month, so I'm going to focus hard on manifesting it via the Law of Attraction," well... good luck with that. But I'd bet against you.

A slightly better vibe is that of hope, but this is still a pretty weak vibe. Hope won't get you very far.

A much better vibe is to come from a place of curiosity and experimentation. Go into a state of childlike wonder. With this vibe you may begin to generate some interesting results.

An even stronger vibe is to generate feelings of playfulness and excitement. This is a great vibe for manifesting money. In the next section, I'll share a story to illustrate how I do this with my daughter.

KNOWING

When you want to manifest money, it's important to know that it's already there. If it's hidden at all, it's hiding in plain sight, waiting for you to notice it and pick it up. This applies whether we're talking about cash found on the ground or opportunities that will generate cash.

Know that the cash and the opportunities are right in front of your face. You just have to adjust your "eyes" to see them. You do this by shifting your vibe—your frequencies of thought and emotion—to one that's capable of detecting the money.

It's fun to think of this vibe-shifting process as shifting dimensions, as if you're tuning in to a different perceptual frequency spectrum. That other reality was there all along. You just couldn't see it before because you were tuned in to incompatible perceptual frequencies, frequencies that made the money invisible and undetectable by your senses. Maybe you were stuck on the red part of the spectrum, while the money was hanging out in the blue part.

Obviously your senses pick up a lot as you go about your day, but you only notice a puny fraction of all that input. In order to manifest money, you need to tune your senses to bring to your attention useful input that you've been subconsciously dismissing as irrelevant background noise. This tuning process takes some time, but you can definitely do it.

Lately I've been teaching my daughter Emily (age 10) how to manifest coins. I do this by turning it into a game. When we're out walking together, I challenge her to see if she can find more coins than I can.

The first time I did this, she was really bad at it. I found several coins during our walk together, often coins that she walked right past without even noticing. Instead of finding coins, she didn't notice anything. The coins didn't register within her perceptual reality.

Later on she began noticing things that were close to coins, but not coins. She found bottle caps, paper clips, scraps of paper, and coin-like smudges on the floor—everything but coins. I kept pointing out to her that there are coins everywhere, but you have to tune in to the "coin abundance frequency" to see them. Each time I found a coin and showed it to her, I could tell it was gradually helping her tune in to the right perceptual frequency.

One reason she was bad at this game was that she was tuning out the possible existence of coins everywhere she walked. She just didn't think there could be that many coins hiding in plain sight. By demonstrating to her that the coins were indeed there and that she was simply failing to notice them, I helped shift her beliefs. She stopped thinking of the game as something outside her control (relying on luck or chance), and she began thinking of what she could control (her open-mindedness and attentiveness).

At first when she would walk past a coin, and I'd pick it up and say, "Look at this, Emily. There was a nickel there, and you walked right past it! Your eyes definitely saw it because you were looking in that direction, but the coin didn't register in your mind. You still need to adjust yourself to the right vibe. Remember—the coins are everywhere! You just need to command your eyes to notice them."

Initially this surprised her. She could dismiss it as luck, or as some kind of trick, or as a momentary lapse of her part. Then when it kept happening, it began to frustrate her. I helped her shift that frustration to amusement by pointing out that she was really good at finding bottle caps and smudges, and we had some laughs about that. She just needed to adjust her mind a little bit more to notice the coins.

Finally she began to accept that yes, there really are coins everywhere, and she only has to notice them. It seemed like she was beginning to tell her eyes and her mind to get with the program and start noticing the coins.

Emily has a competitive side, so I played to that by challenging her to find more coins than me, which boosted her motivation and desire to get good at it. She knows that technically it's a fair game, and she even gave herself an advantage by walking in front of me, so she could be the first to spot new coins. And since she's only four foot nine inches tall, she's a lot closer to the ground than I am.

Gradually she got better at the game. We went out yesterday and played again. In an hour of walking around some hotels on the Vegas Strip, she found 46 cents: 1 quarter, 3 nickels, and 6 pennies. In that same time, I found only 6 cents. She won the game for the first time and was pretty excited about it. And of course I gave her lots of accolades for it, so as to encourage her to keep improving.

I dare say she's probably better at finding coins than I am now. She now knows there are coins everywhere, but she also really gets into the playful and competitive spirit of the game, which is much more exciting for her than it is for me. I think partly she likes knowing that it's a fair game that either of us can win, and there's no reason she can't be at least as skillful as I am.

When it comes to creating a vibe of playfulness and excitement, children can easily be more masterful than adults. This is the same vibe we need to recreate as adults in order to manifest whatever we desire.

It may sound silly to do this as an adult, but it's a game worth playing. When you're out with friends sometime, have a contest to see who can manifest the most money. You may not get too excited about finding coins, but you may generate some excitement about trying to best your friends in a silly contest. That silliness will actually help you get the right vibe, thereby improving your ability to manifest money.

DETACHMENT

People often get confused about the relationship between desire and detachment. Aren't they diametrically opposed? How can you have both at the same time? Isn't desire a form of attachment?

No, these aren't in conflict. They coexist perfectly.

Let me 'splain.

Desire is about what you wish to create. You could describe this vibe as passion, excitement, or even lust. It's a delicious pool of emotions you summon by focusing on a new target. The stronger your desire, the better, so amp it up!

Detachment, on the other hand, is about *how* those desires ultimately manifest for you. When you become too attached to when and how your desires show up, you screw up the manifesting process. Instead of holding the vibe of playfulness and abundance, you start sending out signals like concern, worry, and stress. Don't do that!

Would you become stressed and worried if you couldn't find enough coins on the ground? Would that vibe improve your performance? No, that would only lower your performance.

When you notice that you're getting frustrated, pause, breathe, and go back to the desire side. Hold that vision of the creation you wish to experience, and wallow in the positive sensations of being there in your heart, mind, and spirit. Know that physical reality will soon catch up, as long as you keep holding the right vibe.

When you feel moved to take action from a place of passion and excitement, not stress, then go ahead and let those actions flow through you. It will seem to be more work to stop yourself—you'll feel like you're chickening out and holding back if you stay still. Follow your impulses. But don't worry about the immediate results of those actions. There may be some twists and turns along the way.

POWER

When manifesting money, it's especially important that you don't give your power away to money. This negates your creative ability, and the money probably won't arrive if you do that. This is a *very* common mistake.

You can't effectively wield the power of manifestation by believing that you can manifest something you desire (i.e. money) while simultaneously believing that something you desire has power over you (i.e. money).

If you want to manifest money, you cannot believe that money is a power source. Money cannot give you wealth or abundance or happiness. It really can't give you anything. Money just sits there—all the power comes from you. If you believe that having more money will give you any additional power at all, then you're actually holding the vibe that says, "I'm too weak to attract money." You'll have to get a job instead.

Think of it like this. If you want to manifest money, but you believe that money is its own power source, then deep down you're giving money the power to say no to you. If money has power, then it can refuse to show up.

Instead of this crazy wrong approach, in your mindset and heartset, you must KNOW that you're completely 100% dominant over money and that money is completely 100% submissive to you. You're in total command of it. If you order it to show up, it must obey you. It has no power of its own. It cannot refuse you.

When you manifest money, you are commanding it to come into your reality. You're the creator. Money has no choice but to obey you, but only if you wield your true power. If you give your power away to money, then you empower money to deny your requests. Money will say, "Well, if you're letting me decide, then no, I'm staying over here."

If you approach money like a power source of its own, then by trying to manifest it, you're really trying to overpower it, and in such a contest you'll usually lose. That contest, however, is completely internal—and pretty much insane. It's like trying to arm wrestle yourself. How can you win? It's a false reality you're projecting because you aren't ready to fully wield your own power yet.

Remember that money is nothing but a number. Or it's pieces of metal and paper. How could it possibly be more powerful than a conscious human being such as yourself?

If you think that once you have money, you will become stronger, you're crazy. Absolutely deluded! More likely—if you actually did manifest money from that kind of vibe—you'd grow even weaker. This would be a bad outcome for you, even though it seems like what you want. You'd be a weak-minded, weak-hearted person with more money, and you'd still see the money as more powerful than you, even while it's in your possession. You'd then become attached to it and afraid of losing it because you'd still mistakenly see it as a power source. It would become a source of security for you, a constantly vulnerable one. The more money you had, the more paranoid you'd become about losing it. This would really mess you up big time. So be very, very glad that you naturally attract less money when you think of money as a power source. If you invite money into your life from that crazy frame of giving away your power, then money will become your Master, and you will be forever its slave. Don't even go there!

If money has no power, then why manifest it at all? In truth, you don't need to. But if you wish to manifest money, then do it as a game. Money is a toy you can play with. Get excited about the experience of manifesting money, but don't put any attention into what you'd do with the money once you have it. It's merely a number.

If you desire something you think money will give you, then focus on that desire directly, not on the money you think you need to get it. Money may or may not be part of the manifestation process.

Only focus on manifesting money directly if you're capable of seeing the money as a plaything, like a video game score. It's only something to manifest for fun, not something to get all worked up and stressed about.

Once again, **do not** give your power away to money. You must know that money is completely powerless. All the power is within you, never out there.

UPGRADING

When manifesting money, start small and work up to larger amounts. See it as a score you're aiming to increase, but don't put larger amounts on a pedestal by assuming they're more difficult to manifest.

I started with manifesting pennies in the Summer of 2006. Then I graduated to nickels, dimes, and quarters. I focused on quarters for several weeks. Then I progressed to dollars to $100 to $1000 to $10K to $50K. Overall it took less than a year to go from manifesting pennies to manifesting $50K. After that point I become more interested in non-monetary manifesting and had some especially fun times with manifesting in my social life—friends, mentors, and other yumminess. In fact, I honestly feel that manifesting money is a bit boring compared to all the other cool stuff you can manifest. It's like playing a video game and obsessing over the score. That can be fun for a while, but eventually you want to focus on more interesting aspects of the game world.

If you can get good at manifesting coins, you can manifest larger sums too. The process is the same. Only some limiting beliefs of yours may stand in the way. But as you gradually upgrade to larger sums, you can collapse those false beliefs.

Once Emily gets good at manifesting coins and feels comfortable and confident with it, I'll start challenging her to manifest larger sums. She may not find money on the ground as often, but it will show up in other ways.

Money comes to you through the filters of your beliefs, but you don't have to change your beliefs radically. You just have to open enough of a portal in your beliefs to allow different sums to come to you.

Coins may be found on the ground while you're walking around. Bills will sometimes be found on the ground too. Larger sums may manifest in the form of exchanges, business deals, inheritances, inspired action, and other ways. Assume that those larger sums are right in front of your face, staring at you and screaming at you to notice them. You just have to tune your vibe to the right frequency to pick them up.

I've noticed that as I've shifted my vibe to manifest larger sums of money and to manifest new experiences in other parts of my life, I seem to fall out of resonance with manifesting smaller sums. I'm not as good at manifesting coins as I was in 2006. That's because my vibe isn't tuned in to the coin manifesting frequency as much. These days I'm spending more time using the LoA to manifest cool social connections and travel experiences. I've tuned my vibe to focus on that part of the perceptual frequency. I also feel more excited and playful about manifesting in these other areas as opposed to adding to my financial score.

CONGRUENCY

Every relationship in your life contributes to the overall vibe you're putting out. This includes all the different ways you relate to money.

For example, if your job sucks and doesn't pay you very well, and you try to manifest money on the side, that probably won't work so well because each time you go to work at your job, you risk re-triggering the vibe of feeling financially under-appreciated.

This is where lots of people get stuck with the LoA. They put out conflicting vibes every day. They may visualize having more money and feeling abundant and grateful, but then they go to the grocery store, and they buy cheap, low quality food because in the back of their mind, they're saying to themselves that they can't afford the good stuff. And that naturally cancels out the vibe of abundance, so the result is no change.

If your current circumstances cause you to emit conflicting vibes, then even as you go through the motions of acting in accordance with a scarcer financial situation than you'd like, keep your vibe focused on that of abundance. The best way to do that is by holding the heartset of gratitude. So even if you buy cheap, low-quality food, hold the vibe that you're grateful for it and that you appreciate it. Feel appreciative that such food exists and that it's within your budget. And then look at the high quality stuff, and emotionally invite it into your life. If possible, find one way in which you can splurge for higher quality items, like buying a few organic apples, and feel grateful that you can do that. And when you eat those apples, really enjoy them, and intend to receive more of the same.

But do not beat yourself up for not being able to afford what you desire. That will only lower your vibe.

Do like I did with Emily when she kept finding bottle caps and smudges. Praise yourself for succeeding at what you're already mani-festing, and then command your senses to adjust to a more abundant part of the spectrum of reality. Be patient with yourself—you'll get it.

Whenever you start feeling bad about your financial situation, see that as a form of feedback. Let it become an immediate trigger to refo-cus on your desires. Say to yourself, "Okay, obviously I don't want this. So what do I want instead?" Then think about happier alternatives; al-low your mind to go there, and let the resulting new vibe flow through you.

Manifesting money is a fun challenge. It's definitely doable if you approach it from a place of playfulness, knowing, and power. It does involve some discipline, but the discipline is mental and emotional, not physical.

You aren't going to let a 10-year old girl kick your ass at this game, are you?

22.
The Smart Approach to Money

A recession is possibly the best time to launch a new business or to expand an existing one. It's also a great time to get ahead in your career. I know this sounds counter-intuitive, so let me 'splain.

First, the media goes nuts during a recession. They turn a little bit of negativity into a mountain of pessimism. This makes a lot of people financially paranoid. People become socially conditioned to expect the worst.

If you buy into this social hysteria, you become a victim, too.

But if you tune out such stupidity (not watching TV helps a lot) and maintain a grip on rational thought, you'll see some amazing opportunities popping up everywhere you look.

During such times people get scared and start cutting back on expenses. They cut some of the fluff from their lives. They stop buying so much stuff they don't need.

This causes some businesses to do poorly, especially businesses that don't provide stuff we really need. We can live without new credit cards and gas-guzzling SUVs for a while. Those non-essentials can be put off.

We also become more sensitive to receiving genuine value. When we spend money, we want to make sure we're getting a fair deal.

Consequently, businesses that provide genuine value can actually do better during a recession. More people will flock to those businesses in tough times, while the fluff businesses will become more and more paranoid.

In the USA there are a lot of fluff businesses. Many are based on the moocher mindset, trying to extract money without providing fair value in exchange. A lot of the dead or dying financial companies are like that. The American auto industry has been contracting as well, at least in part because they've been creating inferior products that people don't really need. (Erin and I own a Honda, despite the fact that we could have gotten a significant discount on GM cars because two of my family members used to work for GM. We looked at some GM cars and quickly concluded they sucked. Other family members weren't so lucky.)

A lot of people have been learning that job security doesn't mean much these days. More than 500,000 Americans learned this lesson last month when they lost their "safe and secure" jobs.

THE STUPID APPROACH TO MAKING MONEY

Lately I've seen a lot of people, some of them friends, do some really dumb things in an attempt to earn more money. They buy into lame money-making programs, join and promote useless MLM schemes, and fall prey to scammers.

The common pattern is always the same—they're focused on trying to make more money. They make it their top priority. They think about it constantly. But they keep getting sucked into trying to make money without providing any real value, and it's unsustainable.

In the end this sort of thing eventually self-destructs. The only way to succeed with it in the long run is to find lots of suckers and basically rip them off in order to enrich yourself. Most people have a strong enough moral resistance to this sort of thing that they'll sabotage themselves from going too far with it. This isn't a path of long-term abundance. It's a path of scarcity.

As a general rule, the people I know who are most focused on trying to make more money this year are doing worse, not better. In some cases they're doing much worse. A few have lost or are in the process of losing their homes.

The exceptions are those that are able to sufficiently kill their conscience, so they can remove any incongruencies about ripping people off. But again, this is a pretty rare exception. Most people would rather deal with scarcity than knowingly rip people off to get ahead, so they just make the bare minimum to meet their needs and avoid getting ahead.

THE SMART APPROACH TO MAKING MONEY

There is a smarter approach, however.

Instead of focusing on trying to make more money, put your time and energy into creating and delivering real value. Find a way to give people what they want and/or need.

Take note that the keywords here are *create* and *deliver*.

Creating value means expressing your unique talents and skills in a way that can potentially benefit others. *Delivering* value means ensuring that other people are actually receiving and benefiting from the value you've created. If you don't do both in some fashion, then it's going to be hard for you to generate sustainable income, especially during a recession. I'll explain why.

If you only create value but don't deliver it, then your value isn't being received by anyone. So how can you receive value (such as money) in return?

I see this problem a lot with creative types such as would-be artists, musicians, and writers. They may spend lots of time honing their craft, but if they don't actually get that value into the hands of sufficient numbers of people, they struggle financially, and this hurts them creatively, too. A goodly number of these people are currently seeing their homes in foreclosure now.

The sad thing is that some of these people work very hard. But they spend too much time creating and not nearly enough time delivering. They watch people they consider hacks pull ahead of them. The hacks may not be as good on the creative side, but at least they're getting their value into people's hands, and on some level people are appreciating their work.

I went down that road myself. In the late 90s, I went bankrupt, even though I was working very long hours and creating a lot of potential value in the form of a computer game my company was developing. My problem was that I didn't do a good job of getting that value delivered. I relied on publishers to do that, and for various reasons the game was never released. That resulted in years of wasted effort, aside from the valuable learning experience that is. So I know where this road leads because I traveled it.

On the other hand, if you only deliver value but don't create it, then you're delivering someone else's value. This isn't a terrible approach in the short run, but it's a short-sighted long-term strategy if this is all you do. There's nothing particularly special about delivering other people's value. Anyone can do it. Anyone can sign up for affiliate programs or join an MLM program or become a reseller. If this is your primary means of generating income, your long-term outlook is weak. The better this works for you, the more it will draw competitors into your field. Eventually everyone will be working harder and harder for scraps. This happens all the time. This strategy can be especially weak during a recession, as more people turn to less expensive sources for the same value you deliver, squeezing your profit margins thinner and thinner.

Bloggers fall into this trap when they rehash other people's content and don't really have anything unique or compelling to say. A year later their niche is flooded with competitors doing the same thing. And hardly anyone is earning decent income from it.

The most viable long-term strategy is to create *and* deliver value. You can mix and match other strategies with it, but this should be your primary method of income generation. If you get good at creating and delivering value, you can basically write your own ticket and enjoy lots of abundance.

A CHOICE OF MINDSET

I know a lot of people are dealing with financial challenges these days. Las Vegas is basically the foreclosure capital of the USA right now. I know people who've lost their homes. I see "bank owned" signs all over the place.

If you're going through something like this right now, I totally empathize with you. However, I have to point out that the pattern of what causes this is so clear, it's getting a bit ridiculous to see it play out over and over again.

Generally speaking, people who create and deliver value are doing just fine. In fact, I'd say most are doing better, not worse. Many of these people are seeing their incomes go up during this time. People who don't create and deliver value are seeing their finances grow progressively worse. This leads many of them to panic, so they head even further away from creating and delivering value (such as by chasing lame money-making schemes), which only quickens the decline to insolvency.

I know it seems logical that if you're seeing your finances decline, then you should focus single-mindedly on trying to make more money as quickly as possible. People fall into this trap all the time. I used to fall for it, too. This is absolutely the wrong strategy though. I know that must sound counter-intuitive. The correct strategy is that when you see your finances decline and you want to increase your income, then you need to focus on creating and delivering more value. If you do that, then you're doing the very thing that will generate a sustainable income increase.

What is money? Money is simply a medium for exchanging value. Money is what you receive in exchange for the value you create and deliver. If you can increase your outflow of value creation and delivery, you can increase your inflow of money received.

If, however, you try to increase the inflow of money without increasing the outflow of value, you're trying to get something for nothing. This approach is untenable and will ultimately collapse. Please don't waste your time on it.

I actually figured this out right around the time I was declaring bankruptcy. I was totally broke, yet I found a way to focus my energy on creating and delivering value instead of on trying to scrape together more money. Within about six months, I was back on my feet financially, and year after year my financial situation just kept getting better. I started on this path about 9 years ago, and I've maintained a nice positive cash flow every year since then.

I know that when you're in a financial crunch situation, six months may seem like a long time. But it doesn't matter if it takes you several months or several years to get in the habit of creating and delivering value. The time is going to pass anyway, and this habit will serve you well for life. Be patient and get started. It doesn't matter what happens to the economy—if you keep creating and delivering value, you'll do just fine.

TURNING VALUE INTO INCOME

So how does one generate income from creating and delivering value? Can't you run into a problem of creating and delivering lots of value and making no money from it?

As it turns out, making money is the easy part. If you can create and deliver value to people, the income opportunities will literally come to you. People will practically line up with ways for you to make money. I'm serious.

Here's how this works.

If you get good at creating value, you can connect with other people who are good at delivering value. They deliver your value, such as by selling it, and they pay you a royalty, commission, or licensing fee.

For example, Hay House offered me a book deal last year, so I wrote a book called *Personal Development for Smart People*. I received an advance for the book, and I'll also receive ongoing royalties based on sales. I might even receive royalties from this book for the rest of my life, especially since the content is timeless. Also, writing a book has lead to other opportunities, such as paid speaking engagements. So in this case I created the value (the book), but others deliver it.

Now suppose you get good at delivering value. In this case you can generate income by plugging other people's value into your delivery system. For example, my blog is great at delivering value. It's a very efficient medium for that. But since I give my value away for free, it doesn't generate income directly. However, I can generate plenty of income by promoting other people's products that I like. Then I split the profits from sales with the publisher. I earn six figures a year just from doing that. The product publishers come to me. I get way more offers for this sort of thing than I can handle. It doesn't require a lot of work to do this. Once you have a system for delivering value, you can plug other people's value into it and generate lots of extra income.

If you have the means to create *and* deliver strong value, you'll have so many opportunities it will be totally ridiculous. First, you can plug the value you create into other people's delivery systems, so you can earn ongoing royalties and such. This is easy residual income. I'm still getting checks every month for deals I entered years ago.

Secondly, you can plug other people's creative value into your own delivery system. You pay them a royalty on the sales, or they pay you as an affiliate. Once again you generate ongoing residual income. As long as you're selective about the products you promote, doing your best to ensure that they provide strong value, everyone is happy, and everyone wins.

Thirdly, you can plug your value into your own delivery system. Strangely, this is something I haven't done yet with my blog, although I used to do it all the time with my computer games business. This is something I intend to explore. It simply means that I could create and sell my own products direct. Many other bloggers have already done this with great success, releasing e-books, audio programs, DVDs, etc. They create the value and sell it directly to their visitors.

A big chunk of the income I received in 2008 was from work I did in previous years. I could do no work for all of 2009 and just live off the residual income I know is coming. That's a nice situation to be in. It's no accident though. Years ago I decided that this is how I wanted to set up my financial life, and then I focused on creating and delivering value to make it work. There's no reason you can't use the same strategy. It isn't trademarked.

AVOIDING DISTRACTION

Once you develop the habit of creating and delivering value, it's pretty hard to fail. However, it's very easy to get distracted along the way. Distraction is perhaps your biggest obstacle. You can't get sucked into every money-making scheme that crosses your plate. Getting sucked into a job, where you have to trade hours for dollars, is just as bad. These are dead ends you should avoid by any means. You have to stay focused on creating and delivering value. Everything that detracts from this focus should be viewed as an expense, obstacle, or just plain evil.

This is so important, but most people just don't get how important it is. Getting a job is such a bad idea if you want to enjoy long-term financial abundance. The odds of success on that path are so low, it's not even worth considering.

Seriously, you are better off being broke and homeless, so you can focus on creating and delivering value from that place. You're much worse off if you have to waste day after day showing up to work for someone else. That won't move you closer to financial abundance. It will only distract you further.

If I had to choose between being homeless and getting a full-time job, I'd go the homeless route. Having a job would be 10x worse. As a homeless person, I could stay hungry and focused on creating and delivering value. I might not have the means to produce much value at first, but at least I could get out there in front of people and deliver something. It would be a good start on the right path.

A job is just a monstrous distraction. In many ways it's a modernized form of slavery.

Homelessness is a huge upgrade from traditional employment. Have you ever talked to a homeless person? Some of them find the idea of having a job insulting—it represents a loss of freedom. Sure you smell better and can get a nicer place to live, but you lose your humanity in the process. Perhaps such people realize something you don't: employment is the ultimate form of destitution.

Fortunately, employment is an easy problem to fix. If you have a job, just stop showing up. The rest will take care of itself. Pretty soon you'll feel some motivation and drive to start creating and delivering value, especially if you happen to like eating.

Genuine opportunities are based on creating and/or delivering value. If you see something that looks like a new opportunity, and it doesn't require you to create value, and it doesn't require you to deliver value, then it isn't an opportunity. It's a total waste of your time.

Is creating and delivering value harder than getting a job? I would say no, not at all. Having a job is a lot harder. With a job you still have to provide some form of value usually, but all the residual benefits you produce turn into residual income for someone else. So you're already doing most of what needs to be done, but you aren't enjoying any of the benefits. In the long run, you'll probably have to work much harder if you have a job, but the bulk of the rewards will go to someone else. On the one hand, that's generous, but on the other hand, it's quite dumb.

I could get a job as a writer and get paid a certain amount for each word I write. But then someone else owns my work, and all the residuals from that work go to them. Alternatively, I could write articles for my own website and retain the freedom to republish them as books someday, use them to generate traffic (and thereby income), license them for various publications, use them to promote my book, etc. The correct strategy is a no-brainer really.

Trying to make money is itself a distraction. When you focus on making money, too many things will catch your eye. You'll run around like a chicken with its head cut off, chasing down all sorts of things that look like opportunities. You'll waste a lot of time and energy if you chase dollars.

Creating and delivering value is simpler. This focus is well-aligned with truth, love, and power.

When you create and deliver value, you can be open and honest about what you're doing. You get to spend most of your time doing stuff you'd naturally enjoy. It's pleasurable to hone a craft you're passionate about, whether it's writing articles, composing music, or planting gardens. It's much harder to do boring, non-creative work day after day. It's also very empowering to share your value with others and to see that you're making a positive difference in people's lives. Once you make a habit of creating and delivering value as your primary career focus, you won't want to go back.

THERE'S MORE TO LIFE THAN MONEY

Of all the things I do as part of my "work," making money plays only a small role. Despite having written some popular articles on the subject, I spend little time thinking about money these days. I don't even bother to set financial goals anymore. That seems totally pointless to me.

Sometimes months go by, and I don't even know how much money I'm currently making. I just know there's always plenty and that I'm earning more than I'm spending. The gap is wide enough that I don't need to do any special budgeting or fussing with figures.

The reason this works for me is that I focus on creating and delivering value. I know that as long as I keep doing that, I don't have to do anything special to try to make money. New opportunities just keep showing up. It's not that difficult to maintain.

I remember when I was at a conference in 2004 where Dr. Wayne Dyer was speaking. He said that people would come up and say, "You know, Dr. Dyer. Some people say you've made a lot of money."

Dr. Dyer's response was, "They would be right."

He went on to say something along these lines: "It's not my fault! I just keep doing what I'm doing, and there's always plenty of abundance there."

At the time it was hard for me to relate to this mindset. It seems a bit too unrealistic and exceptional. But still…I wondered what it would be like to live at that level, where you could just assume abundance and it would be there for you. No striving or struggling. It took a few years, but I'm finally grasping what that sort of mindset feels like.

I'd say it's not really a complete mindset by itself though. I doubt very much that Dr. Dyer focuses a lot of attention on trying to make money. I think most of his attention is elsewhere, wrapped up in the material he writes about. And that's exactly where it should be.

Having written about two dozen books, it's safe to say that Dr. Dyer has internalized the concept of creating and delivering value. I have it on good authority that his books sell quite well too. (We share the same publisher.)

Incidentally, Erin and I finally had the chance to meet Dr. Dyer in October at the speakers' dinner for the *I Can Do It!* conference. We only spoke with him for a few minutes. He was very warm and friendly.

This whole abundance mindset might sound really annoying if you're dealing with financial scarcity right now. I can totally relate. I've been there, and I'm sure I'd have been equally annoyed if someone said this sort of stuff to me back then. I'd have been vehement that making money was *not* easy because I tried very hard to do that and failed big at it. Ironically the real problem was that by focusing on making money, I was making a huge mistake.

The key is where you focus your attention. If you focus your attention on making money, I can virtually guarantee that you'll have a long and difficult road ahead of you, filled with setbacks and disappointments. If money is really what you seek, good luck with that. All you'll do is give more and more of your power away, and you'll end up living a pretty empty and shallow life.

Another corrupt form of thinking is to focus your attention on attracting financial abundance. Law of Attraction promoters often present this as a good idea. I once thought it was a good idea, too. Now I realize it's a dead end. It will just run you in circles. The irony is that in order to enjoy real financial abundance, you want to be thinking about money as little as possible.

I know it sounds like focusing on money is the right idea. I assure you that it's a mistake. If you need to take several years to figure that out the hard way like I did, be my guest. But you'll be really pissed that you could have saved yourself all that trouble if you simply let these ideas sink in a bit deeper. I hope that on some level what I'm saying strikes you as common sense. But I know I'll be getting emails five years from now from a few people who went the other route. I hope you aren't one of them.

Try to recognize the truth that focusing on creating and delivering value is the smarter, more sane approach to long-term financial abundance. You may start out a bit slow at first, but eventually you'll learn how to get good at both pieces of this puzzle. Once you have both aspects working reasonably well, it's awesome. Just plain wonderful. And it leads to a really fun and exciting life too. Lots of freedom. Lots of joy. Plenty of cash. And yet the cash doesn't even matter.

The nice thing about having plenty of money is that you can largely ignore it. You can focus your attention on doing more important, more interesting, and more enjoyable things. The funny thing is that it's this sort of focus that creates financial abundance in the first place. Then you come full circle and realize that you never needed money at all. You just needed the courage to go after your dreams full steam ahead, even when you were dead broke. You needed to stop hiding behind a lack of money as an excuse not to live your best life.

If I could learn and apply this lesson while going bankrupt and having less than $100 in the bank, surely you can apply it today. I learned that I could create and deliver value even when I had no money and few resources. It wasn't the greatest value in the world mind you, but at least it was something. I focused on creating something people would like and enjoy. Then I got it into their hands and made sure they enjoyed it. Back then it was a simple computer game. Today I do pretty much the same thing with blogging. The content is different, but the overall strategy is the same.

The delivering part needn't be complicated. If you just create something and share it online, other people will spread it around if they like it.

If you've been putting your value out there for months and months, and you haven't been able to generate much interest from others, that should tell you that your mistakes are on the creative side. The feedback is that people don't care for what you're producing. You think you're creating value, but the world is saying, "Not good enough; we don't need or want this." So you need to adapt to that feedback and use it to improve. Let it encourage you to go deeper within yourself, so you can be more genuine and authentic. Become more real and less phony. Keep working at becoming a more expressive creator until people start to take notice. Then you're golden.

WHAT ABOUT THE ECONOMY?

Personally I think that economic recessions, including the current one, are a good thing. Recessions help to weed out the crappy companies that aren't creating and delivering value people want. Many of those companies were doing a good job at one time, but they failed to keep pace. As our values change, our companies need to adapt. Companies that can't do that deserve to die off, and the jobs they created should be eliminated. They'll eventually be replaced by new companies that have a better sense of people's current needs and desires. Company that just don't "get it" will be replaced by companies that do.

Consider the notion of bailing out the failing U.S. auto companies by having the taxpayers fund them. Is this a good idea? It's okay except for one small problem—it's STUPID! It's one of the dumbest things our political reps could possibly do with our tax dollars. An auto company bailout is definitely not in the best interests of our country, nor is it in the best interests of the auto workers themselves. It's totally short-sighted. And FWIW I think the whole financial bailout was just as dumb.

I have family members who used to work for GM for years (not in the automobile division of the company though). If they were still working for GM today, I'd sooner see them lose their jobs and have to find new work elsewhere than encourage them to live under the illusion that their company should continue doing business as usual. As I mentioned previously, Erin and I bought a Japanese car in 2006 even though we could have gotten a great price break on a GM model with the family discount. We just didn't like any GM cars.

During a recession some companies are going to die off. That's a good thing. To artificially prop up the proven market losers is just dumb. Sure, it will have some rippling consequences. But those ripples are necessary. We need that sort of self-correction to prevent bigger problems down the road. We need to send a message that if you fail to create and deliver value people genuinely want, your business will ultimately fail, and no amount of political lobbying will save you. Of course we get the opposite result when too many people think that the point of life is to chase dollars, especially our politicians. Can you blame them though? Have you ever been known to fall into the same trap?

THE SMART APPROACH TO MONEY

It's better—and much more compassionate—for millions of auto workers to lose their jobs and be re-integrated back into society, where they can start doing socially useful work again instead of wasting their time doing work that simply isn't needed anymore. If it takes years, it takes years. There are other companies that are doing a better job of providing what people want and adapting to the planet's changing transportation needs. Giving more money to the losers is a stupid strategy.

Similarly, if you work for a company that is falling out of sync with creating and delivering value that people want, you should indeed lose your job. It's better to retrain yourself to do more meaningful work elsewhere than to waste your time doing work that isn't needed. Becoming obsolete is a trap that can be avoided. Even if you're an employee, you still need to make sure you're contributing to the creation and delivery of real value. If you fall away from that, it's only a matter of time before you get the axe, so don't be too surprised when it happens.

A VALUE-CENTERED CAREER

How do you know if you're creating and delivering real value?

Ask yourself these questions: If you stopped doing what you do, who would care? Who would object loudly? Who would revolt?

If you're creating and delivering genuine value, and you suddenly stop, people will notice. People will definitely care. Your contribution will be seriously missed. There will practically be rioting in the streets.

Such people may not even credit the value to you directly, especially if your contribution remains somewhat anonymous, but they'll soon detect that something important is missing from their lives. Even if they don't know your name, the removal of your ongoing value creation and delivery will have a definite effect.

If, however, hardly anyone cares that you stopped, that should tell you something. It means that people just didn't value your creative output—not really. What you were doing was either unnecessary or easily replaced. You weren't yet living as a conscious, self-actualized human being. You held back from shining as brightly as you could have.

You have a choice of whether or not you want this to be your fate. You may have been conditioned from a young age to view your life path in terms of getting a job and making money. Go ahead and live that way for a few years if you think it's intelligent. You'll soon see what a pointless, soulless dead-end it really is.

When you finally begin to hear that subtle inner voice screaming at you, "This is just so wrong," realize that it's still possible to live a life of fun, freedom, and fulfillment—and still make plenty of money and not starve. But in order to get there, you have to focus on doing what really matters. You must clear your head of all that socially conditioned non-sense and stop doing what everyone else is doing.

Start living as a conscious human being, not a mindless minion. Focus on expressing your child-like creativity on a daily basis. Stop thinking so much about making money, and focus on connecting with people and sharing your creations with them instead.

Create and deliver. Create and deliver.

The correct focus for financial abundance is so simple it's ridiculous. You learned it in kindergarten.

You: "Hey, look at this picture I made!" (Value created)

Adult: "Wow. That's awesome! You made my day!" (Value received)

My five-year-old son and eight-year-old daughter pretty much have it figured out. If they just keep doing what they naturally like to do, they'll be able to enjoy financial abundance as adults too.

My job as a parent isn't so much to teach them something new in this area—it's to prevent them from being brainwashed into thinking like everyone else.

It took me about 5 hours to write and edit this 6,000-word article. I wasn't even planning to write an article today. But I got inspired by an idea, so I sat down and wrote the whole thing in a single sitting.

My investment of time and energy on the creative side was fixed. But this article will keep delivering value to people for many years to come. That's a good investment then, isn't it?

It doesn't matter whether or not this article generates income for me. I don't think about it like that. I just know that if I keep creating and delivering value, I'll continue to enjoy financial abundance, and I'll feel really good too. Money is basically a non-entity. It doesn't motivate action, nor does it serve as a reward. It's just something that recedes into the background while real life is unfolding.

I'd love for you to be able to enjoy similar benefits if this is something that appeals to you. It all starts with the choice of where you focus your attention. The more you pursue your own creative self-expression, the less you'll have to fuss over money.

The irony is that this is probably what you tell yourself you'll do when you finally have enough money, but that sort of thinking is a trap that will only keep you stuck. The way you would live if/when you're enjoying financial abundance, start living that way now, for that's the very strategy that will produce the abundance you seek. And when you begin to experience financial abundance, you'll realize that you never needed it to begin with. You just needed the courage to start expressing the real you under the conditions you find yourself in this very moment.

This chapter has taken so many twists and turns, I think I've left the original title far behind by now. But somehow I think it still fits.

23.
How to Create Real Value

Let's tackle the question of how to discern whether or not you're creating and delivering real value.

The simple answer is that you know you're creating value when you can see **tangible positive changes** in the world as a result of your creative output.

WEAK VALUE

Suppose I post a new article, and lots of people send me feedback such as, "Great article, Steve. That was awesome! Thanks for posting it."

Does that mean I created real value? Well, maybe I created some. I can see that some people felt good, but is that a tangible positive change? I would say no, not really. The impact will probably be short-lived. I can't say I delivered much real value.

Lots of bloggers write articles that generate this sort of feedback. You might read such articles and think to yourself, "That was a cool article." But a week later you've totally forgotten about it, and nothing in your life has changed. The only value you actually received was perhaps a moment of entertainment or distraction. There isn't much evidence of **tangible positive change**.

So even though this might seem like positive and encouraging feedback, I would interpret it as an indication that I provided weak value. Weak value is better than no value of course, but if this is all I was able to do, I'd probably be struggling financially.

Take note that I receive this type of feedback every day. For any given article and any given reader, there usually isn't a huge amount of value being transferred. And that's okay. Creating impactful articles is very challenging. I don't always know what will deliver strong vs. weak value.

The value received depends on the individual reader and the circumstances of their life too. Some people receive tremendous value upon re-reading an old article that previously didn't mean much to them.

STRONG VALUE

Now suppose I'm walking around at a conference and someone recognizes me and says, "Steve, I'm so glad to finally meet you! I have to tell you our story. Earlier this year my brother and I read your article *10 Reasons You Should Never Get a Job* (http://www.stevepavlina.com/blog/2006/07/10-reasons-you-should-never-get-a-job/). That article convinced us to quit our jobs as corporate engineers and start our own business this year. Now we design and sell inspirational T-shirts. We're loving it. And our customers are digging the T-shirts too. Thank you so much for the work you do. We're so much happier!" This is followed by a squishy hug.

That new business is something real. This is a **tangible positive change**. That article obviously delivered more than just momentary entertainment value. It had a lasting effect.

This was a true story by the way. I was speaking at a conference in October, and I met Drew and Caroline Yacu at their vendor booth. This brother and sister team started a business creating and delivering T-shirts with inspirational messages on them. The twist is that the messages are printed backwards. This means that whenever you see yourself in a mirror, you'll instantly read the message, so it works as a positive affirmation. However, when someone else looks at your shirt, all they see is backwards writing.

Drew and Caroline gave me a free T-shirt at the conference to thank me for helping them get started on this path. I was delighted to see how happy they were. The backwards message on my shirt is, "I am a creative genius."

Whenever I wear that shirt and see myself in a mirror, it always makes me smile. Since I can wear the shirt again and again, the value Drew and Caroline created keeps getting delivered. It's not just a one-time thing.

I've also noticed that when I wear this shirt in public, people will stare at my chest trying to read the backwards writing. It invites people to walk up and connect with me. I always get comments about the shirt. So the shirt provides even more value by acting as a social opener.

Drew and Caroline said they quit their jobs in January, so they've been going for quite a while. And they still remembered the article that helped tip them over the edge. That's another factor I've seen repeatedly. When real value gets delivered, it's usually memorable.

Am I claiming credit for launching their business? Certainly not. They did all the work. That business is fueled by their creativity, not mine. My article was just a catalyst, perhaps one of many. You can check out Drew and Caroline's awesome T-shirts at *ReflectMyLife.com*.

Most of the feedback I get is on the weak value side, but I give the strong value feedback a lot more weight. An article that helps someone launch a new business is a lot more significant to me than an article that generates hundreds of "cool article" emails.

AIM TO CREATE STRONG VALUE

These days it's pretty easy for me to write something that will generate plenty of positive "cool article" feedback. I can consistently deliver weak value without much effort.

Lots of other bloggers have reached the point where they can consistently deliver weak value as well, and that's where they stagnate. They keep getting "cool article" feedback on every post, but they still aren't getting the results they want. They wonder what's missing since the feedback seems to suggest that they're doing great. The problem is that these bloggers never make the transition from weak value to strong value. They don't raise their standards to the point of creating impact instead of just entertainment.

The Internet is already overloaded with weak value. You could spend the rest of your life soaking up the weak value that's already been posted—reading blog posts, watching videos, etc.—it's endless. But ultimately it's nothing but info-crack.

If you pump out more and more weak value, you aren't helping much. Hardly anyone would care if you stopped since they have plenty of other sources to turn to.

If you can figure out how to create strong value though, you differentiate yourself. You're no longer part of the herd pumping out feel-good drivel. Now you're actually doing something real. I hope you grasp this point because it's an important distinction to internalize.

It is very challenging to create and deliver strong value: *what can I say or do that could permanently change someone's life for the better?* The answer isn't obvious. But you can reach this point by becoming a prolific creator and by seeking to continually increase the value you're creating. Put a lot out there, and gradually figure out what matters and what doesn't.

TANGIBLE POSITIVE CHANGES

Here are some other examples of feedback that represent **tangible positive changes**:

1. My father lost 70 pounds this year after I forwarded him your series on the raw food diet.

2. I finally got a girlfriend after reading your article on soulful relationships.

3. I moved to Las Vegas after reading Living in Las Vegas, and I'm loving it here.

4. I had my first lucid dream after listening to Erin's podcast on Lucid Dreaming. It was amazing!

These are all examples of real feedback I've received.

The commonality is that we can see some kind of evidence that positive change has occurred. Some sort of shift has happened. Someone having their first lucid dream is a positive change. Someone going from no relationship to having a girlfriend is a positive change. Someone moving to a new city and beginning a new chapter of their life is a positive change. All of this goes beyond the "cool article" type of feedback.

It isn't enough to hope that you're creating tangible positive changes. You need to see evidence that you're having this effect. One of the simplest is that people will tell you how your creative work has affected them. Are you seeing any evidence that your work is producing **tangible positive changes?**

Some changes are small and subtle. Other changes are big and create massive ongoing ripples.

Note that the value you deliver to the world doesn't have to be earth-shatteringly huge. It could be something small and simple. You may do something that only benefits a single person in a small way. That's terrific.

Over time you'll learn to deepen the value you're able to share. A song can have a deeper impact than a few minutes of distraction. A comedian can do more than entertain. A T-shirt can do more than clothe you.

WHERE VALUE CREATION STARTS

It's a pitfall to think that you need a super-genius-unique-idea to create strong value. You'll run in that circle for an eternity looking for something that has never been created. From the outside looking in, you would think people like Steve Jobs and Bill Gates whom created the ipod and windows personal computer are freaks of nature, as if they were endowed with a vision of the next greatest piece of technology, like Doc Brown from *Back to the Future* was given the vision of the Flux Capacitor when he hit his head off of the toilet.

Creation does not happen like that, however. The ipod or PC or even the Flux Capacitor wasn't manifested out of thin air. Those creations happened by seeing a relationship between two apparently opposite things.

Steve Jobs saw a relationship between playing music via a CD or Cassette player and existing technology that can essentially "computerize" music into what we know as an Mp3. He saw the possibility to carry around a small, handheld computer that can play many songs from various artists. Steve's value creation was bringing that relationship together into a functioning resource for society to consume.

Bill Gates saw the relationship of a taking a huge computing system—and I mean huge, big enough to fill an entire room—and brought the computer to compact size so it fits on your desk. The technology was there, but Bill made the computer into usable value for the mass population to consume.

271

I created *Big Heart Small Business*. The value creation that Big Heart Small Business provides is a relationship between Zen Buddhism and practical business and marketing strategies so that small business owners can connect with their ideal clients without betraying their heart and values. Zen Buddhism already exists. Effective business and marketing strategies exist as well. I brought the two together, refined the approach from my perspective and experience, and gave small business owners a way to integrate spirituality and consciously grow while making a difference and a healthy profit.

True value creations starts with emulation. This is a lot different than being a copy cat. Copy cats rehash already existing value and slap a different name on it. Some examples are Coke and Pepsi—is there really a difference? A blogger taking one of Steve Pavlina's articles and reposting it verbatim on his blog. Taking a Dave Matthews song and "covering" it note for note, and word for word, at your local bar. There's nothing wrong with *copy-catting* value, a unique difference always exist when it exchange hands, however, being a copy cat is providing weak value. You cannot do it for long or you'll find yourself out of business or generalized amongst the masses.

Emulation is creating or producing already existing value, but finding a unique relationship from your experience with that value.

As far as I know, when StevePavlina.com first came out in 2004, he created a relationship between a new way to communicate—blogging—and his experience with personal development. Blogging was a new tool for online communication and not widely known. Personal development has been around for ages. Steve brought the two relationships together, along with his experience in personal development, and created a valuable website that nobody did in the Personal Growth industry. Steve found a unique medium and message, and combined it with his unique Self.

Another example is how I created Big Heart Small Business. I emulated and practiced effective business and marketing strategies for years. Based upon my results and experience with marketing and doing business, I tweaked some strategies that resonated with my unique qualities. I also practiced Zen Buddhism for years. I meditate, do Koan study (informally), and emulated the Big Mind Process. As my relationship with Zen Buddhism grew, I noticed a unique relationship between business and marketing and Buddhist teachings. I learned through experience that you can be your ordinary, compassionate self and succeed in business at the same time. Other people may provide something similar to what I offer, but the uniqueness that I bring to the table is my experience and creativity. Nobody can steal or copy cat that.

GET STARTED

Where do you start to emulate? How do you figure out how to provide strong value?

You get started by creating stuff that provides little or no value. Then keep experimenting. Keep trying different things. Look for ways to improve. In this manner you'll progress to weak value and eventually to some strong value. With practice you will calibrate. You'll learn to provide more value.

I've written more than 800 articles now, and I'm still figuring it out. It's still hit and miss a lot of the time. But I keep writing. I keep trying new approaches and angles. And every once in a while, I manage to put out something that delivers strong value for a lot of people. I constantly make new distinctions. I deepen my understanding of what works and what doesn't. I learn by doing.

The ability to create strong value is the result of high creative output. The more you create stuff, the faster you'll figure out how to create something good. Every creator has to pump out a lot of crap before getting good.

DO MORE THAN NOTHING

The dumbest approach you can apply is to sit still and create nothing. Stand there and whine, "I don't know what to do!"

That's just lame. I'm sorry for being so blunt, but it is.

If you can't get a clue as to how to get started creating and delivering some value to people, you must be blind.

Go outside for starters. Walk down the street. It shouldn't take but a few minutes to find someone you can help.

If you made an all-out effort, could you make a difference in the life of one person today? Could you create even a little bit of weak value for someone somewhere? Have you ever tried?

If you're really, really clueless, then volunteer. Go help people in need. You'll learn quickly that if you have a pulse, you can provide value to people. If the only benefit you think you can offer is body warmth, then go hold crack babies for a few hours a week. This will help get you out of your head and get into action.

I don't know what to do is simply not a valid excuse. That's just fear and cowardice talking. You know you can do better than that. Seriously, if the *Three Stooges* can create value, why not you? Were they geniuses? Perhaps not. But they took a lot of action.

If you really, really don't know what to do though, simply go outside and walk around. Don't go home until you've figured out something you can do to take a stab at creating value.

This isn't rocket science. If it takes you more than an hour to figure out something you can do to create value, you're being way too anal. And the whole time you're creating nothing. You have to figure this out by doing, not by sulking.

If you think you can sit at home and compute the perfect value-creation formula and then begin taking action from that place of perfect insight and understanding, you're delusional. You're suffering from the delay tactic known as *perfectionism*, a word derived from the Latin *wimpus maximus*.

You'll figure out how to provide strong value when you're in motion. Only the act of creation will enable you to figure out how to create strong value. You'll figure it out as you go along. Your first guess at how to create value isn't going to be perfect. Please rid yourself of the myth that if you just come up with the right idea, you'll be a high-level value creator from day one. It just doesn't work like that.

Each time you create weak value, it serves as a learning experience. Every time you hear feedback like "cool song"—or worse... maybe cricket sounds—you can learn from it. You can say, "Well...that sucked. I'll have to try something else."

This is how you calibrate.

BEGINNERS ALWAYS SUCK

If you want to see a good example of calibration at work, go back and read my very first blog post (http://www.stevepavlina.com/blog/2004/10/first-post/). It's only three paragraphs long. I'll wait.

That was a true masterpiece, wasn't it? It's obvious from that first post that I would go on to have a massively successful blog, right?

The truth is that I feel like such a chode for having written that. It's three paragraphs of absolute drivel. It doesn't even come close to providing real value. It announces a book that I eventually decided not to write (canceling that book was the right decision though). I didn't even get the basic "cool article" feedback for that one. But hey, it was a start. It set me in motion. I could only get better from there.

My second post was a little better. At least it has some substance to it, although it was weak value at best. It wasn't particularly creative. As mentioned in that post, I was mainly rehashing other people's ideas. It's a big improvement from the first post though.

The first blog post I wrote that provided even a small degree of strong value was probably *Dealing With Difficult People*. That was my 27th post. And the next one didn't happen until about 2 months later—*How to Discover Your Life Purpose In About 20 Minutes*.

When I first started blogging, it was a challenge just to create weak value. Creating strong value was quite rare and usually accidental. Over time I gradually improved. Notice that I didn't improve by sitting around thinking about how to write impactful blog posts. I got better by writing lots of crappy posts and figuring out what not to do. And I'm still figuring it out. Give me another four years, and I'll probably be embarrassed by what I've written today.

So here's the rule to follow: Create more than nothing.

That's it really. The only way to totally screw this up is to sit around sulking and feeling powerless. That's the only way to fail. Doing nothing is failure. Creating nothing is failure. Creating something, however crappy it may be, is success.

I know I'm right about this because I have the T-shirt to prove it.

24.
Ignore Lack to Create Abundance

I've been enjoying an abundant year because I focus much more attention on abundance, appreciation, and gratitude than I do on lack, scarcity, and poverty. Some people would say that this mindset is the result of abundance; I recognize the mindset/heartset as the cause of it.

When I did the opposite and paid more attention to what was lacking in my life, I experienced a variety of scarcity-based experiences—sinking deeper into debt each year, being kicked out of my apartment due to lack of rent money, not being able to afford what I wanted, feeling stressed whenever my car broke down, always buying the cheapest items and having them break easily, etc. That place of being was compelling enough to capture my attention for a while, but after a number of years there, I got bored with it and decided to try out the abundance mindset to see what that's like.

I would often read books or listen to audio programs that went on and on about the abundance mindset, but I figured that was easy for them to say because they were already living it. What if you're not living it? Usually their recommendation was to start wherever you are, and some would insist that abundance is a mindset you can create regardless of your starting position. I didn't really buy into that notion at the time, but mainly because I was desperate to try something new, I opted to give it an earnest effort for at least a few days to see if it made any difference. It's not like what I was doing before that was working, so I figured it couldn't hurt, and it might help lead me into new territory where a solution could be found.

I began by focusing on feeling grateful for what I did have, like being able to enjoy running along the beach or watching a sunset. I turned my attention away from lack as much as possible. I did my best to ignore my debt, my unpaid bills, and my creditors for a while. Obviously that created some consequences, and I further dealt with those consequences by largely ignoring them as well.

This is really a key point that I don't want you to overlook: it wasn't that I began to focus on abundance thinking, I also did my very best to ignore anything in my life that suggested lack or scarcity. I stopped looking at my bills. I stopped answering the phone since most of the calls were from creditors. I ignored my debt and stopped making credit card payments altogether. That sounds crazy, doesn't it? But when I paid attention to those things, they would just bring me down and make me start thinking about what wasn't working.

This shift of attention soon created external shifts in my reality. I became more creative, released a new product, and started making a lot more money. A year later I was debt free, partly from going bankrupt, which was a good thing because it wiped out most of my debt, and then I paid off the rest mostly in one fell swoop with an advance I received for a game I licensed to a publisher.

I continued to expand upon this mindset of abundance over time; I imagined enjoying time abundance, too. I imagined being more generous, first with my money, but then I felt even better about being generous with my time and creativity. I donated thousands of dollars and hundreds of hours to non-profits. I wrote articles for free and hosted discussion forums for free. I didn't do these things to get any particular result. I did them because I just felt motivated to do them. When I held onto that abundance vibe, I didn't have to push myself to contribute anything. It just flowed out of me without really trying.

I've since created a massive body of creative work and gave it away to the public domain, and I continue to add to that collection each month. This month I started doing microloans as well and encouraged others to join our team, which has been making new loans every day.

I never would have done these things if I was focused on lack. The vibe of lack didn't make me feel particularly generous; it merely made me project generosity as something other people should do more of, or something I should get around to "in the future" (which of course means never).

There is value in having experiences across the spectrum of scarcity to abundance. I'm glad for the experience of scarcity since it helps me understand and appreciate abundance more deeply. For example, I enjoyed my recent trip to Paris that much more because I know what it was like to not being able to afford such a trip and having it seem like an impossibility. Every day I spent in Paris, I felt grateful to be there. I didn't take anything for granted.

Through personal testing I came to see that overall I prefer the abundance vibe to the scarcity vibe. Abundance is a better fit for who I am.

I neither require nor expect others to make the same choice I did. Lots of people find growth lessons in the scarcity vibe, and I have no doubt they'll continue to explore it. I've tested that vibe and that mindset enough to know that it isn't such a good fit for me. I'm happier and more fulfilled on the abundance side. But I wouldn't be so sure of this if I hadn't had those scarcity experiences first.

Many times when I write about abundance, there are people who will take issue with it. It's interesting to see how they project a boatload of assumptions onto me and then argue with their own assumptions. Some seem to think that abundance is wrong. Others want me to pay more attention to poverty.

I pay little attention to poverty, scarcity, and lack, not just in myself but in others as well. My focus is on abundance, gratitude, generosity, appreciation, etc. If you believe that what I'm doing is not enough, it's because you feel what you're doing isn't enough. If you're in resonance with scarcity, then "not enough" is something you'll see wherever you look.

When you view one side of the spectrum through the lens of the other, your perceptions are greatly distorted. Just as scarcity may look upon abundance as greedy, excessive, selfish, elitist, narcissistic, etc., so can abundance look upon scarcity as lazy, wimpy, foolish, childish, stupid, etc. But these perspectives aren't helpful to us, again, because they're distorted.

You can only understand the options available to you when you experience them from the inside. And yes, this does mean that you can't really understand an option until you've experienced it to some degree. From the outside looking in, you can get curious, but you can't really gain much insight.

You're free to do as I've done and test different mindsets/vibes to learn which set of experiences you prefer. You have laid out before you a whole spectrum of possibilities to explore.

Try to avoid the mistake of judging or condemning someone else's position on this spectrum. Don't expect others to change their mindset just because you have issues. If you feel resistance towards what others are experiencing, look to your dissatisfaction with your own vibe. Then remember that you have the power to make the shifts you desire, if you're willing to embrace those shifts fully and completely instead of resisting them.

I'm quite pleased with my choices thus far, even as I continue to explore new points along the spectrum of possibilities. I'm fully aware that some people object to my choices and would prefer to see me focus more attention on problems like poverty. From the perspective of scarcity, they want me to change what they're unwilling to. They want me to join them in their feelings of being not enough. From within the lens of scarcity, this may seem like a reasonable request, but from the perspective of abundance, it's a rather silly thing to do.

The response to such requests is predictable if you understand how both mindsets work. Scarcity criticizes abundance for being not enough. Abundance finds scarcity's request silly and so enjoys amusement at the entertainment value of it; additionally abundance is appreciative of the reminder of the contrast between scarcity and abundance. Scarcity doesn't get its request satisfied and hence validates its experience of not enough-ness; it can continue to live in its world where abundance is greedy and unresponsive to its needs. Abundance ends the interaction feeling appreciative; scarcity leaves feeling frustrated. This is a perfectly congruent outcome from all perspectives. Each vibe creates the experience that harmonizes with it.

A few people have been amusing me lately, which I'm grateful for, and I in turn have been doing my part to frustrate them.

If you desire to shift from scarcity to abundance, how do you do that? There are many techniques that I've shared in this book, so I won't rehash that same content here. A good place to start is to watch the *Creating Abundance* videos (http://www.stevepavlina.com/blog/2009/11/creating-abundance-video/). I actually apply this to an even greater extent today than I did when I created those videos in 2009. Now I'm spending much more time each day doing this kind of vibrational work because I find it extremely powerful.

This morning I woke up at 3:30 and then spent a good 2 hours imagining different aspects of my life as I want them to be and getting a clear lock onto the vibes that are consistent with my desires—the thoughts, feelings, and attitudes I believe I'd be experiencing if all my desires were physically real right now.

Then throughout each day, I do my best to hold onto these new vibes as much as possible. When I catch myself slipping into a vibe I wouldn't likely experience on the side of my new desires, such as frustration or worry, I stop whatever I'm doing, take a deep breath, and reload the vibe I desire. Or if I'm tired and can't do this very well, I just take a break to distract myself.

I continue to practice this because I find it very effective. Not only do I attract and enjoy more of what I want, but my new vibes also become increasingly repulsive to those whose vibes are incompatible, while becoming more attractive to those with compatible vibes and desires—people with whom I can enjoy co-creating abundantly.

ALLOW YOURSELF TO RECEIVE

The vibe of financial abundance is very similar to that of open relationships. It invites and welcomes from a place of flow, and without attachment to outcomes.

We're surrounded by opportunities to invite and receive love, money, and more. But when we're stuck in scarcity thinking, we squeeze this field of possibilities down to a narrow part of the spectrum. And sometimes our intentions are simply too big to be compressed without losing their essence, so we effectively block them.

We intend to increase the flow of love, and then demand that it must come from our primary relationship partner only. We desire more money and require that it must come from our one and only job—or that we must receive a singular job if we don't have one already. This attachment to such thin bands of reception pollutes our intentions with fear. Yes, we actually fear receiving through other parts of the spectrum, parts that lie outside our comfort zones.

What if getting paid what I'm worth means that I have to quit my current job? What if there are other beautiful relationships to enjoy than just this one?

We resist the consequences of such changes, and so we resist the changes themselves, thereby receiving the perpetuation of stuckness. The universe cannot deliver the full package of your desires if your mailbox is too small. When we open up and allow ourselves to receive through all parts of the spectrum (or at least a bit more of it), we reduce the blocks attached to our intentions, and the flow quickly increases.

Is it really so terrible to welcome multiple income streams, or multiple lovers? Can we not simply relax and allow our desires to show up, without presenting a list of fear-based demands that constricts the flow?

Can you allow yourself to receive through all parts of the spectrum of potential, including the bands that expose your limiting beliefs and make you feel vulnerable and afraid? If you can do that, you will soon forget what it's like to experience scarcity.

25.

Pay Yourself First

I'm sure you've heard about this concept before: *pay yourself first*. Most programs or books about money or financial success advocate that you need to pay yourself first to increase abundance in your financial life. I know this topic is somewhat of a cliché. But I want to look at it from a spiritual and practical perspective—something I have yet to find anyone teaches.

THE PRACTICAL

The principle is simple: wealthy people in a healthy relationship with money manage their money well. People who have a poor relationship with money mismanage their relationship with money well. This is the last chapter of the book. And I hope by now you understand its message: it's about having a healthy relationship with money that makes you wealthy. Poor people focus only on income and spending, and then neglect everything else: spiritual alignment, creativity, producing value, delivering value, and managing money.

The problem with only focusing on income and expenditures is that as your income rises, so do your expenses—at least this is true for those in an unhealthy relationship with money. To the majority of people who see money as an object of power, happiness, and survival, when more income comes their way, they buy bigger houses, fancier cars, more gadgets, nicer clothes, and more possessions. Money controls them, and they do not direct money in a way that will give them freedom.

Pay yourself first takes your gross income and allocates it into separate accounts. I've heard many recommendations on how many accounts you should open and the percentage of income that goes into each account. Some are too complex that involves 5-7 bank accounts. I like to keep it simple: have a tax account, savings account, necessities account, and play account.

I normally put in 20% of my gross income into a tax account. It's too easy to not account for taxes when self-employed. Then at the end of the year I'm scrambling to pay the tax bill. I've learned from my lessons and concluded it's much simpler to take care of taxes right in the beginning. Sometimes at the end of the year I have monies left over, and other times I use the entire account. How do I know if 20% is enough? It's a guess. And as the years go on I learn to calibrate and adjust. If I don't use the 20%, I normally cycle the remaining balance at the end of year into my savings.

The Savings account is for saving money and investing money into appreciating assets. I save money in paper, but I also take my paper money and invest it in sound money: gold and silver coin. The banking system—especially the federal reserve—and fiat paper money (greenbacks) is way beyond the scope of this book, but gold and silver have been the commodity of choice in crisis situations and for investment for thousands of years. It's sound and dependable. I also re-invest my income back into my business and to start other information based businesses. I used to invest in Real Estate for passive income, and I still own property, but for now Real Estate is not my cup of tea, nor is the stock market. It's not that Real Estate and the stock market are bad investment vehicles; I don't enjoy either of those vehicles. I learned the hard way about investing money. If I don't enjoy the process and labor and the price for the reward, I don't do it. I don't care if it's the hottest investment in town. I don't value money. I manage money and steward it and respect my relationship with money, but I value intimacy, simplicity, challenges, and adventures. I don't care about accumulating massive amount of paper. I've been broke before and enjoyed life a lot more being broke than trying to accumulate assets and money through vehicles I don't enjoy. There's a price to pay for that time and attention and I don't want to pay that price. If you do, that's great, I'm not judging. But know that there's always a price to pay for anything, and when you want more and more money that price is going to be your life energy.

What percentage do I put into the savings account? It's not fixed, so it depends. Some months it's 1% or 5% or 10% or even 25%, but I always save something. The percentage doesn't matter; it's the principle of stewardship that counts.

The necessities account is for all of my operating expenses. I keep track of my expenses and income every month. Technology has done wonders to make this incredibly simple. I use an iphone app called "ixpenseit." I have an excellent handle my expenses each month, so I know what percentage of my income needs to go in expenditures. The percentage is variable, sometimes it's 100%, other times it's 60%, and then there are times when it's 40%. I don't stress over percentages. I focus so much on financial abundance and its relationship that I always have enough to cover my basic needs. The necessity account is for my day to day operating expenses: rent, food, utilities, household needs, pet, education etc. I also have a business necessity account and business saving account. Same principles apply to the business.

My final account is a play account. I borrowed this account from T. Harv Eker's *Secrets of the Millionaire Mind* book. The play account is for all of my playful purchases. This has a huge range, but mostly involves restaurants, entertainment, travel, hobbies, gifts, and leisure time. I usually deposit about 10% of my income per month into the play account and spend its entirety every month—that's a rule. The only time I won't drive that account bone dry is if I want to travel this month or the next.

WHY PAY YOURSELF FIRST?

Dividing your income with this method teaches you how to steward money. When you're a steward, you manage another's property or financial affairs. You use your income, but there's a level of detachment and respect to money because it's not your property. Stewardship regains control of your finances by taking back your power and leaving money in its proper place—a commodity for the exchange of goods and services. Money is left to be money, and you are left to pursue your adventures and desires without worrying about money.

What most people do is attach their self worth to the flow of money. Every penny spent is like pulling teeth, but yet, at the end of the month they have managed to spend it all and wonder "where did the money go?" So they get frustrated and complain that they don't have enough blaming the world for their misfortune. This may sound like you right now. I know at one point it was me.

The reason you feel frustrated and wondering "where it all goes" is because the money you spend is out of alignment with your true desires and values. Money is life energy. You invest your precious life creating and delivering value to help others and receive money to live the life you want. When you spend money, you are spending your life energy. Those dollars earned represent the time invested to earn that money. You can always earn more money, but you can never get more time. So when you spend your money on things that are not aligned with your true desires and values, or when you invest your energy in work that you do not enjoy, it feels as if you're wasting your life energy because you can never get it back. This is also the main reason why people hate paying taxes. Essentially, the Government is taking your life energy (money) against your will. So of course you're upset! And you have every right to be. You're spending valuable life energy.

Stewarding and managing your money helps you understand how you're investing your time and where you're spending precious life energy. Once I became good at stewarding money, I realized that I spent a lot of money going out to eat. Probably 50 percent of the out-to-eat expenditures were unfulfilling and out of alignment from my true desires. Because I steward my money well, I was able to make quick adjustments. I said, "Oh, I'm not getting satisfaction from going out to eat so much and I'm spending a lot of money doing something I don't enjoy. Well, I'm cutting back my out to eat expenditures to only date night from now on." Once I made that move, I felt more aligned and true to my values and desires. I invested my money elsewhere and stopped feeding it to something I didn't enjoy.

If you don't steward and manage your money well, you'll spend precious life energy on things that do not bring you enjoyment and value. You will keep working to earn money and not even enjoy the rewards. Aside from stewardship, I believe it's equally as important to find a labor of love. Why go through life doing something that you don't enjoy and then spending money on things that also deplete your life energy? That's a double whammy in my eyes.

THE SPIRITUAL COMPONENT TO PAY YOURSELF FIRST

You are always in debt and can never get out. It's a price that comes with being human. Yes, you can get out of financial debt, but you cannot escape spiritual debt. The person you *are* is a miracle. There are so many factors supporting your life this moment that it's impossible to share your gratitude with them all. Consider who does the beating of your heart, is it you? You better hope not. If the beating of your heart was your responsibility, you'd probably be dead a long time ago. Imagine regulating and timing each heart beat? Imagine putting your entire attention to every waking moment to make sure your heart works? A higher intelligence of life enables you to live. This is why you're in debt, and why you need to always pay your debts.

Debt has a pecking order, too. And when the relationship with money is healthy, paying your debts in a certain way supports your relationship with money. What most people do is pay their debts in an unhealthy manner. They first pay their creditors, then themselves, then Big Mind. If these people ever get out of debt from their creditors, they still do not pay their debts to themselves or Big Mind, and it's not long until they are in debt to paying creditors again. You need to switch the pecking order: pay your debt to Big Mind or the Divine or Your Higher Power or God or whatever you call it, pay your debt to yourself, then pay your debts to the people you owe.

The best way to pay your debt to Big Mind, in my opinion, is to appreciate life as it is. Invest time each day expressing your gratitude and appreciation for the life you are and have. There's always something about your life that you can appreciate. I bet you can appreciate the food on your table, the family you have, the ability to communicate, your health, a roof over your head, an internet connection, and even the beating of your heart. Big Mind doesn't discriminate what or how you appreciate life, it only cares that you know your true essence, Big Mind. As a reward for paying your spiritual debt, Big Mind opens the door for abundance. It will show you how to live a life of virtue, mindfulness, confidence, and skillful effort. With these embodied qualities you have the capacity to live a full functioning life.

Next, you want to pay your debts to your Self. You only have one go at this life. How can you love and nurture yourself? How can you get good at receiving? Too often we neglect our own happiness. We con-

287

tinually put others first and sacrifice our own well-being. Most of the time we do this because of limiting beliefs such as, "what makes me good enough is that people think well of me, family comes first, and without family you're nobody." Thus, you spend an entire life winning other people's approval and fearing rejection; all the while those people, in most cases, are taking advantage of your submissiveness to live out their dreams and desires.

From a distance, paying your debts to your Self looks selfish—it's all about me, me, me. The truth is: *it is all about you.* You're the center of the universe. Life only happens in your awareness. You are number one. How can you genuinely help others and the world if you first don't take care of yourself? It's nonsense to believe that you should put others first. When you truly own and embody that you are number 1, a miraculous consequence happens: you give more love and wisdom to those you care about. Take care of yourself. Go after your desires with confidence. Embrace your ego, rather than getting rid of it. Pay yourself first financially, even if it's a small portion of your income. It doesn't matter if the income sits in your savings for less than 24 hours and then it is spent. The principle of rewarding yourself is what matters.

Finally, when all debts are paid to Big Mind and your Self, which is an on-going process, you pay others and your creditors.

THERE'S NO SUCH THING AS EXTRA

"When I make enough money, then I'll start saving." Have you ever said that? I know I have. But when will you ever have enough? There's always something to spend your money on. Having "enough" is too subjective. You can have one dollar and feel that's enough or you can have a million dollars and feel that is not enough. It all depends on the person. But the truth is: there's always room for more; you will never have enough. When does "enough" begin and end? How much money do you need to have "enough" so you can start saving? Once you reach the top of one mountain, there's always another mountain to climb. The journey is never-ending.

"When I make enough money, then I'll start to saving" doesn't work because there's no such thing as extra. Look through the lens of Big Mind and you see an infinite ocean of on-going life. No discrimination between this and that; there's no up and down, left and right, or "black" and "white." Big mind is all the greed in the world, all of the suffering, and all of the happiness. Big mind has nowhere to go, nothing to get, and is everywhere and every-when. Everything that ever-was and ever-will-be is already here. There's only one moment and that's the present moment. This present moment has countless doings, but only one doer. Big Mind is no-discriminating wisdom, which means Big Mind doesn't divide life into labels, boxes, and compartments. Everything is one; therefore, this undifferentiated and no-discriminating substance permeates and penetrates the interspaces of the Universe making everything perfect as it is—never too much or too little, but just right.

Extra is a made-up egoic Self construct so the Self feels important, worthy, and better than others. For example, if you have ten pieces of chewing gum in your pocket and your friend has one piece of gum, do you have more or extra gum than him? If you let your egoic Self answer that question, yes you have extra and more gum. But the perspective of Big Mind says the amount of gum you have is the perfect amount of gum, nothing more or less about it. The same goes with money—you can never have extra. Whatever amount of money you have is the perfect amount. This doesn't mean you cannot have different dollar amounts flow to you in different moments. If you have ten dollars today, and then tomorrow you receive twenty dollars, do you have extra money? No. You may have more money today compared to yesterday, but that thinking is dualistic and imaginary because there's no such thing as yesterday. You only have the ever on-going of now. Money flows in and it flows out.

The practice is when you receive today's money, you save a portion of today's money because all you have is today. The dollar amount you save doesn't matter, but start saving something right now. If you only received fifty dollars today (which is a lot compared to other countries), save at least one dollar. As you get in this habit of saving and investing every time you receive money, you'll find it a fun challenge to double and triple your savings. But it has to start now wherever you stand with money. If you wait to have extra one day, you will wait for a long time because extra money will never come. Money flows in and money flows out. I can't say it enough.

Paying yourself first is a support structure to sustain a healthy relationship with money. Money is life energy. Rather than income and expense, you steward the money by allocating it into what you value and desire. This way, you feel that you're investing your life energy wisely. Begin now to save your money, even if it's one dollar each time you get paid. Make it a challenge to double your savings figure with every paycheck. There's no such thing as extra, so you must start now.

Epilogue:
Financial Freedom in an Unfree World

Financial freedom is somewhat of a cliché now-a-days. It's overused in the financial industry that promises you lavish material possessions and to never have to worry about money again; you just keep sipping your pina colada on the beach and enjoy the waves. Not worrying about money is possible, but that doesn't mean you do not attend to money.

Freedom equates to happiness. When you are truly free, you are happy with your life. Happiness is not a life in which everything meets your expectations. You will not always have your desired financial situation or perfect relationship or the ideal body. The world will always apply pressure; it will stretch you to your limits. But the world can never break you. Only you can break you.

When you have reached your limit, and your capacity to handle life is maxed-out, you will have two choices: 1) you can resist the situation, stay stuck, and be swallowed in your problems for a lifetime, or 2), you can accept the situation as-is and reorganize to a higher level and greater capacity for handling life. Playing it safe, keeping things together and trying to sneak by in life does more harm than good, for it's in your capacity to handle life that brings you freedom and happiness. The question you need to ask yourself is: How can I stretch my capacity?

The people that grow the most are the ones who take the biggest risks. They continually shatter their comfort zones and expand their capacity to handle life. Sometimes the reward is great for expanding your comfort zone, other times the reward is an internal knowing that you are free and happy. You do not have to indulge yourself in big business ventures, risky, high yielding stocks, or run a two hour marathon to expand your comfort zone and capacity. Nor do you need to pursue rewards such as one million dollars, six-pack abs, three-hundred dollar bottles of wine, enlightenment, or a Bel-Air mansion to be happy, free, and at a higher capacity for handling life. You live in a meaningless world. The rewards that society values are just that—rewards that society values. They have nothing to do with your happiness and freedom. Often times, those rewards will constrain your happiness and freedom. This does not mean you should not have or pursue material possessions or recognition; it's fine to have those things. But are you pursuing "things" to play the game of life, or are you doing it for your happiness and freedom?

Happiness and freedom are under your control; it's in your ability to separate meaning from inherently meaningless events. For example, if I lost my job, I could assign many different meanings to that event. Losing my job could be wonderful because I'm free to pursue what I love doing. Losing my job could mean that I'll be unemployed for awhile and I'll have to deplete my savings. Losing my job could mean I have the risk of not being able to afford my home, have electricity, or pay for groceries. Losing my job could open another opportunity for a higher paying job that is fun to work in. The meanings to losing my job are endless. There are many truths, but not one truth is the Truth. I can pick and choose any meaning I want if I'm a free person.

Being a free person doesn't change the truth to the event that I lost my job. The blinders are not on, I know I'm jobless. What's different is that I do not suffer anymore. I know there are many meanings to the event of losing my job, and not one meaning is the truth. How can I suffer when nothing is 100% true? For in any situation I can find many possibilities and many meanings. This is freedom. When you separate the meaning from the event, you are free to decide which meaning is the most resourceful for you to use. And if you do not want to attach to a meaning, you can rest in "no meaning" and merge with the flow of life. Under this perspective money is probably not important to you, but you know that true safety and abundance do not come from money.

The unfree person doesn't have a choice if he loses his job. He is stuck with whatever meaning was conditioned into him. If he's lucky, he had an empowering childhood and teenage years in which his authority figures conditioned him with resourceful beliefs, thoughts, and behaviors. Unfortunately, most people are not lucky. They are plagued with social conditionings that limit their freedom and happiness. They are taught to be victims and blame the world for their misfortune. Fear controls them. All they know is what the senses perceive. It's as if this person refuses to flip the coin because the unknown frightens them.

Society measures your worth based on what you know. The more you know, the higher you can climb in social rankings. If you ever want to be free, you're better off doing the exact opposite of what society says. Those who know the most are too full to live; it's like trying to exercise after Thanksgiving dinner, you can't do it because you're stuffed. The stupider you are the wealthier your life becomes. If you're stupid, you don't know much, therefore, you are empty. It's in your emptiness that you are free. Allow life to fill you up, but master the skill of emptying your cup to become stupid again.

Society has a new trend, and that's teaching our children and children's children to be free thinkers. But their version of "free thinking" is to believe in "my" perspective and fight anyone in opposition. They call it "the new world," but it's nothing more than a dangerous trap to restrict your freedom. Is gun control in your best interest? Is a monopoly over the legal tender of money in your best interest? Is a monopoly on the mail system in your best interest? Is public education and the common core in your best interest? Is printing money out of thin air and inflating commodities in your best interest? Are your parents acting in your best interest? The answer is no. No one acts for your best interest. They only do what makes them happy and what's best for them. How can anyone truly know what's best for you? They may have good intentions, but the road to hell is paved with good intentions. Only you can decide what's best for you. That's freedom, anything else is Hell.

Do not get angry. It's not a useful ally in this situation. The only exception is if you channel that anger to motivate yourself to become free. Your freedom does not come from fixing the world or your loved ones. Even you are doing what's best for you; therefore you are no different than your parents or society. Fighting wars, getting into arguments, and rebelling against other people's intentions create resistance. What you're really resisting is the meaning you are giving to the event. Let go of resisting—that is, consider many truths to the event—and the problem

293

dissolves. What you're left with is the event. You may decide to oppose gun control and do everything you can to protect the second amendment, but the fight for gun control is removed. Your suffering and gross attachment to having things a definite way are gone. You choose to protect the second amendment because that's what you value and enjoy doing. If your efforts fail, it doesn't matter that much. There's another alternative available for your happiness and freedom.

You may not agree with public education. Rather than resisting and suffering over what's being taught in public education, however, you let go of the resistance and take direct action that makes you happy and free. Removing your child from public schools is one alternative. Additional home schooling after public schooling is another alternative. Nothing is stopping you, except for the meanings you are attaching to.

Being free in an unfree world starts with questioning everything. "Is it true?" are the words you want to remember. *Is it true that I'm broke? Is it true that I'm not good enough? Is it true that mistakes and failures are bad? Is it true that my parents know best? Is it true that if I go to church I will go to heaven? Is it true that creating value is how you earn money? Is it true...is it true?* Whatever you question, it's not true. There are countless possibilities and meanings to any event, thought, feeling, or action. Because it is not true doesn't mean you oppose it. Noticing that everything is not the Truth but *a truth* frees you to pursue the life you have always wanted to live.

A valid definition for financial freedom can be presented now: financial freedom is exploring the possibilities that make you happy and taking money from doing what you love. Let that soak in. The financial part is actually the easy part. There are many strategies and paths to earn a buck. The difficult part is freedom. We want to cling, attach, and grasp for meaning and purpose in the world, rather than coming "home" and stepping more into who "I" really am.

BIG MIND

Every event is meaningless. You are the one giving meaning to the event. How can you appreciate this? The moment you appreciate that you're the one giving meaning to meaningless events is the moment you take full responsibility for your life. A new doorway opens; another side of the coin becomes apparent. What you see is the world of no meaning.

Big Mind is your essence. It is that which comes before meaning. Every form that exists has the essence of Big Mind, the formless. Big Mind has no end, nor does it have a beginning. It is the born and unborn, mortal and immortal, the form and formless. Do not think about Big Mind because it is ungraspable, unknowable. Everything I tell you here about Big Mind is not quite Big Mind, but they are pointers to your essence—Big Mind. When you quite your thinking mind and transcend the meanings you are giving, Big Mind is known. Big Mind is the essence of who you are. It's inseparable from being a human being. When you realize Big Mind you do not even know you are Big Mind, because knowing implies thinking, and thinking is dualistic—not Big Mind.

When you separate meaning from the meaningless event, in an instance you are Big Mind. If you hold onto that presence, you are swimming in the ocean of Big Mind. But soon a wave comes passing by and without a choice you are riding the wave being forced back to main land. If you allow the waves to come and go, you'll rest in the ocean of Big Mind. You are happy and free floating on top the gentle waves of life. If you see a wave that would be fun to ride, you mount it like a horse and take it for a ride. Do not become attached to the wave, however. All waves come to an end. It would be silly to attach to the memory of the wave you've ridden. That would be like playing in the sand while dreaming about swimming in the ocean. The ocean is right there! Go to the ocean, float on top of the gentle waves, and catch another ride when the opportunity comes.

It's when you resist the waves, and try to get somewhere other than where you are, is when the chaos happens. Sure, you'll eventually reach a shore and you're back to another main land of meaning…tired and exhausted. You don't stay long, however. Desire or anxiety creeps in and you want to explore the ocean and another main land. So you swim out to the ocean looking for another land, looking for a different meaning to your life. But this time you've swam too far. There's nothing but blue surrounding you. Which way is the main land? Which way is any land? Where are the waves? Fear overwhelms you. Panic. Everything you've known about yourself doesn't matter. What good is it going to do to think about your net worth stranded in the ocean? You realize that there's nowhere to go and nothing to get. The fear subsides; it's not useful. You relax into the ocean. You are Big Mind.

With or without your intention a ship comes by. The men scoop you up, and take you back to main land. You don't fight or struggle for the ocean, nor do you resist going back to main land. You are happy and free. You've already gone "home" before you get home. You are Big Mind. You give meaning. You are the ocean creating waves so you can live a life.

Money, possessions, and recognition are Big Mind; to have or not to have is of relative importance. When you drop your Self and are No Self, you can see Big Mind and know its Truth. *Your happiness and freedom is that which comes before I Am.* Go for an endless swim in the ocean of no meaning and you'll see.

The path is easy, but the journey is long. How much do you value your freedom? How bad do you want it? Is the freedom to choose meaning or no meaning to meaningless events worth it to you? Here is the path:

1. An event occurs.

2. You have a negative feeling and are suffering.

3. Ask, "Who Am I?"

4. Witness your thoughts and feelings. Witness the intensity of your body. Let them be okay.

5. Notice the event. Notice the reaction to the event. Notice how they are separate.

6. Enjoy your happiness and freedom.\

If you want to take it even further and accelerate the integration of Big Mind (no meaning), continually ask, "Who am I?" *Who am I… (silence)…Who am I…(silence)…Who…am…I?*

Once you've found and mastered your freedom, then go after the money. Because now you are playing a game, instead of a serious version of life.

Acknowledgments

This book was co-authored with Steve Pavlina—*Personal Development for Smart People*. Since 2004, he has written hundreds, maybe over a thousand, of articles on personal growth for financial wealth, increasing your health, having prosperous relationships, productivity, subjective reality, and much more. Out of the hundreds and hundreds of articles, and reading and applying his ideas for over five years now, I've found a handful of articles that directly contributed to my financial freedom and his freedom as well. Then, I saw a relationship to the handful of articles and created a developmental process that guides you through the intention of this book: *how to create a financial breakthrough without losing your heart*. He's responsible for at least 50%, if not more, of the ideas and written materials of this book. Thank you, Steve, for making this book possible and for contributing to my financial breakthrough.

Appendix

Imagine you are a company; and the company's name is Nick (insert your name). This company has many employees and not one employee knows his job description, job title, what the product is, and who's the boss. To make matters worse, each employee thinks he is the boss and everyone works for him—yikes!

What's more, the company is always changing. Your product line has changed numerous times. In the beginning you made cars, then you made trucks, next it was lawn mowers, and now you are back to cars again. Employees have come and go, too—there's not one original employee. New employees are hired on a frequent basis, a handful of CEOs have moved in and out, and even the company has switched owners more than once. What is this company? I don't know. The company is in constant flux: moving, changing, growing, and decaying. No one knows what's going on anymore, therefore, the company is dysfunctional.

Over twenty-six hundred years ago, the Buddha realized that human beings are like a dysfunctional company. He called this dysfunction *Dukkha*, which means a stuck wheel whose axel doesn't rotate. Picture a two wheel oxen cart being pulled along a dirt road. Out in the brush, next to the road, someone throws a javelin between one of the wheel's spokes. The wheel is stuck and is in movable. The cart does not stop, however, because one wheel is free-moving. So the cart moves in circles, never leaving the same spot. The oxen cart is dysfunctional.

Like the oxen cart, human beings have become a "wheel whose axel doesn't rotate." The worst part is, you don't even realize it. If you and the collective human race realized how dysfunctional we've become as a species, the circle of dysfunction and the recreation of suffering would halt.

Big Heart Dialogue is a meditative process that repairs the dysfunctional oxen cart so it moves freely again. The meditation doesn't continually push you to grow and to succeed—it doesn't install rocket boosters on the oxen cart. It will not add-on external features to your life, such as a higher income, attracting your ideal mate, losing weight, or to make you astute, like what most personal growth methods promise. Big Heart Dialogue liberates, therefore you rest comfortably as your true self. What's so special about that? Nothing—and that's the point! The moment you try to be special or better or this or that you are lost and dysfunctional. The Self has usurped the throne, and a small little me runs the show. Which would you rather have: billions and billions of tax free money in the bank, or no need for money at all?—your bills, expenses, and desires are paid for. The latter is nothing special, but it is freedom. Wanting the billions and billions of dollars means hard work, exponential growth, and the need to be special. Why not go for liberation, rather than a lifetime of accumulation and hell to later realize it never brings the liberation you desperately seek? That's why you want money in the first place: to be happy and free. What I'm saying is that you can be happy, free, and your true self regardless of money. Now money is in its proper place.

On a practical level, and back to the dysfunctional company metaphor, Big Heart Dialogue calls in each employee of the company and helps him understand his job description, his role in the company, the purpose of the company, and who the boss is. When each employee is recognized for his role and purpose in the company, it becomes healthy and functional. Imagine having all employees doing what they are supposed to be doing, and loving it? The company, which is you the Self, thrives and lives to his fullest; he shares love and every ounce of his uniqueness.

Big Heart Dialogue has roots in the Voice Dialogue Method and the Big Mind Process. What makes Big Heart Dialogue unique are two things. First, we interview, own, and empower the selves that are causing dysfunction in particular relationship areas of your life. For example, if you are struggling with money and suffering in that area, we look at the Selves causing the dysfunction, and then make them healthy and whole; therefore, making the relationship whole and flowing. Second, Big Heart Dialogue facilitates a conversation with your trusted source for guidance. In other words, you call upon your trusted source, for example, Buddha, and have a conversation with Buddha to receive guidance.

In chapter 9 and 10, you received guidance and practical application exploring the uniqueness of Big Heart Dialogue. That facilitation showed you how to work with Big Heart (your trusted source) and receive guidance for a healthy relationship with money. It also showed you how to move into a healthy relationship with money. What you didn't receive is the ground work for Big Heart Dialogue. The reason is because that's a book in itself. However, I learned an accelerated method to quickly build the foundation. It involves interviewing a few Selves—employees—to awaken your heart and liberate yourself.

HOW IT WORKS

There are a few things to remember when doing this work. If you follow these guidelines, you'll have definite success speaking to a Self.

1. Ask permission to speak to a Self. I like to use, "May I please speak to…" Asking permission is humility. Which do you think is healthier? Demands or permission. I think you know the answer.

2. Speak as the Self, in first person, as if you are looking through his eyes. When you need to refer to you, do so by saying your name or *the Self*. For example, lets say you are speaking to the Controller. First, you would ask permission, "May I please speak to the controller?"

Next, respond as the controller: "Yes, I am the controller." Leave *you* aside and speak as the Controller. The facilitator will ask the Controller questions, such as: *please tell me your function and purpose for the self?*

As the Controller, you would respond, for example, "I control the Self's life. I tell him what to eat, who to socialize with, and how much money to make. I'm the controller and it's my job to control."

Are you grasping the concept? Sometimes the facilitator will be another person, and it is always more effective that way, but you can do this work on your own and still succeed. Essentially, it's a conversation with yourself, if you are doing the work alone. You are playing two roles and having a conversation as the facilitator and as the Self.

The ultimate rule to remember is that being in voice, or in character, is what makes this process work. You need to leave yourself aside and jump into the voice.

3. Before you answer the facilitator's question (this applies to both voice and journal dialogue) it is helpful to pause and identify as the Self. For example, if you are dialoguing with the Controller, and the facilitator asks, "What is your function as the Controller," pause, and then identify as the Controller—*I am the Controller.*

THE WORK

We need to lay the foundation and at least have a glimpse at liberation and an awakened heart. I have found a few big Selves that need owned and empowered because they stand in the way of Big Heart—for good reason. Then there are two transcendent Selves we are going to dialogue with for direct access to liberation and an awakened heart. Below is a sample journal dialogue. I recommend reading through it first, and then mimic the exercise yourself.

THE CONTROLLER

Facilitator: May I please speak to the controller?

Controller: Yes, you may. I am the controller.

Facilitator: Can you please tell me about you and your purpose for Nick—the Self.

Controller: Well, my purpose is to control Nick. I help him function in life and get things done.

Facilitator: What are some of the things you control for Nick?

Controller: I control his finances, his health, what to eat, who to interact with, and basically everything.

Facilitator: Where would he be without you?

Controller: Nick would be dead. He would be running around aimlessly not knowing what to do; he wouldn't be able to help a soul. I keep him alive and healthy and prosperous. He needs me.

Facilitator: How does he feel about you?

Controller: Nick is learning to love me, but often times he sees me as a block to his freedom. All he wants to do is live the life he is meant to live, but he see me, the controller, as the one standing in the way.

Facilitator: What's your greatest fear and why?

Controller: My greatest fear is losing control. If I'm out of control, then there's no purpose for me and I don't exist.

Facilitator: What do you, the controller, offer Nick?

Controller: I offer a way for Nick to coordinate his life and to coordinate others so he can make a difference in the world. I offer him the ability to let go and trust that everything will work out because it's my job to make it work. If Nick would stop trying to do everything, and stop worrying, I could do my job and he would be healthy and prosperous.

Facilitator: Thank you controller.

Controller: You are most welcomed.

THE PROTECTOR

Facilitator: May I please speak to the protector?

Protector: Yes you may, I am the Protector.

Facilitator: Please tell me about you. What's your role and function for Nick?

Protector: I protect Nick from harm. There is a lot of danger in the world, and I'm there to make him aware of it and elicit appropriate selves to contribute and help given the situation.

Facilitator: Why do you protect Nick from intimacy and love?

Protector: Nick puts his heart and soul into people, and it's easy to get burnt and have his heart broken. Two examples come to mind. First, I remember when he did work for someone and they promised to pay afterwards. He did the best he could, met every request, and worked long hours, but she stiffed him of pay. So what I do for the next time is make sure contracts and down payments are in place because I hate to see him get hurt. The other instance was when Nick was in love with his high school sweetheart. Again, Nick gave his best and was intimate, but she ended up cheating the relationship. It broke his heart, and I was there to pick up the pieces.

Facilitator: What do you offer Nick?

Protector: I am that shield that protects Nick. The world can be evil, and there are so many people with their own agenda and greed that they would stomp all over Nick if he was vulnerable and intimate.

Facilitator: Thank you Protector.

Protector: My pleasure.

THE SEEKING MIND

Facilitator: May I please speak to the Seeking Mind?

Seeking Mind: Yes you may, I am the Seeking Mind.

Facilitator: Can you tell me about your role and purpose for Nick?

Seeking Mind: I seek what Nick desires. A few years ago he was seeking liberation through meditation, so I set on the path to find the resources and information to best get him there. Now don't get me wrong, I don't achieve anything, that's not my role. I only seek. Today, I am seeking the best way to present and package his teaching and services.

Facilitator: What do you offer Nick?

Seeking Mind: I offer him paths to achieve his desires. And I never stop seeking paths until he is satisfied.

Facilitator: So lets say he accomplished all of his goals and fulfilled them. Do you go away?

Seeking Mind: Absolutely not. I continue to seek the next thing. It never ends. If it did end, I wouldn't exist, and Nick's life would have no purpose or function.

Facilitator: If you were to climb a mountain , and once you got to the top, what would you do next?

Seeking Mind: I would seek the next highest mountain peak.

Facilitator: Thank you Seeking Mind.

Seeking Mind: You are welcomed.

We are going to transit into the transcendent Selves of Big Mind and Big Heart. Big Mind is liberation, and Big Heart is liberation and love. I want you to picture a triangle. At the bottom left-hand corner of the triangle are the many Selves, like the Controller, Protector, and Seeking Mind. Journey across the base of the triangle to the right-hand corner and you are at the transcendent Self of Big Mind. Climb up to the Apex of the triangle and you're at Big Heart. This is a visual to help guide and make sense of the facilitation for the transcendent Selves of Big Mind and Big Heart. In addition, it will be helpful if you sit up straight and give yourself a moment to identify and rest as Big Mind or Big Heart before you write as those Selves.

BIG MIND

Facilitator: May I please speak to Big Mind?

Big Mind: Yes, I am Big Mind.

Facilitator: Please tell me about you. How big are you?

Big Mind: I'm Big. I'm actually beyond words, symbols, and thoughts.

Facilitator: Can you find an end or beginning to you, Big Mind?

Big Mind: No. I go on and on. No end, no beginning. There's no such concept.

Facilitator: If you could put words to who you are...who are you?

Big Mind: I'm beyond this or that. I encompass everything. There's nothing outside of me, nor is there anything inside of me. I am that which comes before form—that's my essence—but I am also form. You cannot destroy me, I am permanent. You could say I'm universal, Buddha Nature, or Godhead. What's important is that I am nothing, with nowhere to go or nothing to get.

Facilitator: What about the war, jealousy, greed, hate, and violence in the world? Is that you?

Big Mind: Yes. It's all me. I'm not judgmental or discerning. I don't pick favorites or make examples. The so called "negative" qualities are human beings manipulating my essence into their thought forms.

Facilitator: Thank you Big Mind. Would you allow Nick to sit as you, Big Mind?

Big Mind: Yes...I am Big Mind

Sit as Big Mind.

BIG HEART

Facilitator: May I please speak to Big Heart?

Big Heart: Yes, I am Big Heart.

Facilitator: Are you as big as Big Mind?

Big Heart: Yes, I am. I include Big Mind, and I include the Self. I am the Apex of the triangle.

Facilitator: How are you different?

Big Heart: I feel. I am the heart and soul for Nick. I tend to human suffering and also make a difference to heal the suffering. I have full range of emotions: love, joy, peace, happiness, anger, hate, jealous, and righteousness. Big mind just is and is sterile. I am compassionate and understanding. I feed Nick love and purpose and when he listens, he can make a big difference in the world.

I am also appropriate and discerning. I'm not stuck in the Self and attached to impermanent form because that leads to suffering. I'm non-attached, but with a caring touch. This means I value things and people, but I'm able to let go. I'm also not stuck in Big Mind, where there is nowhere to go or nothing to get. I'm liberated like Big Mind, but I have aim and purpose.

Facilitator: How do you handle the war, greed, hate, and violence?

305

Big Heart: I bring love and understanding to those situations. I see them just as they are, but I am available to connect with love.

Now it's your turn. There are two ways to Big Heart Dialogue: voice facilitation or journaling. Since you are reading a book, I recommend that you journal, like the exercise above. Ask the same questions, in the same order, that the Facilitator asked. Make sure that you label who is speaking, for example, *Facilitator or Controller*.

QUESTIONS AND OBJECTIONS

The biggest question I get is how do I know that it is working? The simplicity of the practice makes people skeptic. It works so long as you stay in voice when speaking as a Self or a transcendent Self, such as Big Heart. External feedback usually comes in the form of awareness and peace. The things that used to bother you don't anymore. You have awareness over your thoughts, feelings, and actions. This allows you to have appropriate responses, thoughts, actions, and speech. Think of yourself as expanding rather than growing. Awareness brings expansion and expansion brings peace. You are able to handle more of what life throws at you.

Bibliography

Helminski, Kabir. *The Knowing Heart: A Sufi Path of Transformation.* Boston: Shambhala Publications, Inc., 1999.

About the Authors

NICK PFENNIGWERTH

Nick Pfennigwerth is founder of *Big Heart Small Business*. He helps small business owners who feel pressured and overwhelmed to make their business work. He teaches a unique fusion of heart-centered business practices and spirituality so that any small business owner, independent professional, and spiritual teacher can make a difference and connect with their ideal clients that are fun to work with and pay well. Reach out and say hello by visiting him at: http://bigheartsmallbusiness.com/

STEVE PAVLINA

Steve launched StevePavlina.com on October 1st, 2004 and began publishing new personal development articles immediately. His approach to personal growth is extremely hands-on. He loves to dive in and conduct his own experiments. Some of these are temporary excursions, while others lead to long-term lifestyle changes.

StevePavlina.com quickly took off, and within a couple years it became one of the most popular personal growth websites in the world. He didn't spend any money to promote it, and he had nothing to sell. He simply loved sharing, so he gave away all his best ideas for free. He believes that as long as he kept learning and growing, there would always be new ideas to share and that he'd never run out.

Steve has committed himself to conscious growth. His core philosophy consists of three principles: *Truth, Love,* and *Power.*

www.ingramcontent.com/pod-product-compliance
Lightning Source LLC
Chambersburg PA
CBHW021918190326
41519CB00009B/835